APPLIED ETHNOGRAPHY

D1547249

Developing Qualitative Inquiry

Series Editor: Janice Morse, University of Utah

Books in the Developing Qualitative Inquiry series, written by leaders in qualitative inquiry, address important topics in qualitative methods. Targeted to a broad multi-disciplinary readership, the books are intended for mid-level to advanced researchers and advanced students. The series forwards the field of qualitative inquiry by describing new methods or developing particular aspects of established methods.

Series Editorial Board

Books in this Series

1. *Autoethnography as Method*, Heewon Chang
2. *Interpretive Description*, Sally Thorne
3. *Developing Grounded Theory: The Second Generation*, Janice M. Morse, Phyllis Noerager Stern, Juliet Corbin, Barbara Bowers, Kathy Charmaz, and Adele E. Clarke
4. *Mixed Method Design: Principles and Procedures*, Janice M. Morse and Linda Niehaus
5. *Playbuilding as Qualitative Research: A Participatory Arts-Based Approach*, Joe Norris
6. *Poetry as Method: Reporting Research Through Verse*, Sandra L. Faulkner
7. *Duoethnography: Dialogic Methods for Social, Health, and Educational Research*, Joe Norris, Richard Sawyer, and Darren E. Lund, editors
8. *Collaborative Autoethnography*, Heewon Chang, Faith Wambura Ngunjiri, and Kathy-Ann C. Hernandez
9. *Engaging in Narrative Inquiry*, D. Jean Clandinin
10. *Participatory Visual and Digital Methods*, Alene Gubrium and Krista Harper
11. *Fiction as Research Practice*, Patricia Leavy
12. *Applied Ethnography: Guidelines for Field Research*, Pertti Pelto

Applied Ethnography

GUIDELINES FOR FIELD RESEARCH

Pertti Pelto

WALNUT CREEK, CA

Left Coast Press, Inc.
1630 North Main Street, #400
Walnut Creek, CA 94596
http://www.LCoastPress.com

978-1-61132-207-1 hardback
978-1-61132-208-8 paperback
978-1-61132-650-5 consumer eBook

Library of Congress Cataloging-in-Publication Data
Pelto, Pertti J.
  Applied ethnography : guidelines for field research / Pertti Pelto.
    pages cm. -- (Developing qualitative inquiry ; volume 12)
  Includes bibliographical references and index.
  ISBN 978-1-61132-207-1 (hardback : alk. paper) -- ISBN 978-1-61132-208-8 (pbk.
: alk. paper) -- ISBN 978-1-61132-650-5 (consumer ebook)
  1. Applied anthropology. 2. Anthropology--Research. 3. Anthropology--Field
work. I. Title.
  GN397.5.P45 2013
  301--dc23
                              2012050878

Printed in the United States of America

∞ ™ The paper used in this publication meets the minimum requirements of
American National Standard for Information Sciences—Permanence of Paper for
Printed Library Materials, ANSI/NISO Z39.48–1992.

Book design by Lisa Devenish, Devenish Design
Cover design by Andrew Brozyna

CONTENTS

PREFACE

It has been several decades since I last put together a whole book-length compilation about ethnographic research methodology (Pelto 1970; Pelto and Pelto 1978). In the meantime, a great deal has changed in the world of social sciences research. In smaller pieces that I have written, and in my teaching of research methodology in a variety of contexts, I have made many changes in my approaches to field data gathering. In this writing, I will try to express a synthesis of ethnographic approaches, with special emphasis on applied studies in health, education, agriculture, geography, and other topical areas.

However, first I will emphasize what has not changed since I began my professional work. Already a half century ago I emphasized the importance of "the qualitative-quantitative mix" in ethnographic research. Most applied ethnographic research in the 21st century includes both qualitative and quantitative components, and the distinctions between the two research styles are often blurred. A second basic principle of ethnographic field study is the centrality of in-depth interviews. That has always been a key data-gathering approach in ethnography. Now, in the era of the 21st century, in-depth interviewing has taken on new complexities, as the universal use of personal computers has added new dimensions, especially in the realm of data management and analysis.

Another enduring principle in applied ethnographic research is that our work is a scientific attempt to add to useful knowledge. In many applied research projects the useful knowledge is mainly intended for use in a specific, delimited location—with a particular ethnic group, for a certain geographic region, or perhaps in only one institutional setting. That is still science; it is still intended to add useful knowledge. But today we all recognize that knowledge is practically never a final product. Additional research will suggest modifications in "what we know."

PARTICIPATORY RESEARCH APPROACHES

Participation by members of the communities in which ethnographers do research is not a new concept. However, in recent decades, strategies for developing much more active participation from the researched communities and developing partnerships between researchers and local organizations have taken new forms. The development of PRA—which originally meant Participatory Rural Appraisal—and a wide range of other participatory research acronyms (see Chambers 1997) signaled interesting changes in the styles of applied ethnographic research used around the world. Not that these changes are everywhere—I am sure there are still many research projects originating in the developed countries that involve only minimal real participation from the organizations, researchers, and community people at developing nation research sites. However, in many places the patterns are changing toward more egalitarian international collaboration in research projects.

The set of participatory research techniques developed under the PRA banner is worth exploring carefully, as those research tools, such as social mapping, can be very effective in getting new information relatively quickly. Robert Chambers, the chief exponent of the PRA approaches, notes that social anthropologists and others have developed and used some of these methods for many decades. In my view, the technique of social mapping is the most important and widely used item in the PRA repertoire.

CHANGES IN THE TECHNOLOGY OF RESEARCH

Many people will rightly point to the "computer revolution" as the most striking change affecting everything we do in ethnographic research. Certainly there are large changes, particularly in management of our data. Now it's all in the computer. It is hard to imagine that there might be research groups somewhere on the planet who are writing their data on paper, by hand, and not doing computerized analysis. If you know of any such non-computer operations, please let me know about them.

In this book I will not try to deal with all of the complex changes that computers and other electronic tools have brought about in ethnographic research. We only touch on some main points, particularly in data analysis, in the later chapters. It is interesting to read some of the "up-to-date" writing at the end of the 20th century, in which there were very good discussions about the use of computer programs for data analysis. Many of those discussions are now eclipsed by new and different computer software and data analysis strategies.

WORLDWIDE NETWORKING OF ETHNOGRAPHIC RESEARCH

Very large numbers of ethnographic researchers in South and East Asia, the Americas, Africa, and other parts of the world are getting linked through Internet communications and are using personal computers for managing their ethnographic data. I believe there is a very substantial increase in the numbers of international research teams in which ethnographers from western, developed countries are working together with colleagues in developing countries in much more egalitarian arrangements than were possible in the pre-computer era. Simply the greatly enhanced communications possibilities through email contacts have facilitated collaborative research arrangements.

Even small, resource-poor nations such as Nepal, Malawi and Cambodia (and others) are showing up on the Internet as sites of important multi-disciplinary research, and increasing numbers of researchers from developing countries are receiving training in social science research in Europe, Australia, and North America. At the same time, international teams from the World Health Organization (WHO), the United Nations Children's Fund (UNICEF), the World Bank, the International Center for Research on Women (ICRW), the Population Council, and many other organizations are carrying out research in developing countries in arrangements that enhance the technical research skills of teams at the research sites. The work by those multi-disciplinary research teams usually includes ethnographic methods.

Those collaborative projects are made more effective in part through the hugely increased communications possibilities of the Internet, including, of course, the enhanced access to research literature and to the "gray areas" of literature we find in researchers' websites. One of the driving factors in this spread of international collaborative research has been the HIV/AIDS pandemic, which has required very large financial expenditures for program development, accompanied by extensive funding of a wide range of supporting research efforts. I imagine that HIV/AIDS programs have been the leading contributor to increased international collaborative ethnographic research in the 21st century.

THE HIRING OF LOCAL TEAMS OF FIELD RESEARCHERS

Another factor bringing about changes in ethnographic methods is that many applied studies are carried out by teams that include persons from diverse educational backgrounds. In the current scenes of applied research, there are often multiple sites, and local, bilingual individuals are often hired as part of multi-disciplinary research teams.

The local research assistants are trained to do interviewing—doing fairly complex, in-depth, open-ended interviews. They may also be trained to do some social mapping and other PRA style data-gathering. These local research assistants are often recruited from among local college students who may have some graduate (master's level) education in the social sciences. Often there is a quite limited time frame, and the focused nature of the applied research restricts the scope of training and data-gathering. Since those locally hired research assistants are knowledgeable about certain features of the local cultural settings, they can sometimes add a dimension of partial "participant observation," but in many cases such observations are a very small part of the data-gathering action.

THE AIMS AND SCOPE OF THIS BOOK

By now, in the 21st century, ethnographic research has spread widely, in many forms, into various niches of academic and non-academic organizations and environments. In many applied ethnographic studies the data gathering, analysis of data, and writing of research reports is carried out by persons who have rather scant training in ethnographic research. I have seen many research reports that relied heavily on ethnographic data-gathering, but the authors of the research were unable to produce effect reporting, because parts of the data-gathering had flaws and the analysis and write-up lacked effective use of the ethnographic raw materials. Many applied ethnographic studies could have been strengthened considerably by using certain data-gathering operations of which the researchers were probably unaware.

As already pointed out, much has changed in ethnographic field research over the past two decades, and new methods and data-gathering combinations are strengthening the credibility and usefulness of the resulting data. Therefore, this book presents concrete, mostly recent examples of the main tools of current ethnographic research. I have tried to present examples from a range of different topical areas and geographic regions. Many are from developing countries. Applied projects in South

Asia are especially prominent in these materials, in part because there is such a rich mixture of on-going applied research in the region but also because I have spent most of the past two decades in South Asia. I have enjoyed contacts with a very large number of researchers and organizations involved in social and development programs, particularly in Bangladesh, India, Nepal, Pakistan and Sri Lanka.

I begin (Chapter 1) with an overview of applied ethnography, noting some of the areas of interest in different topical areas. Applied ethnographic research has been particularly important in schooling and education, in various health fields, community development, and commercial marketing. The patterns of ethnographic data-gathering are different in these various topical domains, because the problems to be addressed are so varied.

In the first chapter I also address some of the main terminology and concepts, including the ways in which applied ethnographic research often involves inter-relating of qualitative and quantitative data-gathering and analysis. There is a series of dichotomous terms, with "qualitative-quantitative" leading the list. I also deal with inductive and deductive logic and several other complex terminological matters that you encounter in the research literature.

After that introduction the next four chapters focus on the beginning activities of ethnographic field work, including gaining entry and getting the cooperation of the people in the study communities, followed by the most useful first steps of data-gathering. I particularly focus on social mapping and key informant interviewing, after outlining the basic steps of field research in Chapter 2.

Chapter 6 is a key building block in explaining field work, as it deals with the crucial task of recording the (mainly verbal) field data in detail, and then organizing the data into computer files. In my years of training field teams I have seen many instances in which researchers had excellent interviews and direct observation of actions and events, but their written interview notes and other descriptive materials failed to capture all the concrete details.

Researchers need to remember: If you don't write it, it's gone!

Writing up interview notes is also the main step in which you will present "the voices of the people." In 21st century ethnographic research there is now increased emphasis on bringing the people of study communities directly to the forefront, exploring their ideas, behaviors, and needs, and quoting directly from their statements.

Participant observation (Chapter 7) has in earlier decades been a central, defining feature of ethnographic field research. Some people have considered practically all ethnographic research to be "participant observation." However, with the advent of many "rapid assessment procedures" (RAP) and other types of short-term ethnographic research, there is now less opportunity for participant observation. In some projects, even if they are of short duration, researchers will still do some participant observation—taking part in local social events, mingling with local people in urban and rural gathering places, and seeking out ways to take part in some of the local daily life. When your field research team has a more generous timetable, mingling with the community people and activities in research sites and taking full notes about key activities can generate insights and descriptive data that you can never get from interviews.

Throughout this book I emphasize the importance of sampling and counting—and the use of quantitative tools—in the "mixed methods" framework of modern ethnography. Chapter 8 focuses on several main forms of sampling, as ways of insuring that your ethnographic data are reasonably representative of the variations among the communities and categories of persons that you want to understand and describe.

The collection of samples of "cases" (Chapter 9)—special categories of persons such as long-distance truckers, marketplace vendors, young married women, teachers, and a wide range of others—is becoming a core feature of ethnographic research. This is where you put into action the concepts and strategies from the previous chapters.

Chapters 10 and 11 present some highly useful and effective data-gathering tools that I refer to as "structured qualitative methods." These tools are often used as part of the interviewing of the cases discussed in Chapter 9. They are very useful tools for getting the local peoples' vocabularies, and their ways of categorizing and conceptualizing foods, people, plants, illnesses, crops, and other kinds of information in cultural domains.

The "Analysis of Qualitative Text Data: Basic Steps" (Chapter 12) is another "core chapter" concerning your systematic reading, categorizing, and searching for patterns and "themes" in your interview data and field notes from observations. As discussed in this chapter, the concepts of "coding" are particularly important steps for organizing your data analysis. Fortunately there are now some excellent computer software programs that can help your team in coding and data management.

Chapters 13, 14, and 15 deal with somewhat more specialized ethnographic tools and actions. Structured observation techniques (Chapter 13) are becoming more sophisticated, and are considered to produce highly credible, solid data about peoples' behaviors, as well as special events. Similarly, use of diary methods (Chapter 14) for getting behavioral data has become an increasingly popular and useful way to get systematic data among literate populations. In Chapter 15 we return to mapping, but this time the focus is on more complex, technical work, including mapping of indigenous tribal areas, of place names as part of local cultural knowledge, and of land use patterns.

Chapter 16 presents an overview of one piece of the "bigger picture," namely the extensive development of "rapid assessment procedures" (RAP) and short-term "focused ethnographic studies" (FES), which has contributed to major changes in many sectors of applied ethnographic research. The basic ideas of rapid, highly focused data-gathering, structured to answer specific programmatic questions, are especially prominent in some programs of the WHO and some other health-related programs. The various "participatory rural appraisal" methods are also part of this broad transformation. All of these ethnographic developments are intended to increase the levels of participation of the study populations, and to get better expression of the "voices of the study populations." Each of the different approaches discussed in this chapter has produced guidelines and manuals, most of which are available through the Internet.

Chapter 17 (Research Teams and Training) presents an overview of the different kinds of research team arrangements that are found in applied projects, particularly in the developing countries. These materials are intended to give research project managers and persons from academic institutions a realistic view of how applied research is managed in many parts of the world. Much of the complexity of research team organization stems from the need to incorporate persons with knowledge of the local language and culture in the one-on-one interviewing. Another complexity comes from the integration of several different organizations, in the more complex projects.

All the members of the research team need to have a clear conceptual framework concerning the purposes of the research. In addition, the primary interviewers and data-gatherers must be trained in the practical skills needed to use the specific data-gathering tools. Most locally recruited persons who are fluent in the local languages will not have had training in the specific interviewing techniques. All the field workers will need coaching and supervision concerning note taking and other data management.

Writing up the results of ethnographic research (Chapter 18) should begin early during the data-gathering processes. However, I put this chapter near the end of the book, as most of the chapters deal with the work out in the field and the use of the different ethnographic techniques and tools.

For Whom is this Book Intended?

This book is primarily intended for applied research people in both developing and developed countries. The examples I present are mainly from applied research, although there are usually some academic people involved in the complex international programs. There is, of course, no clear demarcation between academic (theoretical) research and applied ethnographic studies. Some research, for example, in HIV/AIDS programs, is distinctly, immediately aimed at providing needed information for developing new interventions or for modifying interventions to better achieve immediate goals. Some projects are focused on seemingly mundane, practical matters such as study of the utilization of bed nets in malarial areas. On the other hand, applied research on health care seeking in marginal rural areas, while aimed at practical issues, may not be immediately taken up in health programs, and the researcher may be focused on exploring alternative theoretical models for academic purposes.

All the research methods presented in this book are also used by academic researchers, and are useful for graduate students doing master's and doctoral thesis research. In some applied program settings, including programs I have described in various chapters, scholars from departments of education, rural development, health care disciplines, and other social science departments, are welcomed as researchers for their academic projects, particularly if they pay heed to the practical needs of the project practitioners in planning their data-gathering.

Also, persons involved in training programs and providing other technical assistance can make good use of the descriptions of ethnographic tools in this book. I have selected research examples that you can present to illustrate the uses of various data-gathering methods. Persons who are helping to develop plans and protocols for quantitative survey research can use some of the ethnographic techniques for getting locally or regionally specific vocabulary and categorizations, in order to design blocks of questions in culturally appropriate language and formats.

Concluding Comment

As I commented at the outset, my aim in this book is to give some useful information, examples, and guidelines for applied ethnographic research, while trying to reflect on some of the trends and new research situations in the international scene. I try, in my examples, to shift at least slightly away from the focus on Euro-American academic researchers, and to include reflections on the work of non-academic research groups, particularly some who are working in developing countries. My impression is that there is a very considerable growth of research groups and individuals in the less industrialized parts of the world. These developments have been, I believe, greatly enhanced by the advent of low-cost personal computers, plus the greatly expanded access to information and knowledge networks brought about through email and the Internet.

In this book I cannot pretend to deal with all the different developments and research ventures around the world. Some of my reflections and suggestions are undoubtedly biased by the highly unusual "sampling" of research groups and activities that I have encountered, particularly during my past 20 years of work in South Asia. Of course, some of my ideas and suggestions have come out of years of teaching students in North America, as well as extensive contacts with researchers in Northern Europe, particularly Finland.

ACKNOWLEDGEMENTS

I became interested in research methods during my graduate studies at the University of California (Berkeley) during the 1950s. The origins of my interest in ethnographic data collection, including the mix of qualitative and quantitative methods, are now impossible to trace. I am indebted to many researchers, from several different disciplines, for the ideas that formed the basis for my first book on field research methodology. Books and articles by psychologists, sociologists, and anthropologists (and authors from other disciplines) shaped my interests, as they were filtered through the lens of my early interests in "culture and personality" and applied anthropology.

During my graduate studies I spent a year at the University of Helsinki, where I learned about Finnish approaches to ethnography, particularly from Kustaa Vilkuna (the leading Finnish ethnographic scholar in mid 20th century), T. I. Itkonen, Karl Nickul, Martti Linkola, and several others. In later years I learned much from contacts with Juha Pentikäinen, Matti Sarmela, Pekka Sammallahti and Jukka Pennanen.

During 1987 to 1995, I enjoyed the highly rewarding experience of working with Russ Bernard and Steve Borgatti in the National Science Foundation "summer methods camp." That was also the period during which the availability of increasingly powerful portable computers, plus Steve Borgatti's "Anthropac" software for data analysis, transformed our approaches to ethnographic field research. My grasp of the quantitative side of the "qualitative-quantitative mix" was greatly enhanced in the course of those interactions. I am much indebted to Russ Bernard and Steve Borgatti, as well as some of their colleagues, for the new knowledge I gained from those intensive sessions.

My views and understanding of ethnographic research have benefitted greatly from the work and writings of university graduate students over the past fifty years. Their various field work projects, theses, and later writing make up an impressive library of field data plus methodological innovations. The list of those former students is very long, and so I can only mention a sample from the larger enumeration: Stephen and Jay Schensul (who have written an impressive set of volumes entitled *Ethnographer's Toolkit*), John Poggie, Mike Robbins, Bill Dressler; Kathleen DeWalt, Bill DeWalt, Peggy Bentley, Jeff Backstrand, Robert Maxwell, Joel Gittelsohn, Lauren Blum, Bette Gebrian, Mary Gannotti, Trisha Hudelson, Jan Hogle, Kevin O'Reilly, Zibin Guo, Ruwani Jayewardene, Merrill Eisenberg, Peter Guarnaccia, Farhat Sultana, Irene Glasser, John Lozier, Amarasiri deSilva, Robin Devin, and Joyce Millen. I am much indebted to all of these hardworking former students for their contributions to our collective "library of ethnographic research."

In recent times I have had rewarding interactions with many applied researchers in South Asia. These contacts, from 1990 to the present (2012), have introduced me to a rich array of ethnographic projects and researchers. My role has been to provide training and technical assistance, as well as guidance in writing up the complex materials from diverse projects in reproductive health, HIV/AIDS programs, self-help groups, and other topics. I am deeply indebted to the many different research teams, individuals, and organizations with whom I had these experiences. The following several paragraphs present an incomplete listing that gives at least a partial expression of this exciting applied ethnography.

In Nepal I had extensive contacts with the Family Health International (FHI) programs of HIV/AIDS control, directed by the late James L. Ross. Also, I enjoyed many activities with researchers from CREHPA (Center for Research on Environment, Health and Population Activities), particularly Anand Tamang and Mahesh Puri, along with their excellent field ethnographers. Several of my training and technical assistance assignments were in Pakistan, during which the contacts with Dr. Fariyal Fikree and her researchers at Aga Khan University Medical College were particularly rewarding.

My many contacts with researchers in Bangladesh were mainly with the International Centre for Diarrhoeal Disease Research, Bangladesh

(ICDDR,B), the Bangladesh Rural Development Committee (BRAC), and the Population Council. I owe many thanks to A. M. R. Chowdhury (BRAC), Lazeena Muna, Papreen Nahar, Abbas Bhuiya, Ruchira Tabassum Naved (these four at ICDDR,B), and Nurul Alam (Jahangirnagar University). There were many others who contributed to our methodology discussions in Bangladesh. In Sri Lanka I had very interesting and rewarding contacts with Dr. Herbert Aponso, Amarasiri deSilva, Tudor Silva, and several of their colleagues.

Training and technical assistance activities in India, however, constitute by far the largest and most diverse part of my years of work in South Asia. It started with the program "Building Social Science Research Capacity for Women's Reproductive Health in India," funded by the Ford Foundation (India). During the decade of the 1990s, our technical assistance teams worked with a wide range of researchers and research organizations. We are all greatly indebted to Dr. Saroj Pachauri for initiating this wide-ranging training and development activity. Also at the Ford Foundation, the late Michael Koenig played a key role in coordinating the workshops and technical assistance activities. Our "technical assistance team" consisted of Margaret (Peggy) Bentley, Joel Gittelsohn, Moni Nag and me, but we relied on assistance from many Indian scholars. Dr. Saroj has continued her key role in promoting the technical assistance from her position as director of the Population Council in Delhi. I must also express my gratitude for the contributions of many other creative workers in the Population Council who have enriched our understanding of ethnographic field research. I am especially indebted to M. E. Khan, Shireen Jejeebhoy, and Niranjan Saggurti, but there is a long list of others in the Population Council research teams who have also had a part in building new lines of ethnographic work.

The many other persons and organizations in India to whom I want to express my gratitude include: Ravi K. Verma, currently head of the International Center for Research on Women (ICRW) in Delhi; Shalini Bharat and Shubhada Maitra at the Tata Institute for Social Sciences (Mumbai); R. K. Mutatkar, president of The Maharashtra Association of Anthropological Sciences (Pune); Drs. Sharad and Kirti Iyengar, founders of Action Research and Training for Health (ARTH) in Udaipur, Rajasthan; Dileep Mavalankar, Public Systems Group, Indian Institute of Management, Ahmedabad, Gujarat; Renu Khanna, SAHAJ, Society for Health Alternatives, Gujarat; Pallavi Patel, Centre for Health, Education, Training and Nutrition Awareness (CHETNA), Ahmedabad, Gujarat; Rani and Abhay Bang, Society for Education, Action and Research in Community Health (SEARCH), Gadchiroli, Maharashtra; Armin Jamshedji, Family Planning Association of India (FPAI), Mumbai; Dr. Vinay Kulkarni, director of Amrita Clinic, Pune; Jayashree Ramakrishna, National Institute of Mental Health and Neurosciences (NIMHANS), Bangalore; Akhila Vasan, freelance researcher; Annie George, free-lance researcher; Rajendra Singh, ICRW Mumbai; Archana Joshi, director, Deepak Foundation, Vadodhara, Gujarat; Aruna Lakhani, formerly director, Deepak Foundation, Vadodhara, Gujarat; Dr. Vikram Patel, co-founder of SANGATH (NGO), Goa, and faculty member at London School of Hygiene and Tropical Medicine; Gracy Andrew, SANGATH, Goa; Dr. Abraham Peedicayil, Christian Medical College, Vellore, Tamil Nadu; Braj Das, Asian Institute for Marketing Studies (AIMS), Bhubaneshwar, Odissa; Dr. K. A. Narayan, Jawaharlal Institute for Postgraduate Medical Education and Research (JIPMER), Pondicherry; Asha Kilaru, Belaku Trust, Bangalore; Dr. Geeta Sodhi, director of Swasthya (NGO), Delhi; T. Narayan, formerly program manager of VIMUKTHI (community-based organization of sex workers), Bellary, Karnataka; Shagufa Kapadia, Director, Women's Studies Research Center, Maharaja Sayajirao University of Baroda , Gujarat; C. K. George, director, The Institute of Health Systems, Hyderabad, Andhra Pradesh.

Among the many field ethnographers in India, Lakshmi Ramachandar has been the stellar performer that I have relied on as a role model for ethnographic research. From her extensive experience in field research I have learned many subtle features about the conduct of interviewing and other data gathering. To me it is very impressive that she can carry out in-depth interviews in four different languages. I owe a great debt of gratitude to her for sharing many field work insights (and interview transcripts) with me.

Many researchers from outside South Asia have contributed to the development of applied ethnographic work in the region. I want to express my personal indebtedness to Dr. Jose Martines of WHO; John Cleland of the London School of Hygiene and Tropical Medicine; Martine Collumbien, from that same UK institution; and Dr. Sarah Hawkes, Institute of Global Health, University College London—all of whom have made important contributions to ethnographic research in South Asia. I must also express my appreciation and thanks to Robert Chambers, Institute of Development Studies (UK), whose concepts of participatory rural appraisal have influenced many of the ideas I present in this book.

In writing this book I have received much encouragement and technical help from my daughter, Dunja Pelto, who did much of the first round of copyediting and created all the sketches. Technical formatting of the text was done by Ragnar Müller-Wille, and I received much moral support and technical assistance from my long-time friends Linna Müller-Wille and Ludger Müller-Wille. Gretel Pelto contributed important technical information about her recent research. I extend my sincere thanks to this highly supportive and competent "team."

The players at Left Coast Press, Inc. have also been highly supportive and technically responsible. Many thanks to Janice M. Morse, Jennifer Collier, Ryan Harris, Louise Bell, and Mitch Allen.

Introduction to Ethnographic Research

This book presents concrete examples of practical ethnographic research and provides guidelines for using this type of research in intervention programs relating to health, community development, education, agriculture, and other applied topics. The data-gathering methods I describe should be useful to researchers from various disciplines, including anthropology, education, epidemiology, geography, nursing, psychology, public health, sociology, marketing and others. It is also intended that the explanations of ethnographic data-gathering methods should be useful for non-academic applied research organizations in developing countries. Although the focus on methods in this book is primarily "non-academic," all of the basic techniques presented here are also widely used in academic studies, including that centrally important genre—master's and doctoral dissertation research.

ETHNOGRAPHY: WHAT IS IT?

The common definition of ethnography in earlier times was simply: Ethnography is the branch of anthropology that deals with the systematic description of specific human cultures. That definition reflected a bygone era in the social sciences. There was, indeed, a time when the word ethnography was found mainly in anthropology, and most cultural anthropologists would say that they did ethnographic research. However, research of exactly the same type was also well established among many sociologists, notably the Chicago School, beginning in the 1920s, although they didn't use the label ethnography very much for their research paradigm. In European countries there were many researchers who referred to themselves as folklorists, folk culture researchers, and

Pertti Pelto, "Introduction to Ethnographic Research," in *Applied Ethnography: Guidelines for Field Research*, pp. 21-42. © 2013 Left Coast Press, Inc. All rights reserved.

various other labels, but much of their research could easily be considered ethnography.

On the other hand, the term ethnography has been in use in European academic circles at least since the middle of the 19th century. One of the very earliest ethnographers in Finland, Mathias A. Castren, gave the following definition:

> [Ethnography] is a new name for an old thing. It means the scientific study of the religion, society, customs, way of life, habitations, of different peoples, in a word, everything that belongs to their inner and outer life. Ethnography could be regarded as a part of cultural history, but not all nations possess a history in the textual sense; instead, their history consists of ethnography. (Castren 1857: 8; quoted in Niiranen 1992: 23)

I am quoting Castren here, because the case can be made that he was the first "real ethnographic field researcher." The scope of Castren's ethnographic field work in Siberia is given in the following excerpt from a bulletin of the Russian Academy of Sciences at the time of his field research:

> The Academy's wish is that Mr. Castren has as his main object the study of languages and major dialects of all the peoples roaming over the above mentioned territories [southern part of Yenisei Province].... Mr. Castren will pay attention to the oral traditions and legends of those peoples....
> His long contacts with the aboriginal peoples will make it perfectly easy for him to study their physical constitution, daily life, clothes, rites, rituals and customs, standard of education and their opinions about faith as well as everything that makes it possible to describe these peoples and all their specific features. (Russian Academy of Sciences, quoted in Sokolova 1992: 11)

Castren carried out four years of field work in Siberia (1845 to 1849), in accordance with the instructions from the Russian Academy, and collected a wide range of linguistic data from a number of different tribal groups, as well as folk songs, ethnic and geographical names, and other ethnographic data.

There were other "heroes of ethnographic research" in the 19th century, in many lands, but I will leave those histories for someone else. For example, H.R. Bernard (2011) commented that the 19th century sociologist, Beatrice Webb, was doing qualitative ethnography, including participant observation and informant interviewing, in the 1880s.

W. P. Handwerker provided a useful definition of ethnography in *Quick Ethnography*: "Ethnography, as I use the word, consists of the processes and products of research that document what people know, feel, and do in a way that situates the phenomena at specific points in time in the history of individual lives, including pertinent global events and processes" (Handwerker 2001: 7).

That definition gives us the following features:

- Ethnography is not confined to people's idea systems (knowledge, mores, values, emotions) but also includes documentation of behaviors, events, and actions.

- In Handwerker's theoretical orientation, "culture" (knowledge, systems of ideas and beliefs, etc.) is first of all a system of properties "in the history of individual lives." To me, that means that he considers individual, unique mental patterns to be culture—personal culture.

- "Ethnography" refers to the process of doing research, but the word is also used to refer to the products of research, as in "an ethnography of the Andaman Islanders." The word is often used as a subtitle, as in Ogbu (1974) *The Next Generation: An Ethnography of Education in an Urban Neighborhood.*

- Ethnography does not "belong" solely to anthropologists, but is found in a wide range of disciplines.

Concerning "ethnography as product," LeCompte and Preissle noted that "Ethnographies re-create for the reader the shared beliefs, practices, artifacts, folk knowledge, and behaviors of some group of people" (LeCompte and Preissle 1993: 2–3).

In recent decades, the word ethnography has spread throughout many areas of sociology—studies focused on schooling and education, various sectors in health care and nursing, marketing research, and urban geography—as well as to a number of other disciplines.

ETHNOGRAPHY IN EDUCATION RESEARCH

The word and methodology of ethnography found a comfortable home in the field of education many decades ago. In 1982, G. Spindler put together a collection of papers entitled "Doing the Ethnography of Schooling," in which his first sentence refers to the "meteoric rise in the past decade..." [of ethnographic research in education]. Margaret LeCompte and Judith Preissle produced a widely used textbook, *Ethnography and Qualitative Design in Educational Research*, in 1984 (second edition in 1993). Also, together with W. I. Millroy, they produced *The Handbook of*

Qualitative Research in Education (1992). These works show that ethnography has deep and impressive roots in education. They pointed out that in 1913 M. Montessori wrote a book called *Pedagogical Anthropology*, which discussed the importance of anthropological (ethnographic) methods and theory for understanding educational processes, including the training of teachers (LeCompte and Preissle 1993: 10).

A large number of publications feature ethnographic research in the field of education. Here is the statement of the journal *Ethnography and Education*, as found on its website:

> *Ethnography and Education* is an international, peer-reviewed journal that publishes articles illuminating educational practices through empirical methodologies, which prioritize the experiences and perspectives of those involved. The journal is open to a wide range of ethnographic research that emanates from the perspectives of sociology, linguistics, history, psychology and general educational studies as well as anthropology. The journal's priority is to support ethnographic research that involves long-term engagement with those studied in order to understand their cultures; uses multiple methods of generating data, and recognizes the centrality of the researcher in the research process. (Ethnography and Education 2012)

ETHNOGRAPHY IN COMMUNITY HEALTH, NURSING, AND OTHER HEALTH FIELDS

Anthropologists were undoubtedly among the first to carry out ethnographic research in aspects of health and illness, beginning with descriptive studies of traditional beliefs and practices of healing and healers in various traditional societies. Around the middle of the 20th century, a number of anthropologists were doing research in health and nutrition issues, including applied projects. One of the first collections of these studies, put together by Benjamin Paul in 1955, is *Health, Culture and Community*. Included are descriptions of people's reactions and behaviors in a cholera epidemic in China, diphtheria immunization in a Thai population, a nutrition research program in Guatemala, and several other informative applied studies. This collection is interesting because, among the 16 papers, only two or three present any quantitative data. This reflects the strongly qualitative approach of ethnographic research methods in the first half of the 20th century. Within a few years after that book appeared, medical anthropology became a rapidly growing sub-discipline. Today, research articles in medical anthropology are found in many research journals, and include large numbers of studies based on mixed qualitative and quantitative data gathering, often including complex statistical analysis.

In the mid-20th century, anthropologists were turning their attention to "peasant societies" in India, Mexico, South America, the Caribbean and other areas. Many of the "new style" studies involved research on "pluralistic health care," which examined people's patterns of resort to combinations of traditional treatments and "modern" allopathic medicines and practitioners.

During the 1950s, Alan Beals made three field trips to south India, where he carried out ethnographic research that included in-depth study of villagers' lists of illnesses, their explanations concerning treatments, available health practitioners, and treatment-seeking behaviors. He found that there was a wide range of different traditional beliefs and practices concerning treatment of illness, and that very few people believed it was useful to seek "modern medicines," partly because of the costs, including transportation costs (Beals [1976] 1998).

James Young conducted a particularly interesting study of treatment decision-making among Mexican families in the 1970s, in a small town (Pichataro) in the west-central state of Michoacan (Young 1981). During the year of field work, he and his wife collected 323 illness episodes, in which he identified the range of different treatment possibilities as recognized by the individual families, and collected information concerning people's criteria and motives for their choices of health care providers. The study showed that the available sources of treatment were:

- self-treatment (home remedies and "modern medicines");
- traditional curers (*curanderas*), who were almost all older women using mainly herbal remedies;
- unqualified practitioners of "modern" medicine, referred to as *practicantes*; and
- a small number of trained medical doctors, available at the city of Patzcuaro, located about one hour's bus ride from Pichataro.

Young used a number of structured qualitative research tools, including paired comparisons, hypothetical scenarios, and rank ordering, in order to examine the people's choices of providers and treatment-seeking patterns.

As a "typical anthropological study," Young's work took a full year and resulted in the publication of a widely cited book. It should be noted, however, that the main data-gathering tools of the study could be trimmed down considerably for applied purposes. Thus, a useful assessment of treatment-seeking, decision-making processes could be achieved in a much shorter time period, if needed for planning an intervention program.

Ethnography in Nursing Research

In contrast to the long-time commitment to qualitative ethnographic study of health care in anthropology, the nursing profession in the mid 20th century experienced considerable conflict and confusion about basic orientations to research methods. Leininger and McFarland commented that researchers in nursing "...*prior to 1965 were relying heavily on quantitative research methods as the only means for 'scientific' knowledge and methods acceptable to science, medicine and nursing as a discipline*" (Leininger and McFarland 2002: 75 emphasis in original). The nursing profession was developing rapidly in that time, but it was not primarily oriented to research. Nursing was seen as a pragmatic profession: training people to do effective health care in hospitals, clinics, and community health programs.

In the 1960s, United States government policymakers increasingly realized the importance of research in the field of nursing practices and related health areas. They recognized the need to support nurses to take doctoral degrees in research disciplines outside of nursing. The program of Nurse Scientist Training Grants (1962) and the Nurse Training Act (1964) offered fellowships for nursing students to gain advanced degrees for research purposes. While many of the students in nursing programs chose to go into supposedly more scientific studies in biology, physiology, and other "hard sciences," some of them opted for social sciences—sociology and anthropology. That choice led to the creation of an active group of nursing researchers who developed ethnographic research approaches for addressing issues in health care.

Among those early pioneers, M. Leininger carried out research in a remote area in New Guinea in the 1960s, in which she developed her theoretical approaches for "transcultural nursing," which focused on qualitative methods of data gathering. Other key phrases in her theoretical writings include "ethnonursing," "culturally congruent care," and "culture care theory." Leininger's *Qualitative Research Methods in Nursing* (1985) was among the first major publications devoted to describing ethnographic approaches for nursing research. During that seminal period, a number of other individuals, partly influenced by their studies in anthropology, also contributed to the growth of what has become a multi-faceted field of ethnographic research by nursing professionals.

Some of these nurse-researchers, including Leininger, have argued that qualitative field research should not be mixed with quantitative methods. "Still today some nurse researchers and others are mixing and using both qualitative and quantitative methods.... Such practices seriously violate the integrity and philosophical purpose of each paradigm" (Leininger and McFarland 2002: 87).

J. Morse has written that "We owe a tremendous debt to this cadre of nurses who fought for the introduction of qualitative research into nursing. Madeleine Leininger, Margareta Kay, Eleanor Bowen, Pam Brink, Noel Chrisman, and Melanie Dreher prepared course outlines, and taught the first courses. They monitored journal editors, insisting on fair reviews by qualified reviewers" (Morse 2013).

The struggles for increased acceptance of qualitative ethnographic research in nursing led to the founding of new publication channels, particularly journals more friendly to ethnographic research papers. In 1979, the *Western Journal of Nursing Research* began publication, with Pamela Brink as editor, a role she continued for more than two decades. This publication accepts research from diverse methodological orientations—phenomenology, historiography, grounded theory, quasi-experimental design, controlled experiments, and others. In 1991, another important ethnography-oriented journal, *Qualitative Health Research*, was initiated; it is currently edited by J. Morse. Of course, there are now many journals in the field of nursing research, publishing a wide array of quantitative and qualitative studies.

Many of the ethnography-oriented researchers in nursing have carried out studies in non-Western societies, thus broadening the scope and theoretical understanding of health issues and treatment styles in widely different cultural settings. Brink studied health care issues among the Northern Paiute Native Americans and carried out ethnographic field research in the Annang ethnic group in the Cross River area of Nigeria. Her paper entitled "Value Orientations as an Assessment Tool in Cultural Diversity" (Brink 1984) presents interesting data about cultural ideas among the Annang people, as assessed with a research instrument designed by F. Kluckhohn in the 1950s. That study is an interesting blend of qualitative and quantitative research methods, as it includes the statistical analysis, for example, of the Annang people's preference for "collateral relations" rather than "individualism" in interpersonal relations, along with other components of their value orientations. Brink commented that "Health care givers should self-administer the schedule prior to administering it to patients in order to discover their own value profile to contrast it with that of the patient under care" (p. 202).

J. Morse and P. A. Field published an overview of qualitative approaches in nursing research in 1985, with a revised edition in 1996. In the preface to the second edition, they commented as follows on the widespread acceptance of qualitative research methods in the last two decades of the 20th century:

> While in some disciplines, such as anthropology, qualitative methods have always been the norm, other disciplines have been dominated by quantitative methodologists. In quantitatively oriented disciplines or departments, qualitative researchers felt alone and stigmatized. While there may still be enclaves of quantitative researchers, the most significant change is that qualitative methods have gained legitimacy, are now fundable by grant agencies, and publishable in many journals. (Morse and Field, 1996: preface)

More recently, Morse has put forth the argument that qualitative health research is a separate, distinct discipline, an argument based partly on the strength of large numbers of research articles submitted to the journal carrying that name. She states, "In this book, I make the case that qualitative health research is a discipline in its own right, with unique methods, subject matter, concepts and theories, practices, interventions, and standards of evidence" (Morse 2012: 13). There are now dozens of journals in various branches of community health and related fields that accept qualitative ethnographic articles, as well as studies with various mixtures of qualitative and quantitative research. However, *Qualitative Health Research* stands out as the exemplar of the new discipline (or sub-discipline) that Morse has highlighted.

Concerning the importance of ethnography in nursing research, Morse and Field wrote, "Ethnography is a means of gaining access to the health beliefs and practices of a culture and allows the observer to view phenomena in the context in which it occurs...." For an example, they wrote, "Researchers might ask 'What is it like for a person to live in a nursing home?' The researcher wants to find out whether a person can actually shape his or her life in a nursing home, and how they cope..." (Morse and Field 1996: 21).

Although it appears that research reports concerning health and illness appearing in the news media are predominantly from large-scale, multi-site quantitative studies, it is clear that ethnographic research in health care issues is a broad and expanding arena, with extensive contributions from nurse-researchers, along with the wide range of other social scientists.

ETHNOGRAPHY IN MARKETING RESEARCH

It is interesting to note that there is now the field of "ethnographic market research." One enterprising marketing research firm advertises:

> Welcome to Ethnographic Insight, Inc., where qualitative marketing research provides your business with the ultimate vantage point—a close-up of your company's products and services through the eyes of your consumer. (Ethnographic Insight, Inc 2011)

It appears that there has been a veritable explosion of "ethnographic research" in marketing in the first decade of the 21st century. Also, the term "ethnographic" appears to have taken on a more specialized meaning for some people in the field of marketing. The following statement gives a broad clue:

> Focus groups, anthropologists argue, set an artificial stage, while ethnographic research reaches much deeper into the social fabric. If companies understand a group's social context, they can better understand and even predict their product needs and attitudes towards products in the future. (McFarland 2001)

That statement is meant to say that "focus group discussions" are not ethnography. The same theme is evident in this piece from Asia Market Research:

> The strength of ethnographic research is in reducing the sources of error associated with more artificial and secondary qualitative methods such as focus groups. (Asia Market Research, 2012)

Several other sources carried the same message, namely that, whereas focus groups had been widely touted in marketing research in the 1980s and 1990s, there is now disillusionment with that form of data gathering, and marketing research firms are turning to methods of studying people's shopping and product-use behaviors through contacts directly in the home and other "natural settings."

An article from the Australian School of Business states that, "A key tool for the ethnographer is the video camera, along with diaries, which the researchers ask consumers to fill in.... We video record in 80% of our ethnographic work, and often leave consumers with cameras to use themselves" (Australian School of Business 2011). The article also mentions that the Australian School of Business has a new course in ethnography.

ETHNOGRAPHY: QUALITATIVE AND QUANTITATIVE

Some of the definitions one finds in social science literature equate ethnography with qualitative research methods. It is true that "traditional ethnographies" done by anthropologists (including myself), particularly in the first two-thirds of the 20th century, were largely qualitative works. By "qualitative" we mean that the data gathering generally did not include structured quantitative surveys, and statistical operations were seldom included in the data analysis. Ethnographies in earlier times consisted of extensive textual and photographic depictions of housing, material goods, economic activities, rituals, and other aspects of daily life, along with kinship terminology, illness concepts, and other beliefs and behaviors of a particular (usually non-modern) community.

Quantitative Components in Ethnographic Research

Many writers have pointed out that all ethnographies, however devoid of quantitative analysis, nonetheless contain a great many quantitative statements. All ethnographic descriptions include language such as "most of the people," "they seldom....", "quite often...", "a small minority," "much of their time is spent..." and other quantitative statements. Additionally, many ethnographic accounts have included a few actual numbers, but they have been secondary to the verbal descriptive materials.

Some social theorists have argued that the "qualitative paradigm" is both fundamentally and philosophically different from quantitative scientific research. A few researchers have gone so far as to claim that "Only quantitative research is true science." That puts Charles Darwin's *The Origin of Species*, which contains no statistical analysis, and many other important works of the 19th century in the category of "non-science." Especially in earlier times, large areas of the biological sciences and medical research, for example, were based primarily on qualitative, descriptive empirical research.

The claims for two separate and incompatible paradigms, "quantitative versus qualitative," have been largely dismissed in recent times, as more and more scientific research is seen to encompass "quantitative-qualitative integration" (Pelto and Cleland 2003; Reichardt and Cook 1979; Schensul, Schensul, and LeCompte 1999).

The sociologist Hammersley has examined the "two paradigms" issue in depth, saying:

> "Qualitative" and "quantitative" are sometimes used to represent fundamentally opposed approaches to the study of the social world, one representing the true way, the other the work of the devil.

He went on to say:

> I want to challenge the widely held idea that there are two methodologi-
> cal paradigms in social research: the quantitative and the qualitative... I
> shall argue...that the distinction between qualitative and quantitative is
> of limited use and, indeed, carries some danger. (Hammersley 1992: 159)

He is right to say that the distinction "carries some danger." The main
danger is that the characterizations of both qualitative and quantitative
research are presented as stereotypes, or caricatures, far removed from
what is actually happening in real research projects.

Here it is useful to add a note from Bernard: "Qualitative description is a kind of measurement, an integral part of the complex whole that
comprises scientific research" (Bernard, 2011: 20). In thinking more carefully about the meanings of qualitative and quantitative, it is important to
remember that all branches of science got their beginnings in the form of
descriptive, qualitative data. Some of the physical sciences—notably geology, paleontology, botany, and other areas of biology—depend to a considerable extent on qualitative descriptive data, including descriptions of
group behaviors, growth patterns, and (in geology) specific rock and soil
formations and successions.

Reichardt and Cook (1979) have critically examined the "two paradigms" argument in relation to evaluation research, and summed up
their view of the qualitative-quantitative "debates" as follows:

> There is no need to choose a research method on the basis of a tradi-
> tional paradigmatic stance. Nor is there any reason to pick between
> two polar-opposite paradigms. Thus there is no need for a dichotomy
> between the method-types and there is every reason (at least in logic)
> to use them together to satisfy the demands of evaluation research in
> the most efficacious manner possible. (Reichardt and Cook 1979: 27)

REALISM AND POSITIVISM VERSUS RELATIVISM AND INTERPRETIVISM

Closely linked to the "qualitative versus quantitative" philosophical arguments are the major issues concerning the nature of scientific knowledge and our relationships to the world of phenomena about which we
have "knowledge." In that series of philosophical arguments, the term
"positivism" has come to play a complex, often confusing role.

Some social scientists have presented intensely negative views of positivism, often adding features that "positivist researchers" do not generally include in their assumptions. H. J. Rubin and I. S. Rubin have presented one of the more extreme anti-positivist characterizations:

> Positivist social researchers look for the uniform, precise rules that organize the world, much as physicists try to do. And just as positivists in the experimental sciences do, positivists in the social sciences examine simplified models of the social world to see how a small number of variables, for instance, gender and education, interact.... A positivist model extracts simple relationships from a complex real world and frequently examines them as if time and context did not matter, and as if social life was stable rather than constantly changing.... Positivists assume that knowledge is politically and socially neutral and that such knowledge is achieved by following a precise, predetermined approach to gathering information. (Rubin and Rubin 1995: 32)

This negatively charged view of positivism ignores the considerable variations in the meaning of the term among different philosophical and scientific writers. Each point in the above statement can be found in some "positivist writings" and variously disclaimed in other descriptions and philosophies.

This is not the place to get into lengthy discourse about positivism, except to note that it is extremely difficult to live our daily lives and to carry out research projects, without making some fairly strong assumptions concerning the usefulness of our acquired knowledge, our methods for acquiring new knowledge, and our various abilities to form and use generalizations about the world around us. Bernard has discussed various meanings and permutations of positivism in relation to ethnographic research. He commented:

> The central position of positivism as a philosophy of knowledge is that experience is the foundation of knowledge. We record what we experience—what we see others do, what we hear others say, what we feel others feel. The quality of the recording, then, becomes the key to knowledge. Can we, in fact, record what others do, say and feel? Yes, of course we can. Are there pitfalls in doing so? Yes, of course there are. To some social researchers, these pitfalls are evidence of natural limits to a science of humanity; to others, like me, they are a challenge to extend the current limits by improving measurement. The fact that knowledge is tentative is something we all learn to live with. (Bernard, 2002: 17)

T. Schweizer has written a useful, brief review of the various strands and sectors of positivism and of the different, more or less "anti-positivist" philosophies that are currently found in the social and behavioral sciences (Schweizer 1998). Some of the main points to keep in mind with regard to the positivist versus anti-positivist debates include the following:

- The origins of positivism were basically an attack on metaphysical and religious explanations of human behavior and socio-cultural systems. It was not a movement constructed to maintain the political and economic status quo. Quite the opposite.

- Compared to the physical sciences (and parts of economics and psychology), anthropology and other "ethnographic social sciences" have been much less oriented to developing theory, as the aims have, much of the time, been to develop better (more useful) ethnographic descriptions.

- Compared to other branches of the sciences and humanities, ethnographically oriented social science, practically by definition, is oriented to empirical research, often with a strong element of inductive research methodology. This has resulted in a great deal of low- and middle-level theory, much of it unrecognized as such.

- Most of the theoretical generalizations in ethnographic works are probabilistic, rather than fixed, immutable "laws."

- Large parts of "theory" in ethnographic works are "theory at the local level," rather than global principles. We refer to this as "ideographic theory."

- In much of practical, applied social sciences, the goals of research are not to develop new theoretical frameworks, but rather, to use already existing theoretical principles for developing effective descriptive information needed in programmatic interventions.

Realism and Relativism

Realism is often mentioned as an essential attribute of positivist scientific philosophy, although not all "positivists" agree. Hammerley, in discussing problems of epistemology in ethnographic thinking, wrote, "... [one problem is] the doctrine of realism, by which I mean the idea that there is a reality independent of the researcher, whose nature can be known, and that the aim of research is to produce accounts that correspond to that reality.... It is a philosophical doctrine on which much ethnography is founded." Further along, he notes that "From this point of view the goal of ethnographic research is to discover and represent faithfully the true nature of social phenomena. And the superiority of ethnography is based precisely on the grounds that it is able to get closer to social reality than other methods" (Hammersley, 1992: 43–44).

A major critique of realism comes in the form of "social constructivism," according to which people's beliefs, interpretations of reality, and resulting behaviors are socially constructed, and hence are at least one step removed from any "reality." Hammersley goes on to note that the ethnographer who takes the philosophical view that "reality is socially/culturally constructed" should assume that the products of ethnographic research are also "social constructions."

J. Maxwell (2004) offers a somewhat different picture of positivism and realism. From his point of view, realism is a middle ground between positivism and constructivism. Maxwell builds his argument around the fundamental differences between "variable-oriented" and "process-oriented" analysis of ethnographic data. This is an important distinction, which all ethnographic researchers should recognize.

In the supposedly standard practice of proving causality (positivist model), there needs to be an "experiment," with an experimental group and a control group, with measurements pre- and post-experiment, and statistical analysis of the key variables about which causal relations are hypothesized. In the stereotyped definitions of "positivist science," that is the only way to "prove causation," namely, by testing a hypothesis through statistical analysis and deriving a positive theoretical generalization. Never mind that in many developments in the physical and biological sciences, the "experiment" model was not their road to knowledge.

In the developing philosophical realm of realism, there is now increasing support for the view that "Realists typically understand causality as consisting not of regularities but of real (and in principle, observable) causal mechanisms and processes, which may or may not produce regularities" (Maxwell 2004: 247). Translated into ordinary language, this means that some causal processes can be directly observed in specific events and actions—observed by researchers. In contrast, the statistical procedures for comparing experimental and control groups are not close to actually seeing and describing the "causality" in action; they deal only with the statistical regularities between presumed causes and the hypothesized (expected) outcomes. Maxwell argues that there is a growing positive awareness of the possibilities for direct observation of processes, including causality.

He notes that realism is compatible with many of the claims of postmodernists and relativists but that, "Where it differs from these is primarily in the realist ontology—a commitment to the existence of a real, although not 'objectively' knowable world—and its emphasis on causality (although a fundamentally different concept of causality than that of the positivists) as intrinsic to social science" (Maxwell 2004: 247).

I expect many researchers who call themselves positivists would accept Maxwell's portrait of "realist social science" and say that it is a branch of "modern positivism."

Again I emphasize that research groups with a job to do—"go and find out what is happening in that program" and, perhaps (more challenging), "identify the factors that led to the success in community A, compared to the failure in community B"—will not waste time pondering the meaning of "realism versus constructivism," but will consider Maxwell's arguments concerning the identification of processes through intensive data collection.

Not many social science researchers will lose sleep over the issues concerning realism. In fact, it is common now to hear researchers saying, "Of course, there is no way to prove that there is an ultimate reality out there. We can continue to carry out our daily routines and do research projects just as always. We don't have to assume there is an ultimate reality." The aims of ethnographic research, then, are to discover and represent faithfully the constructed social realities of various groups and communities in order to make better practical programs of change.

INDUCTIVE VERSUS DEDUCTIVE RESEARCH

Another dichotomy that has excited a great deal of discussion and soul-searching (and overdrawn arguments) is the contrast between inductive and deductive procedures. Some theorists in the social sciences have insisted that "true science" consists of the hypothetico-deductive process, in which hypotheses are developed from theoretical systems or models, followed by data gathering to test the hypotheses. That means that a theoretical proposition, or a theoretical "system" and specific relevant data, should be defined in advance, and data collected accordingly. The logical structure of deductive research is often portrayed in the form of simple syllogisms.

The following is an example of a hypothetico-deductive syllogism:

1. If a student is sick, then she or he will be absent from school.
2. If the student is absent, then he/she will miss the class work.
3. Students L, M, and H are sick, so they will miss their class work.

In general form, deductive research is portrayed as a "top-down" set of steps:

1. Statement of a theory (set of theoretical propositions).
2. Deducing a hypothesis from the theoretical formulation.
3. Obtaining data corresponding to the key terms or variables in the hypothesis.

Thus, in the example above, we need to get empirical data about the students who are sick: find out if they are/were absent from school and get data on whether they missed the class work.

Just as there have been theorists of methodology who claimed that only quantitative research is "true science," there are those who have insisted that only the deductive method (or the hypothetico-deductive method) produces true scientific conclusions and builds useful theory. Here again there are dangers of oversimplification and "reification" of certain principles as well as a failure to see the multiple approaches—the great varieties of research that have contributed to current scientific knowledge.

Returning for a moment to Charles Darwin's famous development of a "theory of biological evolution," it is notable that Darwin himself, and a great many other biologists and botanists in the early 19th century, spent large amounts of time in collecting and describing specimens in various environments. I think it is fair to say that, in all areas of physical, biological, and social sciences, early phases of knowledge accumulation have generally depended on a great deal of inductive discovery and description of phenomena, often with very little concern about developing theoretical systems. In the flourishing of debates about biological evolution versus the "fixity of species" in mid-19th century, Darwin, Wallace, and others were developing complex theoretical formulations that had emerged from their inductive data gathering.

Darwin's own writings point to the great amount of inductive fact collecting in his research. In 1844, his letter to Joseph Hooker included the following:

> Besides a general interest about the southern lands, I have been now ever since my return engaged in a very presumptuous work, and I know no one individual who would not say a very foolish one. I was struck with the distribution of the Galapagos organisms &ct &ct...and with the character of the American fossil mammifers....that *I determined to collect blindly every sort of fact* which could bear in any way on what are species. I have read heaps of agricultural and horticultural

books, and *I have never ceased collecting facts.* At last gleams of light have come, and I am almost convinced (quite contrary to the opinion I started with) that species are not (it is like confessing a murder) immutable. (quoted in Eldredge 2005: 58–59, emphasis added)

According to Eldredge, Darwin wrote in his autobiography that "he saw himself as working 'on true Baconian principles, and without any theory collected facts on a wholesale scale,' such that 'my mind seems to have become a kind of machine for grinding general laws out of large collections of facts" (Eldredge 2005: 55). That is the clearest exposition of an inductive research strategy we are likely to find in the writings of scientists.

INDUCTIVE RESEARCH AND GROUNDED THEORY

As noted in the statement above, the founder of inductive method was Francis Bacon (1561–1626). Inductive procedures in science are sometimes referred to as the Baconian Method. Although he was much involved in governmental duties in England, Bacon wrote a number of essays about the need for systematic investigation "of all things natural." His book, *Novum Organum* (1620), presents the main principles of the scientific method he developed.

Qualitative (ethnographic) research in sociology got a big boost in the middle of the 20th century with the advent of *The Discovery of Grounded Theory* (Glaser and Strauss 1967). The authors wrote:

> In this book we address ourselves to the…important task of how the discovery of theory from data—systematically obtained and analyzed in social research—can be furthered. We believe that the discovery of theory from data—which we call grounded theory—is a major task confronting sociology today, for, as we shall try to show, such a theory fits empirical situations, and is understandable to sociologists and laymen alike. (Glaser and Strauss 1967: 1)

The paradigm of grounded theory, especially in their original work, represented a thoroughly inductive approach to research. In the ideal form of this approach, investigator(s) should not even do a review of the literature in the topical area, and thus should have no preconceptions, no beginning assumptions, and no hypotheses whatsoever.

Various writers and researchers have pointed out that it is virtually impossible to carry out data gathering if the researchers have no "hunches," or "pre-conceived notions." Many psychologists and other researchers believe that the human brain is constructed to explore hypotheses, and to develop hunches about causal connections and related explanatory information.

Even today, there are advocates of grounded theory in various disciplines who try to maintain a fully inductive approach, and some people argue that the inductive approach is a defining characteristic of qualitative research. However, the super-inductive approach in the grounded theory literature is often totally unsuited to practical, applied research and is seldom found in the applied literature.

ABDUCTION: A COMMON FORM OF RESEARCH LOGIC IN THE SOCIAL SCIENCES

Some modern researchers argue that, especially in the social sciences, the logical paradigm of abduction is what actually happens in most research—and is productive. This paradigm was developed by Charles Peirce at the end of the 19th and beginning of the 20th century (Douven 2011).

The paradigm has the following form:

A surprising fact, C, is observed;

A likely cause, X is hypothesized, that would certainly be a cause of C.

If X were true, C would be a matter of course;

Hence, there is reason to suspect that X is true.

The following is an example from common experience:

I am surprised to find that the grass is wet this morning. It must be that there was rain during the night.

In the various discussions of abduction, the point is frequently made that the evidence might be quite weak concerning the "prior cause" and much of scientific research consists of further data gathering to get more evidence and to examine alternative explanations: "I will ask my neighbors (and check the weather reports) to find out if it rained last night." There are alternative possibilities. Douven concluded his discussion about abduction with the following: "It is remarkable that there is no reference in Peirce's writings on abduction to the notion of *best* explanation. Some satisfactory explanations might still be better than others, and there might even be a unique best one. This idea is crucial in all recent thinking about abduction" (Douven 2011).

In the best social science studies, researchers will explore a series of alternative explanations for the phenomena, even though one's first discovery of a probable cause for a "surprising finding" appears very plausible.

Much of applied ethnographic research, in relation to initiating and maintaining intervention programs or suggesting changes in social and economic policies, is a complex mixture that is best described as abductive in the sense outlined above. Applied researchers generally do not have the spare time and resources to engage in "pure inductive" processes. At the same time, most applied research is not intent on developing theory. The aim is to get information that will help improve programs of change. To an increasing extent, funding agencies are expecting that action programs will make active use of theoretical principles that have been developed in other projects. For that purpose, abductive research would appear to be ideal. In some respects, applied social sciences research resembles medical practice and some legal decision-making, particularly in the fact that "the evidence is never complete." In this view, "the crucial function of a pattern of abduction … consists in its function as a search strategy which leads us, for a given kind of scenario, in a reasonable time to a most promising explanatory conjecture which is then subject to further test" (Douven 2011).

A medical diagnosis is a typical application of abductive reasoning: Given this set of symptoms, what is the diagnosis that would best account for the patient's illness? That is largely parallel to some applied research in which there is a problem: "Why don't these students manage better marks in their academic work?" There are several possible explanations, but researchers must go out and find which ones are the best hypotheses, and (continuing abductively) look for the best solutions. Some writers have noted that cogent inductive reasoning requires that the evidence that might shed light on the subject be fairly complete, whether positive or negative; abductive reasoning is characterized by a lack of completeness in either the evidence or the explanation, or in both (Butte College 2011).

It is useful to view the concept of abductive research as the reality of much applied research. Most field research, regardless of some elegantly structured proposals and equally elegantly structured descriptions of the resulting analysis, is really a mixture of discoveries, suggesting some possible explanations, and a back-and-forth between theoretical thinking and getting more information related to the hypotheses. Pollnac and Hickman have commented on this process:

> In the…research process the next step would be one of deductive hypothesis, then inductive theory building, followed by another round of abductive hypothesis generation. (Pollnac and Hickman 1975: 29)

IDEOGRAPHIC AND NOMOTHETIC THEORY

An ideographic theory (or theoretical system) is a system of explanation and description that applies only in specific situations—perhaps only in one community or region. Nomothetic theory, on the other hand, is more generally applicable, and ideally we would like to develop theoretical systems that are "universally" applicable. As we contemplate those definitions, we are immediately struck with the likelihood that theoretical systems about human behaviors may vary from completely ideographic (unique in this one place or situation) to "applicable in many situations/locations similar to the study area" and on up to "broadly applicable to many cases or situations." Of course, we recognize that in physics and chemistry a wide range of theoretical systems are truly nomothetic. In biological sciences, on the other hand, we are likely to find many theoretical models that are "intermediate," as they apply only to a certain category of plants or animals or only in certain special environments. For example, some of the processes of developing new subspecies and varieties among the birds in the Galapagos Islands (made famous by Charles Darwin's study) could only happen in that special environment of multiple island environments.

In applied social science research, we are likely to find some important research objectives to be "very ideographic." In some cases, applied research is carried out to find out why one particular part of a specific program is outstandingly successful. One (abductive) possibility is that a highly unusual, resourceful local leader has been in charge of the program. At the same time, researchers interested in broader theory-building have identified recurring patterns in ethnographic descriptions, including "very ideographic studies," that led them to develop at least partially nomothetic models that can be applied to understand programmatic outcomes in several different places. Sometimes we refer to that as developing "mid-level theory" or "middle-range theory." For example, some middle-range theoretical models of social interactions may be applicable only in rigidly fundamentalist religious communities; other examples of middle-range theory may make sense only among nomadic peoples.

CONCERNING MIXED-METHODS RESEARCH

As I pointed out in the Preface, most applied ethnographic research nowadays is a mixture of qualitative and quantitative data gathering and analysis. In many of the ethnographic techniques described in the following chapters, the data gathering is qualitative, but quantitative procedures are important in the analysis of the resulting materials. This is particularly the case when you do the same qualitative data-gathering procedure with a sample of 25 or more informants. In many studies there are separate moments of analysis for the free list sample and the pile sorting, and then a more complex mix of qualitative and quantitative analysis with a sample of "cases." The mix is in both data gathering and various steps of analysis.

In *Mixed Method Design* (Morse and Niehaus 2009), ethnography is mentioned as one of the varieties of "mixed method" research, usually with a qualitative methodological core. The authors also note that there are many varieties of ethnographic research. In this book, my examples of individual studies will show that in modern ethnographic research there are many different patterns, many different mixtures. In particular, we need to distinguish the qualitative methods used for developing variables or collecting vocabularies that will be incorporated into the next steps of both qualitative and quantitative data gathering.

For example, you are advised to use free listing in relatively early stages of research in order to identify the contents or items in the topical areas about which you want to get more information. If your task is to understand women's use of microcredit for income-generating investments, you should collect lists of "things women invest in to get income." If you are studying successes and failures in the local schools, then one important free list might be "all the reasons why students drop out of school." You may need to collect several different kinds of lists at different stages of your research. From those lists, and related interviewing, you can go on to design more complex interviews and observations, as well as revising your research questions because of new, unexpected, information.

CONCLUSION

In my comments about positivism, realism, and constructivism I have pointed out that most of the philosophical issues concerning the "scientificness" of social science research in general are not of much concern in applied ethnographic research. Those are mostly "academic issues," and need not interfere with the practical concerns of applied, problem-solving studies.

Applied ethnography is, however, a scientific activity, and for the research to be useful, the data gathering and analysis must be as rigorous and thorough as time and resources permit. On the analysis side, I and most of my colleagues believe strongly that ethnography should make effective use of quantitative analysis wherever it can contribute to interpreting and understanding the qualitative materials.

Sometimes the ethnographic research can include some real contributions to more general theoretical models. But that is not usually the main objective in applied studies. Often the first objective is to provide descriptive information about processes and situations for making positive changes in ongoing schooling, health care, community development, reducing poverty, and other practical matters.

If your research identifies ways in which intervention programs can be improved, or "what went wrong" in some situations, that information needs to be communicated to people involved in the relevant programs. In some cases, researchers will be asked to sit down with the program people and work out some practical programmatic modifications. The chances for immediate practical application of research findings are much better if some program people have been involved directly in the research operations. That strategy in applied studies is increasingly being adopted in some research sectors.

In the following chapters I will present the more common ethnographic tools and provide examples of how they were used in some actual research situations. The examples are not necessarily the most sparkling and successful ones; in some cases, the particular research question might have been better addressed with a different data-gathering technique. My main aim is to describe as concretely as possible how these techniques are used in field research situations.

Many research groups will have access to some of the printed versions of the studies that I describe. Also, you can find many examples of these research tools on the Internet. I suggest that ethnographers who are preparing for a specific research assignment select the research tools most likely to be appropriate for their study situation. Then, in addition to the examples that I give in these chapters, you should find additional studies in which your selection of data-gathering methods have been used.

The ethnographic tools that I include in the following chapters have all been utilized in a wide variety of research situations, and have been used by researchers in many disciplines. If your research focus is, for example, in agricultural development, don't limit your exploration of research methods only to agricultural research. Most of these ethnographic techniques have wide applicability to different research topics and situations.

Finally, if any of your advisers, mentors, or funding agency experts tell you that you have to do hypothetico-deductive research, or if someone says you should do purely inductive research, tell them your model is that of abductive research strategy, which includes both deductive and inductive procedures. Then, refer them to literature containing descriptions of this widely known research paradigm.

Main Steps of Applied Ethnographic Field Research

There are a great many different forms of applied ethnographic projects. In the past two decades the diffusion of ethnographic techniques into widely varied issues, programs, and disciplines has created a truly complicated mosaic of types of studies. Nonetheless it is possible to describe main steps and pathways that we see repeated in various research projects, big and small.

This chapter begins with a "bare-bones" outline of main steps you are likely to follow in an applied ethnographic study. There will, of course, be many research projects that take a different shape, and you will face tasks that are not included in this outline. When you are ready to begin research in a new field site, you can use this set of suggestions and selectively examine chapters that are related to specific research steps and components. In exploring these chapters, particularly look for descriptions of studies that resemble the project you are just beginning. Also, contact some of your colleagues in your network, to find out if they know of particularly useful studies along these same lines.

Later in this chapter I present a review of the main ethical issues in ethnographic field research. You and your field researchers should be well informed about these issues, particularly concerning the anonymity, confidentiality, and safety of the informants and other people you work with in the research setting.

OUTLINE FOR ETHNOGRAPHIC FIELD RESEARCH

You should keep in mind that ethnographic field research is intended to be flexible and exploratory, especially in the beginning phases. In the following steps of research, I am assuming that you have developed a statement of

Pertti Pelto, "Main Steps of Applied Ethnographic Field Research," in *Applied Ethnography: Guidelines for Field Research*, pp. 43-57. © 2013 Left Coast Press, Inc. All rights reserved.

basic research aims and objectives—perhaps spelled out by the host non-government organization (NGO) at the research site, or else developed at your home base and already negotiated with the organization (or community) within whose program you will do the research.

Literature Review

Probably you did most of your literature review in the initial phases of planning and negotiating the research. In some cases, however, your research group has been invited (contracted) to carry out some stipulated research in a situation with which you are not familiar. You need to get acquainted with the main topical area and the theoretical and practical issues. In many applied projects with specific goals, your "literature search" might best be focused on information about the project region—geographical, economic, social and demographic details. Who lives in that area? What are the different languages? Religions? Ethnic groups? If your research is sponsored by, or connected to, a local organization, ask the leaders to give you their annual reports and other data about their NGO, including its aims, scope of coverage, and other details.

Making Initial Contacts

Your next step is contacting the program people, local government officials, and other key people in the research site(s). In many contemporary ethnographic projects, the research team is invited or contracted by a local action organization (NGO or government agency). Another common process is that a research group contacts an ongoing social, educational, or development program and asks for entry to conduct some research that will be useful for them. For example, in many developing countries with large-scale HIV/AIDS programs (and other internationally funded health programs), research teams are invited, or can seek out contacts with, the HIV/AIDS program headquarters. Your research team may be referred by the headquarters people to a specific local branch office of the program. That's where it all begins.

If the local branch of the program is well organized, the leaders are likely to plan an orientation meeting for you and your team. You will need to find out immediately if the local organization has field researchers or other qualified persons that you can add to your research team. In most cases you need those local researchers, because the local language—even if it is the "same as yours"—will have many dialectical peculiarities. In some projects, most of the field interviewers are recruited from the local areas. For example, as I point out in Chapter 17 (Teams and Training), in South Asia, many research groups hire some local persons for conducting interviews, and for helping the team to get acquainted with special features that are important to know about when working in that specific area.

Training the Research Team

Many of the people recruited for doing ethnographic interviewing at project sites have had little training and experience in the data-gathering methods that are described in the following chapters. The initial training should be at least five days, with plenty of role-play and practice in interviewing people from the study area. Chapter 17 provides an in-depth discussion of training. Usually the people in the local branch of the intervention program (often a local NGO) can take your team out to community sites for "practice interviewing." After spending most of the day interviewing community people, your field team should spend several hours writing up those interviews. Chapter 6 includes instructions and examples for writing up interview notes. In most projects we have found that training the field workers to write out full interview notes, and full details of their observations, is our most important task. If the "trainees" have spent most of the day in practice interviewing and then several hours in writing (expanding) their field notes, you can devote the following day to examining the products, as well as hearing feedback from the team members. That leads to revision of your interview guidelines.

In projects with short timeframes, research needs to begin after five or six days of training, but the research coordinator or director must provide close supervision, often with daily team meetings to discuss the results of interviews and observations, to insure data quality.

Social Mapping and Key Informant Interviewing

These first steps of data gathering are mainly to get acquainted with different sectors of the local communities and to get a good initial picture of the socio-cultural geography of the research area (see Chapters 4 and 5 for a thorough discussion of these steps). You should also get acquainted with the outreach workers (if any) of the local program or NGO. Usually your first interviews are with people in the NGO or other personnel of the intervention program with which you are working.

Social mapping—first with the program people and then with some groups to which they provide introductions—is now recognized as the best way to get acquainted with many features of the local community

Figure 2.1. Women making a map of all the health facilities and providers in their community. © Dunja Pelto 2013.

and region and, at the same time, becoming acquainted with persons who may be good key informants (see Figure 2.1).

If your research is about agricultural practices, try to meet with some farmers. If it is about schools and education, get some parents of students, and also groups of students, to do some social mapping and describing.

In addition to social mapping, you and your team should tour the area (see Figure 2.2). Transect walks (see Chapter 4) are a good learning process if the area is small. If your study area is large, then touring and observing will require a vehicle.

First-Round Data Gathering

First-round data gathering is exploratory, preparing for a more focused set of operations later on. This information about the different kinds of people in various neighborhoods, hamlets and villages gives you a framework for planning sampling strategies.

There are now many ethnographic projects (e.g., the Focused Ethnographic Studies described in Chapter 16) in which the first round of data

Figure 2.2. Researchers sometimes stroll around the study area, to get a "feel of the place." © Dunja Pelto 2013.

gathering is intended to get the vocabulary, geography and socio-cultural details needed for planning specific steps and ethnographic tools that will help to answer the questions detailed in your research plan. At that point, you and your team will put together the sampling design and specific interviewing guidelines for the next, more advanced part of the study. Often the second phase of your study includes some structured qualitative techniques, such as sorting cards for categorizing and rating qualities, paired comparisons and other techniques (see Chapters 10 and 11 for examples of those techniques).

Developing your Start List

The "start list" of topics/labels is used for coding text data from interviews and other written materials. In some cases, research groups come to the field with a prepared list of codes for analysis of text data. However, such code lists should always be modified to include locally relevant features that emerge in the early stages of the research. (Coding of text materials is discussed in Chapter 12.)

Revising your Conceptual Models and Objectives

Early in the exploratory phase, you and your team should be revising some of your conceptual models and objectives, based on analysis of the new information obtained in the preliminary phases of work. In many applied projects, the local action organization will have given you a mandate for a specific focus of study. However, those specific mandates often encounter unexpected complexities that raise new issues, and perhaps require that the research questions need to be revised.

For example, suppose you have been invited to study the feeding practices of young children 12 to 24 months of age. The NGO asks you to find out what are all the weaning foods and complementary foods given to that specific age group, including costs and sources of supply. As you and your team explore this research topic, you find that in this set of communities there are many different "feeders"—because the mothers are often involved in selling in the marketplace or out doing agricultural work. Feeding the small children is done by other children, by grandparents, and sometimes household males.

You may need to meet with the NGO leaders and discuss with them about expanding and modifying the data-gathering plans to make full use of this new information.

Writing Preliminary Descriptions and Conceptual Frameworks

It should now be clear that data analysis in ethnographic work begins at the beginning of data-gathering. Also, it is a good idea for researchers to begin writing descriptive materials about the first steps of the research, as well as about new concepts and information that emerged in the first, exploratory phases of the project.

Developing Sampling Strategies for the Next Phases of Data Gathering

Sampling strategies in ethnographic research take many shapes—and sampling is not just one operation. Often there are several different "samplings" for different research components. In your social mapping operations (described earlier in this section) you should have already "sampled" from different sectors of the research area. In many studies there are multiple sites in which you will need to have some sampling strategy. (Sampling strategies are discussed in Chapter 8.)

Protocols and Approaches for Data Collecting

Ethnographic research needs carefully designed protocols and approaches for the collection of "case interviews" or "structured qualitative observations" or other systematic collection of qualitative data. Depending on your overall applied objectives, you may need to get "samples" of adoption of home gardens, treatment seeking for children's illness, income-generating projects of rural women, or persons in innovative school programs. In many projects there are several different samples.

Pilot-Testing your Interview Instrument

You should always pilot-test your interview instruments with a small number of cases to check to see that the language of open-ended questions is clear and suited to the local cultural vocabulary. Also, the pilot-testing will show whether your interview team members fully understand the goals of the data-gathering. Check to see that the interviewers are doing thorough probing in connection with the informants' responses.

Quantitative Data

Possibly the program people will expect you to do at least a modest quantitative survey. They may insist that you put more numbers on the main patterns and variations that you found in your qualitative interviews and observations. On the other hand, if you have a substantial sample of in-depth case interviews (at least 40 or 50 cases) then you can do considerable quantitative analysis with those materials.

Larger Quantitative Surveys

If you must do a larger quantitative survey, use the information from your qualitative data gathering to select appropriate language and questions for the survey instrument. Your aim will be to get more credible numerical descriptions and testing of specific hypotheses about patterns of behaviors in the wider population of the area.

Combining Quantitative Results with Qualitative Information

Analyze the quantitative results to see how they "fit" with the qualitative information and previous ideas concerning the topics of interest. Write up a draft of the quantitative data, and insert descriptive examples from qualitative materials.

Box 2.1. A Note on Quantitative Research

In this book concerning ethnographic methods, I am not presenting guidelines or examples for quantitative survey research. There are plenty of books and manuals concerning various forms of survey research, and the statistical approaches for quantitative analysis. The combination of ethnographic research with quantitative surveys is now a common practice. In all cases it is recommended that at least part of the ethnographic research should come first in order to develop the vocabulary and fine-tune the questions for more effective surveys. Also, ethnographic research is often recommended for getting data about special populations and ethnic groups in the area for use in developing effective sampling strategies.

Collecting Additional Qualitative Data

If time and resources permit, after your quantitative survey, collect more qualitative data from key informants, observations, and "selected cases" in order to get explanations for some of the quantitative results. Then, revise and expand your write up of the basic descriptive materials and conceptual framework.

Developing Policy and Program Recommendations

For any applied program, the researchers should be developing "policy and program recommendations." Those products should be developed through joint meetings with the program people.

Writing the Report and Papers for Publication

Continue writing the report and perhaps papers for publication, interrelating the qualitative and quantitative materials and identifying important statistical and qualitative results that relate to the programmatic recommendations.

POSSIBLE FEATURES OF A BIGGER PROJECT

In some cases a "bigger project" means only that you have more sites in which you will be carrying out the same ethnographic steps. That will give you a chance to use the lessons learned in the first site and improve the products of the research, as you go on to those additional locations.

It may be that you must expand to additional schools or more rural health centers, or perhaps you are finding out what works and what doesn't work in women's income-generating projects, so you must go to more self-help groups. If all the different sites are in the same governmental and cultural area (and they speak the same language), you may be able to keep your original research team members, so the training requirements are fewer when you move to new sites. In many developing country situations, however, you are likely to need to recruit fresh trainees in at least some of the new research locations.

Another possibility is that your task of formative research is to explore the feasibility of a suggested intervention program and to develop guidelines for a complex multi-partner project. In some projects, the sponsors want to include many different stakeholders—several different kinds of organizations in a public-private partnership (PPP). Partners in the project might include government personnel at local and district levels, government health center personnel, private health practitioners, NGOs, and community-based organizations such as women's groups.

Faced with that sort of challenge, you might consider that the various categories of "partners" are somewhat like ethnic groups, as each category has a distinct vocabulary and distinct organizational norms, and that they have different types and sources of economic and political influence. Some of the steps and guidelines above can be modified for use in this complex PPP situation, but you will have to invent some new ways of keeping up communications among the different partners, and much more of your research structure will be devoted to administrative and communications activities.

ADDITIONAL SUGGESTIONS AND RESOURCES

If your project deals with health issues, I recommend that you get a copy of *Rapid Assessment Procedures (RAP): Ethnographic Methods to Investigate Women's Health* (Gittelsohn et al. 1998). The data-gathering suggestions in that manual can be adapted to a wide range of different health issues. For example, this RAP manual has been utilized in nutrition programs and HIV/AIDS prevention research. The manual is especially useful because it includes a large number of data-recording forms and protocols that you can adapt for your specific research needs. For many types of structured ethnographic methods it is advisable to use ready-made data formats, such as those presented in the manual. The Gittelsohn et al. manual (1998) is available online at http://archive.unu.edu/unupress/food2/UIN01E/UIN01E00.HTM.

The data-recording forms in the Gittelsohn RAP manual can be adapted to many other research topics, if you are using some of the same ethnographic methods as detailed in that book. There are a great many such practical manuals and guidelines. You can also find many useful resources in the Internet.

Most of the research examples included in this book can be regarded as mixed-method studies. As I noted in Chapter 1, "mixed methods" is a complex subject. Basically it deals with issues and strategies for interrelating qualitative and quantitative data gathering and analysis. In many studies the basic data-gathering operations are done using qualitative techniques. The qualitative methods are carried out with a sufficiently large sample that you can do some numerical analysis of the resulting data.

I also recommend S. C. Weller and A. K. Romney's *Systematic Data Collection* (1998), which is Volume 10 in a series entitled *Qualitative Research Methods*. This little handbook has excellent, easy to follow instructions for free-listing, pile-sorting, paired comparisons, and many other structured qualitative tools (see research examples in Chapters 10 and 11).

ETHICAL ISSUES IN FIELD RESEARCH: BASIC GUIDELINES

Although this chapter is primarily devoted to the main practical steps in field research, it is essential that persons in charge of research operations and field researchers at all levels understand the basic standards for ethical conduct of research. The main points about ethical issues should be incorporated in training researchers, including the training of teams recruited in the individual field sites.

Ethical issues in field work have become much more complex and important in the 21st century. Now, in the era of widespread use of electronic communications technology, social networking systems, worldwide transmission of photos, videos, and other communications in many different channels, the possibilities for serious distortion and misuse of research data are greatly magnified. Even honest, well-intended, positive information can be distorted and cause harm to individuals and groups in study populations.

In the current era, most applied ethnographic research must be reviewed by some kind of institutional review board (IRB) before data gathering can begin. Indeed, it is an ethical requirement that your intended research be subject to a thorough review before the inception of field work. In many cases, the planned research is reviewed by the IRB of the principal investigator's institutional or organizational "home base," and quite often another review is required in the realm of the study community. As described in some of the cases in the following chapter, reviews and permissions for carrying out the research may be required by several different organizations and political entities in the project area.

GUIDELINE 1

The main principle concerning ethical practices in ethnographic research is to protect the privacy, anonymity, confidentiality and safety of your informants and all the information you get from them. That means that researchers must not disclose the names or identities of individuals (informants and others), and they must insure that their research data—interview notes, audio recordings, photographs, and all other materials—cannot fall into the hands of persons who might misuse that information.

GUIDELINE 2

Researchers should be aware that their field notes, audio recorded materials, photographs and other materials can be subpoenaed by legal authorities in most countries (including the United States). Also, in many cases all of the field data belong to the sponsoring organization, and therefore can be requested by them. This means that ethnographic researchers should examine carefully the written terms of contract research they undertake for government agencies, NGOs, or other entities. Researchers based in academic institutions should note that many universities now stipulate that all research data and related materials collected by university researchers belong to the university and can be requested by university authorities. (DeWalt and DeWalt 2010: 177)

In order to protect against the possibility that your data might be improperly used by others, including legal authorities, I strongly recommend that no names or identities of individuals be retained in field notes, audio recordings, and other raw materials. Pseudonyms or codes should be used in place of real names or identities, and your list linking names or identities to their codes must be in a separate file, kept in a safe place.

Whenever a research team is involved in study of illegal or sensitive, socially disapproved activities, a good precautionary measure is to avoid all audio-recording of interviews and other information and to use only pseudonyms for persons, organizations, and places in the field notes. In Chapter 6 I have quoted from an ethnographer who reports these kinds of precautions in her research on illegal abortions.

GUIDELINE 3

The competence of the research design and researchers is another important element in ethical research guidelines. Because field research inevitably invades and, to some extent, disrupts the daily lives of the people in study populations, it is unethical if such invasion of people's private lives is done in an incompetent fashion, resulting in questionable and/or useless information. To be ethical, the research should be sound, be well carried-out, and produce valuable information. DeWalt and DeWalt (2010: 211–212) in their discussion of ethnographic field research note that the ethical guidelines of major professional organizations of the social sciences, such as the American Anthropological Association and the American Sociological Association, emphasize the importance of competence in the research. That means that researchers should have sufficient prior training, research plans should be carefully designed in order to insure effective data gathering, and there should be adequate supervision of field researchers, particularly any data gatherers who may have had less exposure to research training.

This last point deserves special attention, as we have encountered many research projects, especially in multi-cultural, multi-language regions, in which data-gatherers were recruited on the basis of their proficiency in local languages. In some cases, these local-based researchers had had little social science research training or experience and needed strong supervisory guidance.

GUIDELINE 4

The principle of informed consent is another cornerstone of ethical field research. This means that, for all semi-structured and structured interviews and direct observations, the informants and/or other participants should receive an explanation of the nature and purposes of the research, and they should be assured that participation is voluntary and they can refuse to participate. They should also understand that during interviews they can refuse to answer any specific questions, if they wish.

The best way to handle informed consent is to have a written form, in the local language, which is read and explained to the person. The statement describes the purposes of the research, and assures her/him of anonymity, confidentiality, and voluntariness of the participation. After reading and explaining the statement, the researcher asks if the individual consents to the interview or structured observation, or other data-gathering.

Some research sponsors (and IRBs) require researchers to ask each informant/participant to sign a written consent form. However, in communities where there are many illiterate people, such signing (or thumb printing) is itself ethically questionable, and verbal consent is sufficient.

Researchers should insure that people in the research communities are aware that they (research team) are gathering data, observing activities of people, and will be reporting about the community (without naming the community) in the ensuing report writing.

GUIDELINE 5

At a more general level of ethical conduct, researchers should at all times show respect and egalitarian attitudes for people's cultural practices, attitudes, and beliefs. Researchers should not criticize, try to correct, or make any moral judgments directed to persons in the research communities.

I have a particularly vivid recollection of a general group discussion in a rural village, in the course of which one of the researchers, a medical doctor, loudly criticized a woman because she had been working out in her crop land when her labor pains were starting. The medical doctor said "How many times do we have to tell you people....etc., etc." Unfortunately these kinds of unethical criticisms are still common occurrences in some research groups.

GUIDELINE 6

Major ethical issues can arise when researchers go on to write up their results. First, in many research projects it is nearly impossible to disguise the location of the research and thus to protect the anonymity of certain types of informants. This is partly because of the greatly expanded scale of access to published and unpublished information through electronic channels. Yes, if you give pseudonyms for the research sites, in some cases you can make it difficult for people to identify individuals and organizations mentioned in your research reporting. But in many cases such anonymity and protection of individual identities is now increasingly difficult.

SPECIAL ETHICAL ISSUES IN APPLIED ETHNOGRAPHIC RESEARCH

Whyte and Whyte (1984) reported a situation in which extensive ethnographic research was carried out in a prominent hotel in the Midwestern United States. Although pseudonyms were used for the hotel and all the individuals in the written materials, the research was sufficiently well known that the researchers realized that the specific hotel and many of the individuals described in the report would be identifiable. The researcher and mentors held off publication of their book for nearly 20 years! By the time their ethnographic report was published, almost all of the administrators and other personnel in the hotel had retired or moved to other locations, so there was no longer any ethical problem about the possible identification of the research site and certain key individuals.

Another example of avoiding ethical wrong-doing was reported by C. Fluehr-Lobban concerning her own research career. She had carried out research in Islamic communities and learned Arabic in the course of field work in Sudan, Egypt, and Tunisia. She intended to carry out further study of Islamist movements, but became aware of the serious ethical dilemmas she would face. She wrote, "I struggled with the ethical dilemma of being open with national research boards, disguising my interest in fundamentalist Islam and other research objectives, or resolving the dilemma by not conducting the research. In the end, I decided not to carry out the research on the subject and to postpone or altogether avoid research in the country I had chosen" (Fluehr-Lobban 1998:187).

E. Chambers has described participation in evaluation research in a large, multi-site housing scheme developed by the United States Department of Housing and Urban Development. He noted several difficulties for which ethnographic researchers would need to develop special approaches in order to avoid serious ethical dilemmas.

Working in an evaluation project, mainly producing qualitative, descriptive materials, there is almost no way to preserve the anonymity of individual administrators in a project, particularly if the ethnographer is to report on meetings and decision-making processes. Chambers recommended that "Individuals who undertake this sort of work should understand from the start that there may be instances where confidentiality cannot be guaranteed. As noted above...this was the case in reporting on the activities of upper level management staff. It became impossible to report effectively on agency operations and policies without identifying key individuals" (Chambers 1977: 264).

Chambers also noted that ethnographers have tended to be biased against administrators and agencies in complex programs. He wrote, "Where research has been conducted on, for example, administrative agencies, it has generally been highly critical of the processes and personalities involved. Our bias is nowhere in greater evidence" (page 265).

It is very important, in complex applied data gathering involving government agencies and other administrative bodies, that ethnographic researchers maintain a balance of objective, neutral reporting in order to provide useful, policy-related information. Ethnographic researchers who have done most of their research among the (often low-income, marginal) recipients of government and non-government programs can have difficulties in maintaining attitudes of neutral, sympathetic understanding when doing research in complex bureaucratic structures.

Researchers should be well aware of all of these ethical issues, and should develop plans for dealing with these matters of ethical conduct, including preparation of informed consent forms and other instruments, before beginning the ethnographic research. In studies dealing with complex bureaucratic structures, researchers should review the ethical issues, including problems concerning confidentiality, with some of the administrators among whom the research will be conducted. Finally, discussion of the main points of ethical data-gathering standards should be incorporated into training agendas before research begins, and research teams should review their work for any ethical problems that may have developed in the course of data gathering.

Gaining Entry to a Study Site: Getting Started

In some research settings it is easy to gain entry and find key informants. There are research settings in which the study population is receptive to outsiders, including researchers. That is particularly likely if the researchers (and their sponsors) have a relationship with local community organizations in the study population. For example, for many years, beginning in the 1970s, social scientists at the University of Connecticut have had working relationships with the Puerto Rican community in Hartford, CT, through an action organization, the Hispanic Health Council. The social science researchers at the university have mainly been interested in community health research, which was also a felt need among the Puerto Rican individuals they met with when the Hispanic Health Council was established. Social scientists and community people have worked together to develop research proposals to explore health issues in the Hartford urban area. That university-community partnership has included research on reproductive health issues, substance abuse, asthma among Puerto Rican young people, and a variety of other health topics. Because of the long-term collaboration, graduate students and faculty from the university have generally experienced few problems in gaining access to Puerto Rican neighborhoods, families, and informative individuals (LeCompte and Schensul 1999; Schensul et al. 1999).

Many university-based social science departments have developed collaborative relationships with community organizations and "study populations" as field sites are established, including research bases in other countries. Some decades earlier, the Vicos Project area in highland Peru was a research base for Cornell University social scientists and their guests. Such collaborative relationships between researchers and study communities can significantly reduce the problems of "gaining access and getting cooperation" for individual research projects.

Pertti Pelto, "Gaining Entry to a Study Site: Getting Started," in *Applied Ethnography: Guidelines for Field Research*, pp. 59-71. © 2013 Left Coast Press, Inc. All rights reserved.

DIFFICULT RESEARCH POPULATIONS

A great many factors can result in serious difficulties for gaining entrance and initiating research in certain communities. Most refugee communities are likely to be sensitive about outsiders, particularly if there are major differences in religion, cultural backgrounds, and other characteristics differentiating them from the "host populations." Also, sub-groups involved in illegal or socially disapproved activities (sex worker groups, injection drug users, smuggler communities, illegal immigrant groups, etc.) can be highly resistant to researchers prowling about, asking questions.

Research in a Red Light District in India:
Linking with a Local Community Organization

Bhattacharya and Senapati (1994) have described research among sex workers in brothels in Kolkata (formerly Calcutta). Access for research in the brothels would normally be very difficult, but The Child In Need Institute (CINI), a local NGO, linked up with a local residence-based social club in order to facilitate intervention activities on behalf of the sex worker population.

> CINI has been rendering services to the children of the Rambagan sex workers for the last two years. The Institute has opened a drop-in-center for the children to keep engaged in different educational and recreational activities while their mothers are at work. Involvement of a local club has helped to gain confidence of the sex workers in Rambagan. A club in West Bengal is usually a registered body consisting of influential persons of the local area.... The main activities of such a body is to organize pujas [religious ceremonies]... festivals, sports events, and cultural programmes for the local people. They are also engaged in welfare activities.... The club members are duly respected by the sex workers. (Bhattacharya and Senapati 1994: 548)

In the data-gathering among the sex workers, some of the club members volunteered to help in collecting a census of the sex workers in the area. Thus, the relationship with the local club was a key factor in the research project. The project was able to get highly sensitive data concerning the numbers of clients of the sex workers, types of sex acts, and condom use. The data about these specifics was possible because of a unique system of self-report cards (see Chapter 14).

The CINI research team members were able to gain entry to the brothels and to develop good relationships with the sex workers because of two factors—their own system of services and actions on behalf of the brothel women and their collaborative arrangement with the local social club. Without these two connections to the brothel neighborhood, they would not have been able to get the levels of trust and cooperation necessary for their sensitive research aims.

Research in a Somali Refugee Population

The Somali refugee population in Finland is a small Islamic contingent, adapting to a northern European cultural system that differs from theirs in practically every human aspect—religion, skin color, gender norms, marriage patterns, education—in addition to the environmental challenge of long, cold winters. The intercultural contrasts have led to serious racial discrimination and tensions between the refugee and host populations, although there are some signs that the overt social conflicts may have lessened slightly. Given those problems, the entry of a Finnish woman ethnographer into research among Somali women was not an easy matter.

Marja Tiilikainen (2002) has described her initial difficulties in undertaking research among the Somali refugee women. Somali people, although their numbers are not large, are the biggest refugee group in Finland (about 10,000 persons in 2010), and they are highly visible because of skin color, their Islamic religion, and the differences in dress and language. Tilikainen pointed out that the economic depression in the 1990s sharpened some of the tensions between Somalis and the Finnish population. Trying to initiate her research, she found: "As a researcher I was not always welcomed, but faced... resistance and suspicion. I had to answer many questions: Why was I interested in Somali women? What was I going to write? What would I do after I finished my studies?" (Tiilikainen 2002: 275) Her description probably reflects a Finnish-style understatement of the actual difficulties.

In addition to the problems of tensions between the host population and the migrants, she faced another problem that many researchers have encountered in urban areas—the study population in the metropolitan area (Helsinki) is scattered about the city, so it is difficult to find an entry point with sufficient numbers of persons.

After some negotiations with the public health bureaucracy, including clearance from their ethics committee, she got permission to do research at an urban health center that served considerable numbers of Somalis. She carried a letter, written in the Somali language, which she showed to the women seeking services at the center. In most cases it was women bringing their small children for check-ups, and some of them gave her permission to observe and interview. Her second point of contact was with a newly formed Somali women's group, to which she was admitted as a regular participant. However, they only met once a month, so it was not a source of intensive contacts, particularly in the early phases of the research. Her third method for contacting a wider range of women was what she referred to as the "snowball method."

> A Somali woman whom I knew and who happened to live in the same area [near the researcher's home] promised to help me. In fact, she became one of my key informants. She took me to many social happenings and with her assistance I became acquainted with many more women. Later I realized that these different ways of searching for contacts…made it possible to reach different kinds of women. In the neighborhood and in the women's groups I met mostly women with children who stayed at home. Through other connections I…met women who worked or studied. This helped me to see a great variety of Somali women and differences [among]…them. (Tiilikainen 2002: 277)

As Tiilikainen gradually expanded her network of contacts beyond the immediate neighborhood, she began to visit mosques, other neighborhoods, and Islamic seminars, and occasionally she was invited to weddings. She also began to spend much time sitting in the homes of some women who agreed that she could come to visit and chat.

Telephone conversations were another major source of contacts and data, and Tiilikainen noted that "The telephone was a comfortable way to have lengthy discussions…. The telephone was the means of communication the women used with their friends and relatives in Finland and abroad…" (p. 279). In Finland, as in most other parts of the world, cell phones have become an important technological means for data-gathering, in addition to their role in increased social networking.

During two years of research Tiilikainen collected a great deal of data about the women's many emotional and social problems, their dealing with health issues and beliefs about illness, and the styles of interaction between the Somali women and health providers as well as other social services. She also collected considerable data concerning the health care practices in Somalia, as well as information about the women's contacts with friends and relatives in their former homeland.

Her description of entry to field work and methods of data collection included discussion of the various ethical issues in research with marginalized refugee groups. Although she noted that some of the ethical issues are not yet resolved, it is clear from her descriptions that part of the "paying back" for the data she was collecting involved being a resource person for some of the women she was studying:

> For some women, I became a Finnish friend. For some of them I was more like a resource person who could help them, for instance to explain difficult language, to give them information or help them in their studies. Furthermore, I was a mediator between Finnish and Somali people. Surprisingly, sometimes I was a mediator between Somali women and Muslim men, too; as a non-Muslim I did not need to be shy of men and could concretely act as a protecting shield. (p. 275)

Based on her research data, she has written about the communications problems between the Finnish health providers and the Somali women, including the fact that the women are continually frustrated in finding little help for their many difficult-to-define health problems.

The data from her research show that, although the Somali women had some respect for the Finnish doctors' treatment of physical conditions, there was great frustration concerning the lack of communication and of any useful treatment for all their psychological problems. Sometimes the women found relief if they had access to Somali healers, whose treatments included passages from the Quran.

Tiilikainen's entry to the research community and development of contacts with key informants was a slow and difficult process. She had very little help from community-based organizations, though the access through a community health center opened a few doors for her. Her description of gradual acceptance and wider contacts in the research community points to the need for patience and perseverance, which is particularly evident in many cases where a lone researcher seeks to develop a project without organizational support, in a marginalized community experiencing many kinds of economic and interpersonal tensions.

Gaining Access to Multiethnic Metropolitan Neighborhoods

We might assume that it would be relatively easy to gain entry to urban neighborhoods in which there are government agencies involved in development work. With appropriate formal contacts—letters and personal visits—gaining entry should be easier than in the case of the scattered Somali refugees in Helsinki. However, if the government agency people are not responsive, difficulties may arise.

Paul Maginn has described in detail his difficulties in getting access to his intended research sites in London, England. He wanted to work in three different neighborhoods in which there is ethnic/racial diversity and in which there are local "urban regeneration partnerships and community forums." The first step in seeking access to his tentatively selected communities was to write formal letters (on university stationary) to local officials (directors of Housing, Planning, and Regeneration). Those officials were very slow to respond, so after a few weeks he sent out a follow-up letter, to which he received ambiguous, lukewarm replies.

At the same time, he initiated informal contacts with persons working in urban regeneration and community development, beginning with contacting an Afro-Caribbean male who was working in a black-led housing association. Soon he had a fairly broad network of contacts, developed through the usual "snowball process." Maginn described that he emphasized two different identities in meetings with the various people working in urban regeneration programs. With researchers or others familiar with research, he emphasized his credentials as a professional researcher. On the other hand, with ethnic/racial minority persons he emphasized his origins (North Ireland), where he had plenty of experience and understanding of community organization and discriminatory practices.

Maginn makes it clear in his descriptions of letters, informal contacts, and formal meetings that his first success in gaining access to a research site came about because of positive support from a key individual. "After almost 8 months of intensive networking and several failures, I had finally secured access to...my first case study" (Maginn 2007: 434). Six and seven months later he finally got permission for research in the two additional sites that he wanted.

He summed up the experience, noting that gaining access (and maintaining access) in the three sites "were secured as a resulted of a complex mix of factors. In particular, access would not have been possible without the complex network of contacts I had developed and knowing when and how to emphasize...my different social and professional identities." However, he added that there is "no simple formula guaranteeing successful entry" (p. 438).

This story has an important feature that researchers are likely to encounter in many urban settings: gaining entry for research required dealing with two different types of gatekeepers—the government officials and the decision-makers in the local populations. In some areas both types can be difficult. The difficulties are likely to be particularly serious if the researcher must approach the gatekeepers on her or his own, instead of having full organizational backing. As the example of the CINI research in Kolkata shows, developing relationships at the organizational level is likely to gain more rapid cooperation from multiple gatekeepers, as compared with contacts made by solo researchers.

Gaining Entry, but How to Get Cooperation?

The experiences of trying to gain entry for field work in London described by Maginn remind us that in many situations there are multiple gatekeepers, at different levels or in different bureaucratic settings. One common pattern has the government officials who must give clearance and then local community organizations which may have very different views about research. In school systems there is usually a complex hierarchy: at the top is the district superintendent, then perhaps a middle level in the bureaucracy, and then the most sensitive gatekeepers—the principals at individual schools and the teachers in their classrooms.

Wanat (2009) has described experiences at four different school research sites where she and her students had official permissions for research from the top levels of bureaucratic gatekeepers. When they tried to initiate the research in the individual schools, they encountered various levels of cooperation and non-cooperation. In one of the projects, she and her student researchers gained entry to an elementary school, at which they carried out semi-structured interviews with 48 parents concerning "meaningful parental involvement." The local gatekeeper provided them with the list of parents, and most of the parents were cooperative about agreeing to be interviewed. That was the most positive research experience.

The second school project also involved interviewing parents about barriers to parental involvement in the schooling of their children. The study called for interviewing of parents with positive experiences, and corresponding interviews with parents having negative experiences with the schools. The local level gatekeepers cooperated in providing lists of the "positive parents," but there was much less cooperation concerning the "negative cases." The same type of local-level non-cooperation was encountered in the third study, which was intended to focus on parents with little involvement in the school situation.

The fourth study was designed as interviews of teachers concerning their perceptions of a new program for students defined as "struggling readers." In that case, the principals in the schools provided the names of teachers, but then prohibited the researchers from directly contacting the teachers. All contacts were to be arranged by the principals, but there were delays, "forgetting," failure to communicate, and other patterns of non-cooperation. In that situation it was impossible for the researchers to have casual conversations with the teachers and develop rapport and trust.

Wanat described a considerable range of obstructionist tactics used by the gatekeepers at the lower levels of the school hierarchy, which were apparently motivated by the principals' fears that the research would result in negative publicity for their school. Also, some of the teachers were concerned that the research projects somehow contained evaluations of their teaching performance.

The research situations described in Wanat's paper would appear to be highly vulnerable to obstructions at the local school levels. The studies were designed around qualitative interviewing, with little opportunity for participant observation, such as spending time around the schools to develop rapport with the school authorities, teachers and students. In addition, as Wanat noted, the advent of the "No Child Left Behind" program aroused anxieties at all levels of the school system, raising fears of evaluations, negative publicity, and other threats.

This example of research in various schools, like the previous example of seeking entry for research in urban neighborhoods, suggests the need for stronger organizational networking from the researchers' institutional base. Of course, the research situation in schools is particularly sensitive in the United States (and perhaps many other countries) because of growing political conflicts concerning "privatization" and other components of "educational reform."

Permission for Research in Arctic Canada

In some areas, governmental or quasi-governmental bodies control the access to research in restricted areas, in addition to which local community organizations may also exercise control. Collings (2009) has described the complexities involved in getting permission to do research in native communities in Canada's arctic areas.

> By law, before research can be conducted in Native communities, the project in question must be licensed. In the Northwest Territories, applications for a research license are made to the Aurora Research Institute (ARI), which reviews applications and grants licenses to researchers. The application process is relatively straightforward with one caveat. ARI encourages community consultation for all projects that will be conducted with Native peoples, in Native communities, or on Native-controlled lands. It is generally expected that research projects will receive community approval before the application for a research license is filed with ARI. Even so, ARI conducts its own community consultation with the

local municipal government and community corporation about the suitability of a project before it grants a license. (Collings 2009: 137)

Collings refers to the ARI, the local government, and the (native) community as a "three-headed gatekeeper" that can sometimes be a serious obstacle to gaining research permission, particularly if there are any individuals in the local community who are opposed to the proposed study. He goes on to describe the difficulties in getting acceptance in the Inuit community context, and the ways in which the researcher must learn special techniques of interaction with the people who have had much experience with researchers and generally dislike interviews.

Expected specific benefits for the local community and participating community organizations are important factors in most applications for research permissions. The "expected benefits" should not be vague generalizations about "more community development," but something much more specific such as assisting and counseling students in their applications to advanced education, working with the local organizations to reduce police harassment, or other locally relevant actions. In India, an attractive benefit in many areas is "counseling and helping local people to gain access to citizen entitlements such as ration cards, voter identification cards."

LONG-TERM COLLABORATION AND PARTNERSHIPS WITH COMMUNITY-BASED ORGANIZATIONS

I believe there are important advantages for academic departments and other research organizations in developing long-term relationships with specific community entities such as NGOs, schools, community development organizations, and government bodies for maintaining "research, development, and experimental action programs." Many such collaborative relationships already exist in various areas. Such arrangements need not have large amounts of funding, although it is of course much more attractive for any community organization if your research people can offer to bring in some funding to the community side of the partnership.

Those kinds of partnerships work best if there are individuals in the community-based organizations (e.g., people in local schools or community organizations) who are committed to the collaborative arrangements and who have the administrative flexibility and authority to make such programs work for the benefit of the community.

The Haitian Health Foundation:
A Friendly Site for Public Health Researchers

In 1986, the Haitian Health Foundation (HHF), a Connecticut based non-governmental organization, established a major public-health activity in southwestern Haiti, based in the town of Jeremie (Grand Anse Region). In the first phase of operations the HHF served a collection of 23 rural villages, but in the 1990s the coverage was expanded to a total of 104 communities. Although the headquarters in Jeremie includes significant inpatient and outpatient facilities, a major part of the activities take place as outreach services in the villages, carried out by trained, resident Community Health Workers (CHWs). In recent years the program has served approximately 200,000 people, most of whom are in the rural, hard-to-reach villages (Lewis and Gebrian 2009).

The HHF public health system in Haiti has had a regular flow of researchers throughout its 25 years of activity. Many of the researchers are public health master's students from the University of Connecticut, plus a few students from other universities. Because of the close ties between the HHF and these academic institutions, research results are regularly introduced into the public health program. For example, in the early 1990s, ethnographic research indicated that males in households are surprisingly active in the health care of their children (Devin and Erickson 1996). Based on that finding, the HHF began to establish Fathers' Clubs in the villages.

> Fathers' club participants meet regularly to learn about child and family health. They discuss how to best support their wives and mutually care for their children. Fathers' clubs are run by the men themselves and are open to all men in the village. Health education sessions occur with input from the nurse or village health agent. Education formats include discussion, songs, and skits. The ultimate goal of the fathers' clubs is to improve child health through education. (Sloand et al. 2010: 201)

Recent research has shown that the fathers' clubs have had a positive impact on children's health—particularly in raising the percentages of immunizations, vitamin A supplementation, and weight monitoring of infants (Sloand, Astone, and Gebrian 2010).

The collaboration between the HHF community health program and academic researchers is an example of how partnerships between academic researchers and community-based organizations can be beneficial to both sides. At the same time, these arrangements make the process of "gaining entry and getting cooperation" much easier for researchers.

In the 21st century both academic and non-academic researchers often have little time for drawn-out negotiations and slow, patient networking for gaining entry to research sites. Those problems are much less bothersome when collaborative arrangements are already in place.

Recently (2007) another interesting multi-partner arrangement between academic researchers and community organizations has been developed in Florida. Social scientists at the University of Florida, Florida Agricultural and Mechanical University, and Florida State University have entered into a collaborative relationship with organizations in Tallahassee, FL, to develop a "community-academic partnership" called the Health Equity Alliance of Tallahassee (HEAT). This research and action organization includes community members, academic researchers, and local policy makers. The policy statement includes the following:

> HEAT believes that active collaboration between researchers and community members enhances the validity of scientific research. (HEAT, 2012)

The partners in the HEAT organization include the Greater Frenchtown Revitalization Council, Tallahassee Memorial Hospital's Faith Community Health Ministry, the Leon County Health Department, the Florida Department of Health, and researchers from three large universities in Florida.

These examples illustrate the principle that researchers should make themselves familiar with the structures of potential community-based partner organizations. Some structures (organizations) may be difficult to work with; others are more flexible and "user friendly." In the HHF and HEAT coalitions there are several different types of organizations with varied resources, which enhance the possibilities for productive and practical research.

The examples I have sketched in this chapter suggest that in some communities, such as small refugee populations and special ethnic minorities (e.g., Inuit communities in the Arctic), negotiating acceptance for research activities should probably be done by individual ethnographers. The researcher must be patient and careful in learning effective ways to gain the confidence of the local people, including local gatekeepers.

In other settings, such as schools, health care systems, multi-ethnic neighborhoods, and others, it may be more effective if the researchers' home organization negotiates an agreement for collaborative activity, preferably a longer-term arrangement. Without such a "partnership" at the organizational level, the individual researchers are constantly vulnerable to arbitrarily uncooperative gate-keepers.

The following suggestions are especially important for researchers when "seeking entry" to a study site, but they are also important throughout your stay in a research location. Getting good cooperation and rapport in a study community or institutional setting is not a one-time action. Researchers must be careful to maintain "appropriate behavior" and interaction styles, as the cooperation and goodwill of the local people can always be jeopardized if complex "researcher norms" are violated.

GUIDELINES FOR INDIVIDUAL RESEARCHERS SEEKING ENTRY AND RESEARCH COOPERATION

GUIDELINE 1

You should try hard to get detailed information about the political, economic, and social situations in your proposed study sites. There are always political cleavages and varieties of factionalism, including turf struggles between local organizations, subtle conflicts between governmental and non-governmental entities, localized ethnic rivalries, and other socio-political issues.

GUIDELINE 2

In meeting with government officials and leaders of NGOs it is useful to have a short, well-prepared statement about your research intentions.

GUIDELINE 3

Researchers seeking entry and cooperation in study sites should carefully study local dress codes and other culturally shaped behavioral expectations. In South Asia we have seen several instances of researchers' "inappropriate dress style," to which local people reacted negatively.

GUIDELINE 4

While seeking entry to a study site, researchers should observe strict ethical standards from the very beginning. Maintaining confidentiality of all received information and respecting the privacy of individuals begins on the first day.

GUIDELINE 5

In many situations the would-be researcher should avoid asking too many questions. W. F. Whyte (1993) commented about the ways in which researchers should learn how to use indirect methods of conversational probing.

That caution applies to general researcher behavior, but it is especially important in the early phases of seeking acceptance in study communities.

GUIDELINE 6

Always start learning the "local language," or the "local dialect," but avoid showing off by using the local dialect too early while seeking acceptance and cooperation in a research site. That initial learning should be focused on learning usual forms of greetings, thanking patterns, and other elements of local etiquette.

GUIDELINE 7

Try to develop a network of friendly contacts. Search out individuals and organizations that seem to accept the main aims of your research. However, you should avoid being too closely identified with (spending too much time with) any particular individual or group.

GUIDELINE 8

The example given by Maginn concerning finally getting some progress with gatekeepers (described earlier in this chapter), emphasized the influence of one important person who supported his proposed study. For many researchers, gaining effective entry to a research site has hinged on finding the right (influential) person to speak on behalf of the proposed research activities.

Although that last suggestion—finding the "right sponsor"—sounds attractive, researchers should be careful to avoid being identified too much with a particular local leader or local group, unless there is clear evidence that the "potential sponsor" (individual or organization) is truly neutral and acceptable to the different possible factions or "rival entities" in the community. At the beginning of your research you are especially vulnerable to being labeled as "attached to such and such special interests."

Social Mapping and Sketch Mapping: Getting the Lay of the Land

This chapter discusses mapping—an important method of data gathering that has a variety of uses.

SOCIAL MAPPING

One of the first activities for a newly initiated formative research project can be a series of social mapping sessions. This activity consists of gathering small groups of local people—at an NGO, a women's group, and other settings—and asking each group (preferably four to eight persons) to draw a map of the local community (or their section of the city) in order to show the locations of key features, landmarks, social services, and other information. If the research is about schools and education reform, the local map-makers can be asked to mark all of the locations of government and private schools, areas of ethnic minorities with language learning problems, and other salient features. If the research is focused on health, mapping can show locations of clinics, doctors, hospitals, and other health providers. In practically all applied projects it is useful to find out the locations of different ethnic groups, occupational categories, local organizations and other socio-cultural and economic features.

Social mapping is the most widely used research tool in the series of formative research operations known as "participatory rural appraisal" (PRA). Robert Chambers, in an extensive series of publications, has been the leading exponent of PRA, particularly in community development and agricultural program activities. He described several cross-check studies in which the products from social mapping were compared with survey data, and the social mapping results were found to be more accurate than the surveys. A study in a series of communities in India, carried out by the National Council for Applied Economic Research in 1992, found that "the demographic data derived from the participatory mapping were much closer to the recent national census than those derived from the...questionnaire survey" (Chambers 1997: 144).

Although Chambers and others have recommended the PRA social mapping and related techniques for getting detailed, accurate demographic data, they have also emphasized the use of social mapping for developing relationships with local people to involve them as information sources and possible research partners. I especially recommend social mapping as an effective activity for identifying potential key informants in the early phases of research, in addition to getting "the lay of the land" in the research communities (see Figure 4.1).

Participatory (social) mapping, like other ethnographic mapping, encompasses a wide range of different topics, geographical areas, and styles of operation. Many of the social mapping examples in the PRA literature describe situations in which village people were asked to do a mapping on some open ground (perhaps in the village square). Whoever was present at the village meeting was free to contribute to the mapping.

Figure 4.1. Three villagers making a map in a social mapping exercise.
© Dunja Pelto 2013.

In South India, the colored powders (rangoli) used by most households for ritual drawings on their doorsteps were often used for doing elaborate mappings, with different colors representing special landmarks and features.

Social mapping is an excellent opening for introducing community people to your research activities, and is also effective for rapidly learning about the various social groups, economic activities, and other special features in research locations. In many intervention projects focused on HIV/AIDS, social mapping has been an effective way to develop preliminary mapping of sex work sites, as well as drinking places, drug-dealing sites, and other key locations.

Mapping and transect walks are also useful for preliminary mapping of soil types, cropping patterns, watershed characteristics, and other important data in agricultural and resource development projects. Data concerning relationships among local herding collectives, social networks of entrepreneurs, local political leaders, and other important features of social organization can be effectively derived from participatory mapping operations.

Participatory (Social) Mapping in an HIV/AIDS Program in Four Countries

Suzanne Maman and associates have reported using participatory (social) mapping in four countries—South Africa, Thailand, Tanzania, and Zimbabwe—in formative research for Project Accept, which was "designed to test the efficacy of a community-based model of HIV counseling and testing" (Maman 2009: 371). The actual map drawing, as described in their report, followed the classic steps found in the PRA literature:

> To develop the maps, six to thirteen members of the community who represented various community constituents—including youth, women, men, and elders—were selected by community leaders to participate in the mapping exercises.... In selecting the mapping participants, leaders were asked to identify individuals who were knowledgeable about the community and who they felt best represented these different constituencies....The team identified an open location for the community members to draw the maps, often outside or in an empty classroom.... (Maman et al. 2009: 373)

After the team had explained the mapping task to the community mapping team, the mappers were asked to select one of their members to do the actual drawing, which was usually drawn directly into the dirt, using a stick or sometimes with chalk. Various items such as rocks, leaves, bottle caps, shells, and different colors of chalk were used as markers for special features in the maps. The materials used, and the time required for the process, varied considerably in different communities.

Individuals from the research teams were assigned the task of taking notes about everything that was said by the mappers during the process. After the maps were completed, each research team copied the dirt-maps onto paper, as well as expanding their notes to give full descriptions of the entire process. The mapping sessions were reported to have taken three to four hours in each community. Several communities were mapped in this fashion in each of the four countries.

After the participatory/social mapping activities were completed, the formative research teams in each country selected small groups of three or four community persons to accompany the researchers on "transect walks" through various parts of the mapped communities in order to see firsthand some of the mapped features and to learn a great deal more about the communities. Not all of the transects were done by walking, as some of the communities were quite large and it was more efficient to travel by vehicle.

The researchers felt that the participatory mapping and transect tours were highly effective in developing detailed plans for the intervention program. In addition to initiating relationships with local community persons and identifying key facilities that could be utilized in the counseling and testing program, the teams learned valuable information for avoiding serious mistakes in the implementation of the programs in the four countries.

- They found that the boundaries of several communities on available maps were not representative of current population subdivisions. That information was essential for delineating the experimental and control sub-populations.

- The mapping and transect information was essential for identifying places that would be unsuitable for locating counseling/testing facilities.

- They developed considerable preliminary information concerning persons and organizations that could play central roles in community mobilization work.

- The relationships with the mapping teams and contacts with individuals and groups during the transect tours laid the groundwork for making further contacts with various sectors of local populations and service facilities, whose cooperation would be essential to the success of the intervention program.

TRANSECT WALKS

The idea of "transect walks" is part of the repertoire of data-gathering methods developed by Rapid Rural Appraisal (RRA) researchers in community development projects, and is often associated with participatory (social) mapping activities. The procedure is "... systematically walking with local guides and analysts through an area, observing, asking, listening, discussing, learning about different zones, soils, land uses, vegetation, crops, etc... and mapping and diagramming the zones, resources and findings" (Chambers 1997:117). Chambers references guidelines written by Mascarenhas (1990), which provide a particularly useful description of this data-gathering technique as taught by the MYRADA (NGO) people in India. Mascarenhas describes several types of information-gathering walks, including "village transects," "resource transects," and "cultural transects." Although this technique has been especially utilized in rural development projects, it can be extremely useful in urban environments as well. In metropolitan areas, and in projects that are spread out over many kilometers of territory, transect walks can be done by vehicle.

Of course, a great many ethnographers have done some sort of "local tours," with varying degrees of thoroughness and varying depths of discussion with key informants along the way. The methodology is particularly useful in agricultural and other environmental development projects, because much of the important data of interest is physically visible, in the form of soils, water sources, crops, wild and not-so-wild vegetation, fuel resources, and other physical features. On the other hand, researchers in projects dealing with sex workers, injection drug users, and other special populations have learned a great deal from "guided tours" in sex worker locations, brothels, and other "hot spots" (see Figure 4.2).

In some areas, such as drug-dealing hot spots and marginalized ethnic groups, openly taking notes during transect walks may arouse suspicions and hostility among the local populace. You can try various alternatives, including stopping in secluded places to quickly write up the observations from the area you just walked through. Another alternative might be that, as you walk along, you dictate into a hand-held recording device. Almost everywhere nowadays we see persons talking to their cell phones, so people might not pay any special attention to the researcher dictating field notes into a "telephone."

Figure 4.2. NGO workers identifying sex work locations. © Dunja Pelto 2013.

USES FOR SOCIAL (PARTICIPATORY) MAPPING

Participatory mapping activities in different projects vary greatly in the degrees of accuracy and extensiveness of data expected from these operations. In the project(s) described by Maman and colleagues, each mapping produced an extensive inventory of data (including revising the boundaries of several communities) that was felt to be essential information for selecting the specific sites for the program activities. In some of the examples cited by Chambers concerning participatory (social) mapping in South Asia, the mapping and interviewing was used to get accurate demographic data, including physical locations of all the households in the study villages.

In other projects, including some HIV/AIDS interventions and explorations of abortion services in South Asia, social mapping has been intended primarily to identify sex work locations and to establish initial contacts with local persons and groups. Dimensions and distances in the maps are not an issue in many social mapping activities, as long as the research teams can get the help of local people, including NGO workers, to find the specific sites that were marked on the maps. In some small-scale studies of abortion practices and services in India, the social mapping was carried out mainly to obtain a preliminary inventory of the various health providers, particularly those who are involved with abortion services. The maps themselves only served as a vehicle for collecting the data (Ramachandar 2009b).

Research teams should plan to do several social mapping sessions in each community. The products of individual social mapping sessions will vary considerably in quality, and each mapping group is likely to omit some important features. In many cases, it will be useful for the team to use the products from several social mapping groups to compile a cleaned-up, composite map. That composite map can then be examined by NGO workers and other key informants, particularly if a fully developed map is needed in later steps of the research.

The participatory mapping activities always involve considerable discussion among the local people doing the mapping, and researchers can sometimes enter into the discussion to ask for clarification of local terminology or for specific cultural information. However, the mapping facilitators and note takers should avoid interfering very much with the mapping operations. When the mapping is completed, it is essential to "interview the map," raising questions about individual features on the map and getting further information about some locations and culturally important points that came up during the map-making.

Box 4.1 Instructions for Social Mapping

1. The essence of social mapping is that you ask persons in the research community to do the actual mapping—drawing features of their local environment onto large blank sheets of paper that you provide for the purpose.

2. It is best to have at least three or four persons (or more) as a small group of informants.

3. You (the facilitator) give instructions about what you would like them to put onto the map. Perhaps you would like them to "put onto the map all the different health care providers—the people and facilities you go to for treatment of illness or other health problems." Or, if your focus is a project regarding schools and education, then you ask the mappers to "show the locations of all the different kinds of schools in the communities."

4. Ask the mappers to select one of their group to do the marking on the paper, though others can also do some of the mapping.

5. It is often useful to start with a few streets, or the "main road," and a few other primary landmarks. (At this point some groups become very enthusiastic, and start putting in all kinds of features of their local environment—temples, marketplaces, police station, and others.)

6. You can introduce additional instructions as they continue the mapping. "OK, now that you have the general mapping of the town (or village or larger unit), please put in all the places people go for recreation, entertainment, or other fun activities."

7. Be sure to have one or two note takers, writing down all the comments that people make as they continue marking on the map.

SKETCH MAPPING OF KEY LOCATIONS IN THE RESEARCH AREA

In addition to the participatory social mapping, it is useful for researchers themselves to do various kinds of mapping in the early phases of ethnographic research. If your team has recently arrived in a research area, you can expand that concept of "transect walk" and tour the area, preferably with one or two local informants, to get firsthand understanding about various special locations pointed out to you by NGO outreach workers and/or other persons. In some important locations your team members can draw sketch maps in order to better understand the activities and kinds of people in some of the sites. Field researchers often make sketch maps of special locations such as market places, religious sites, meetings (seating patterns), health center spatial layouts, and other "action settings."

LeCompte and Preissle, in discussing ethnographic methods in educational research, described the "initial stages of an ethnographer's entry to the field or the interviewer's approach to respondents as an informal process of...getting a picture of the social, as well as the physical, environment" (LeCompte and Preissle 1993: 113). They commented further that "Ethnographers commonly initiate field residence with mapping procedures that establish the range of possible informants and participants in a group and the variety of situations in which they are found" (p. 114).

It is a useful practice to do informal mapping of special places and special events throughout the course of a field project, although here I am emphasizing activities that can help your team to quickly gain familiarity with features of an unfamiliar local environment.

K. DeWalt and B. DeWalt, in *Participant Observation* (2010), discussed the importance of small-scale mapping and using "sketch mapping" to study social interactions and also to help to remember details of local spatial arrangements. The DeWalts described some of the note-taking and sketch mapping they did in a study of "women's social power in Ecuador":

> We also made sketch maps of who was sitting, and standing, where men and women were seated, where specific individuals we believed were community leaders were seated, and where speakers were sitting or standing....Our notes regarding who spoke showed equal participation by men and women. However, the sketch map shows an all-male cluster seated apart from other members of the community...it became clear that all the decisions were being made within that cluster of men. (DeWalt and DeWalt 2010: 83)

S. L. Schensul, J. J. Schensul, and M. D. LeCompte, in *Ethnographer's Toolkit* (1999), presented an example of sketch mapping at a community health fair. The sketches show a series of different booths and other points of interest, and the numbers of individuals at each of those locations. The same sketch map, at two different time periods, shows how the numbers of people at the different locations greatly increased later in the day (p. 108). This example demonstrates the possibilities for introducing important dimensions of process and change into sketch mapping.

Researchers should make it a general rule that whenever they or their research assistants attend any gatherings—community meetings, market places, festive occasions, or other events—to always do at least a rough sketch map of the ways in which different people are located in the physical space, and also put in any important environmental features. It is always useful to make estimates of numbers of people and their sociocultural characteristics (age, sex, ethnicity, etc.). Notes concerning people's behaviors (special activities, speeches, etc.) at the events should be coordinated with the sketch maps. Mapping of spatial relationships can, of course, include a wide variety of useful ethnographic information. That is why I have put such emphasis on participatory social mapping in this chapter. In practically all communities, different social categories of people have different sectors or niches in geographic space. Also, in most communities there are hidden, or not so hidden, conflicts concerning "territoriality."

It should be evident that a research team's mapping activities, as suggested here, should be a combination of participatory social mapping, as delineated by Robert Chambers, interrelated with various degrees of sketch mapping carried out by the researchers—often through visits to some of the specific areas or action settings that emerge from the social mapping exercises.

LOCAL REACTIONS TO MAPPING

Mapping is sometimes looked on with hostility. In their discussion of ethnographic mapping, Schensul and colleagues pointed out that in some locations, mapping activities, or even casual "observing" in the area, can arouse suspicions and hostility among the local inhabitants. They described a situation in which one of the authors (LeCompte) carried out educational research in a town in the southwestern United States that was characterized by strong ethnic segregation. She found it easy to map most parts of the town, but when she went to the residential area of a Native American ethnic cluster, she encountered serious hostility. "Rocks were thrown, and feedback from local people made it clear that non-locals should not venture out of their designated areas. Doing house-to-house mapping was out of the question..." (Schensul, Schensul, and LeCompte 1999: 110–111). Similar problems of suspicions and overt hostility regarding "reconnaissance" and mapping have been reported from many other research projects. In some rural areas, people become suspicious of any mapping because they are afraid that the government or other people are going to seize their lands. Another fear is that they are going to be taxed.

That takes us back to the advantages of participatory social mapping. The processes of social mapping are much less likely to generate hostility and opposition, because local people are the primary map-makers. Also, social mapping is most often done without the need for touring all around the community, as the local people construct the maps from their recall and intimate familiarity with even minor features of their local area.

OTHER VISUAL DEPICTION IN FIELD WORK

Chambers, in his discussions of PRA techniques, pointed out that practically all people can do mapping and other visual displays of information, and that mapping and diagramming can be useful "equalizers" in which illiterate persons can present information and participate in discussions on a par with their literate, educated neighbors (Chambers 1997: 149). Diagramming of information in some of the participatory data-gathering techniques can include depiction of the annual cycle of rainfall and agricultural practices, flow diagrams of the causes of hunger, presentation of the socio-economic "wealth" hierarchy of families in rural communities, ratings of the severity of different illnesses, and a wide range of other information.

The "visual depictions" of information in various PRA techniques are sometimes done with easily available physical materials found in local communities. "Bar charts" showing "severity of illnesses" and other "ratings" can be done with small stones, bottle caps, or sticks of varying length. The same materials can be used to depict rainfall variations or agricultural actions. On the other hand, many of these same operations are done—even with illiterate informants—using cards with various illustrations. For example, informants are asked to sort the cards into categories of "high, "medium," and "low" according to some locally relevant dimensions. Some of those card-sorting operations are described further in Chapter 11. These same visual depictions are also often done on paper, using various styles of drawing groups, pie charts, and other pictures.

Even in your first days of field work, if you have good contact with an active NGO, a women's organization, or other informants, you will be able to get important preliminary data that expand your knowledge from the social mapping to more detailed information. For example, your social mapping group has pointed to several main "sex worker hot spots" in the area. The mapping work is finished, so you can ask some of the informants: "Can you give us some estimates of how many sex workers there are in these different locations? Now let's consider the five 'hot spots' you marked on the map. Just as general estimates—which of these five has the most sex workers? And which are very small in terms of numbers? You can use these small stones....You can show the biggest hot spot with a longer row of stones and then smaller numbers of stones for the others, so we get an idea of their relative sizes." Figure 4.3 shows a bar chart (hypothetical) that illustrates this method. This kind of preliminary PRA style of data gathering has been very effective, even in the early stages of research. Of course, your research team will need to get more concrete data later on in the research to check some of these initial numerical estimates.

Conclusion

The data-gathering activities presented in this chapter are particularly designed to get your research team acquainted with the geographic and social "lay of the land" in your project area. Of course, your use of these

Figure 4.3. Women making a bar chart of the relative numbers of sex workers in five hot spots. © Dunja Pelto 2013.

methods will vary, depending on the nature of your particular research project as well as your time frame and available resources. In many applied projects I have seen, especially in South Asia, some sort of NGO or other local organization is doing a program for which the applied research will provide new ideas, an evaluation, and/or other important data. The other model is that of a larger "host organization," such as the International Center for Diarrhoeal Disease Research, Bangladesh (ICDDR,B), to which researchers from other countries can come to do short-term or longer-term research, provided it is reviewed by the host institution. As mentioned in Chapter 3, various types of "local host organizations" are important for your gaining entry to research sites, and they are also your first sources of information and help for getting an understanding of local geography, economic conditions, and other useful orientation to the research area.

During these early steps of data gathering you should be especially attentive concerning the ethical issues outlined in Chapter 2. As you meet new groups and new informants, it is essential that you explain your research and get people's informed consent whenever you do some semi-structured interviewing, photography, or audio-recording. Be sure that you have clearance and approval from local authorities, and if, during mapping and other explorations, you venture into neighboring communities, be sure to explain your project to any important local community leaders. As noted in Chapter 3, "gaining entry and cooperation" is an ongoing process. Even if you have received permissions from the "authorities," in many cases you will need the help of your key informants, and perhaps a "respected local sponsor," to get introduced and gain the support at different levels and sub-groups of your study site. Often it is useful to have a letter of permission and support from some "authoritative source" that you can show to "gatekeepers" at various sites of your study area. In your beginning phases of research you should be especially cautious concerning use of photography and audio-recording.

Learning local cultural "rules and styles" is another important aspect of your data gathering in the first days and weeks of field research. You can ask your key informants for guidance concerning appropriate greetings, special salutations, cultural observances such as (in South Asia and other places) removing your shoes on entering people's homes and religious places, how to signal to a taxi or other vehicle, and other cultural practices. Some of these cultural practices can be learned during your first transect walks in the communities. Of course, you should have the local "dress codes" clearly in mind before you get to the research area.

Early Phases of Research: Key Informants and Group Discussions

In many ethnographic studies, the first contact with the study community involves meeting key informants. Often, the research is connected with one or more NGOs involved in an intervention project, so the first contacts are likely to be with the NGO staff people. On the other hand, if the research is connected with a program to improve schooling in a district, or some other complex institution, your first key informants are likely to be government administrators or other officials.

Often, in addition to contacts with key informants, meetings with groups can be useful in the beginning phases of data-gathering. In some cases the "host organization" will want to hold an orientation meeting in order to introduce the research team to their staff people and to give your research team information about the structure of the organization. Other types of group meetings will include social mapping sessions (see Chapter 4) and perhaps so-called "focus group discussions," which are discussed later in this chapter.

Box 5.1 The Ongoing Role of Key Informants

Whenever there are available resources, including research personnel, as well as good contacts with a small number of key informants, multi-method ethnographic research benefits from getting new information from three or four key informants throughout the duration of the study, including into the report writing. In many cases, when resources are available, at least two key informants can be paid an appropriate honorarium for their comments and reactions, perhaps even for adding bits of new information to the final reports.

Pertti Pelto, "Early Phases of Research: Key Informants and Group Discussions," in *Applied Ethnography: Guidelines for Field Research*, pp. 87-102. © 2013 Left Coast Press, Inc. All rights reserved.

KEY INFORMANTS: WHO AND WHAT ARE THEY?

In earlier times the concept of "key informants" was used mainly by anthropologists. Since the research was often intended for getting rich data about past cultural patterns ("before the coming of the white man"), a common practice was to find the older informants, provided they remembered much of the detail about the food-getting patterns, kinship rules, marriage customs, and other information about the past culture of their people. Another basic principle was that key informants were the ones researchers talked with many times. The ethnographer met individually with a small number of key informants regularly and conducted interviews, perhaps over a period of months, to record the wide range of cultural lore from the available knowledgeable persons.

Key Informants: Definitions from the Literature

H. R. Bernard wrote, "Key informants are people who know a lot about their culture, and are, for reasons of their own, willing to share all their knowledge with you." He goes on to say that "Good key informants are people [who]...can talk to you easily, who understand the information that you need, and who are glad to give it to you or get it for you" (Bernard, 2011: 150).

S. L. Schensul and coauthors stated, "Key informants are people with recognized special expertise in a topic of interest to the researcher..." (Schensul, Schensul, and LeCompte 1999: 74). Farther along, the authors present a useful listing of "Local Resources, Gatekeepers and Key Informants" (p. 82). It is likely that in practice, so-called "gatekeepers" can become good key informants. Some of the categories of people in their list include teachers, factory floor supervisors, local politicians, taxi drivers, hotel personnel, and community health workers.

M. J. LeCompte and J. Preissle wrote, "Key informants are individuals who possess special knowledge, status, or communicative skills and who are willing to share that knowledge and skill with the researcher.... [Furthermore] they frequently are chosen because they have access—in time, space, or perspective—to observations denied the ethnographer..." (LeCompte and Preissle 1993: 166).

There are, of course, a great many kinds of key informants. However, one important feature of key informants is that they are people who can give researchers information about the research community and the people's cultural behaviors and beliefs—not just about themselves. A second type of key informant is that of a "specialist," who can tell about some special area of information that is not general in the community. Thus, a key informant could be a traditional healer, who may be the only local person who can describe the various illnesses, special herbs and other treatment materials that he or she uses.

It appears that there has been a subtle change in the definition of "key informant" in recent decades, as a consequence of the changing patterns of ethnographic field work. Bernard's definition appears to reflect the older, classical, "cultural expert," whose expertise would help the researcher in a wide-ranging exploration of many aspects of "the culture." In the older, classic concept of key informants, the following have been essential:

- Persons who can systematically describe with much detail, and can explain so-called "cultural rules and patterns"

- Someone who was witness to some special event—she was there at the big conflict between Group A and Group B that resulted in a major break-up in the community—or perhaps was one of the founding members and an "officer" of a community organization that is still active in the study area

- Persons with whom the ethnographer should have many contacts (especially in the older, classical days of ethnographic research)

- Each interview with a key informant is meant to be very open, usually relatively unstructured, and the interviews with each key informant are uniquely different.

- One important, defining feature of "key informants" is that we cannot really specify how many key informants we will need and how many times we will meet with each of them. Most interviews with key informants are not subjected to statistical analysis, except in the special case of some structured interviews about lists and ratings (see Chapters 10 and 11).

Famous Key Informants

In modern times, probably the most famous key informant has been "Doc," the star gatekeeper-key informant who was a major factor in the production of *Street Corner Society* by William F. Whyte (originally published in 1943). Russ Bernard, in his discussion of that famous "local resource person," wrote:

> Doc was straight up; he told Whyte to rely on him and to ask him anything, and Doc was good to his word all through Whyte's 3 years

of field work. Doc introduced Whyte to the boys on the corner; Doc hung out with Whyte and spoke up for Whyte when people questioned Whyte's presence. Doc was just spectacular. (Bernard, 2011: 151)

Bernard went on to point out that, although Doc is a widely cited example of an exceptional key informant, a great many ethnographers have benefitted from similar long-term relationships with key persons.

Purpose of Key Informant Interviews

As noted previously, key informant interviews are especially important in the early phases of research for giving you general information about the research site, the study populations, and the current programs (if any) being carried out in the study sites. In addition, key informants can be important sources of information and insights at various stages of research for some of the following:

- Explaining events and actions currently taking place in the community. Perhaps researchers observed a community meeting in which a number of people spoke about matters that were difficult to understand. What was the gist of the meeting? Who were those people who spoke? And what sorts of social sectors or subgroups do they represent?

- Explaining unexpected new information. Suppose the team has carried out a small survey with a sample of households. The survey focused on attitudes about education and the local schools. Several of the results in the survey are puzzling, and they appeared to focus on one particular school, and something that happened (or is happening) there. Perhaps the story is a complex conflict that involves two quite different points of view about the teaching in the school. Researchers will need to get new information from more than one key informant to explore conflicting interpretations.

- Commenting on researchers' interpretations. Often it is useful to ask key informants to comment on the first drafts of report writing. Also, if you have done some pile sorting, paired comparisons, or some other structured data gathering, you can ask key informants to comment on some of the interesting patterns of results.

- Commenting on tentative results at every stage of research. In many cases key informants will suggest gaps that researchers have overlooked, which need to be explored before the conclusion of the study.

Box 5.2 Triangulation

Triangulation is checking on the accuracy of some data by referring to and comparing multiple data sources, multiple informants and/or use of multiple methods, for example, comparing the qualitative interviews with survey results concerning the same information. This subject is discussed further towards the end of Chapter 8. It's a good rule to do plenty of triangulation in your research.

Types of Key Informants

Some years ago I suggested that we should distinguish three main types of key informants (Pelto 1994).

Type One: Officials in government offices, police, administrators in NGOs, school administrators, and other persons in authority. These are often the gatekeepers that we need to meet in order to be allowed to start the research. We have to explain our research aims to them, and then we may get a chance to interview them about the local community and the specific population that they are connected with.

Type Two: Street-wise outreach workers. If they are outreach workers of a health service or NGO, these are the kinds of people who often have a great deal of good information, and it will be useful to maintain a continuing relationship with at least two or three such individuals in order to gain in-depth descriptive data about the local communities. They are also likely to be able to introduce researchers to good informants and gatekeepers in the study population.

Type Three: Members of the study population. "In research for HIV/AIDS interventions [for example] it is essential that data-gatherers develop strong contacts with members of the target population and the various types of actors and actresses in the relevant behaviour settings. In gathering information about the vocabulary of commercial sex workers, for example, it is essential to get information directly from users of that vocabulary" (Pelto, 1994: 596).

In some studies it appears that inexperienced researchers believe that key informants should always be persons in authority (Type One key informants). However, often the people who are most helpful are the outreach workers (Type Two), and some of the most vocal individuals in the study communities (Type Three), particularly those who happen to have the most knowledge and experience in the local research settings. If researchers pay attention to the informants' work schedules and avoid interfering with the usual daily rhythms of activity, it is often rewarding to have repeated contacts with those best key informants. It is only through repeated contacts that you begin to get "the real picture."

Of course, there can be many other types of key informants, depending on the characteristics of the research and the specific details to be covered in the data-gathering. In some cases you will need to find key informants who are specialists in some focused, unusual aspects of local culture. Thus, in some studies an important key informant may, for example, be a local religious leader, from whom you can learn about the beliefs, the deities, and other aspects of spiritual/religious knowledge and practices. In research on agricultural practices, you may need to find specialists who are "experts" in cultivating certain special crops or perhaps have unusual skills in recently introduced agricultural techniques that most of the other farmers have not yet tried.

Interviewing Key Informants

With Type One key informants, it is a good idea to plan a semi-structured interview using a checklist. This is particularly true if the person is a government official, officer in an NGO, principal of a school, or other person in authority who may have limited time, so you will not have the luxury of developing an easygoing, conversational style. You should be able to get a sense of the time limits in the interview within a few minutes after the introductory formalities are completed.

Never use a prepared, structured interview questionnaire in key informant interviews. Remember that key informant interviews are intended to be a discovery process. With Type Two and Type Three key informants particularly, the aim should be to develop an informal conversational style (see Figure 5.1). That does not preclude your planning a set of topics—as a checklist. That checklist should be at least partly committed to memory. Perhaps two-thirds of the way through the interview, you could have a glance at the checklist.

Figure 5.1. Key informant explains herbal remedy to researchers. © Dunja Pelto 2013.

EXAMPLE: Interview with an unlicensed village-level practitioner in rural India (mid-way in the interview): "Could you please describe to me the most recent childbirth that you have conducted in this village?"

FIELD NOTES: The recent delivery that he conducted was in January. He described to me that the mother-in-law came and tapped at his door and said that her daughter-in-law was in labor. That was her fourth delivery. Within ten minutes he reached her house. He continues the narrative:

> During my visit the mother-in-law, two children and her husband were all present. The delivery was taking place in her mother-in-law's house. She was lying on the bed. I examined her lower abdomen. I could feel the movement of the infant. I administered an injection for strength. They were wage laborers and extremely poor. She was 27 years old. I returned to my clinic. After an hour the family members sent word for me and they were very anxious. I went there and the labor had just then started and it was very slow. My first visit to her house was at 5:00 pm and the second visit as at 7:30 pm to 8:00 pm. Within half an hour she delivered a male child. There was a dai [traditional birth attendant] who was monitoring her pain and keeping the family members informed about her condition. She did the cleaning and other routine work. I gave instructions

to the dai and left the place. I visited her two times in a fortnight for post natal care. She had complaints of abdominal pain after the delivery and I gave an injection to control the pain. (Ramachandar 2009a: 8)

Generally the narrative opens up a series of questions as you ask for further details.

INTERVIEWER: "Do you sometimes administer any injection to induce labor pain?"

PRACTITIONER: "We should be careful administering oxytocin or epitocin for inducing labor pain. Any excess dose can be harmful to the unborn fetus. Therefore I do not give any oxytocin."

If the informant gives a long narrative, many questions will come to your mind, but most of the questions should wait until the informant has finished "the story."

Usually your next question should be based on something the key informant told in the narrative, for example, "You told me that you suggested they should take the daughter-in-law to the hospital. What did they say to that?" "Why did they refuse?" "How did they state those reasons?"

Even if you write your expanded notes in English (or your native language), include key words and phrases and words in the local language in your expanded notes, as in the following statements by another unqualified village practitioner in India:

Sometimes the newborn infants have respiratory problems. I administer artificial respiration from mouth to mouth. "Adhu ondhu jeeva naanu ondhu jeeva" [translation from Kannada: 'That is a life and I am also a life']. In case of such problems if I am not satisfied with the breathing I take personal care and accompany the family to the nearest government hospital. (Ramachandar 2009a: 17)

After each key informant interview, expand your jotted notes fully and make lists of "next questions/topics." Sometimes you go to another key informant for triangulation—cross-checking on a key point of information (see later in this chapter for a discussion of triangulation). Some of your next questions, however, are asking further details about the narrative, for example, the key informant's story about dealing with a corrupt government official.

If you have had a good interview with a key informant during the first or second contact, you will surely have many more topics to explore after you have reviewed that first set of notes. For every topic that she or he described, more in-depth questions will occur to you, as you go over your

Figure 5.2. Interviewer is careful to get key words in the local language.
© Dunja Pelto 2013.

notes and expand the initial interviews into fully developed transcripts.

A likely opening line for your next interview would be: "Last time when we were talking, you mentioned that the _____ usually ask for money (bribe). Can you tell me more about how they ask, and then what happens?" Again, the interview strategy is to try for another story or part of a story, or else to flesh out with more detail the narration just completed.

The main objective in interviewing key informants is to get useful, accurate information, but it is also important to get clues about new areas of information that you need to explore (see Figure 5.2). Of course, in the first days in the research site, you would like to get quick information about the place, the community, and the kinds of people who are the principal actors there.

Often your important key informants are the ones who give you a social mapping of "where things are, and what is happening there." That is why I always suggest that you start with mapping, asking some locally available informants to do the actual drawing of maps—the social mapping. That initial session of mapping, with local persons drawing on the map, can be one of the most eye-opening and exciting first moments in field work.

Phased Assertion: A Special Interviewing Technique

Sometimes in talking with key informants, we put forth a piece of supposed "key information," in order to sound as if we already know something about a topical area, hoping it will get the key informant to be open in giving new information. I recall one moment of revelation in my very early field work among the reindeer herders in Finnish Lapland. I had had an interesting talk with some herdsmen about their extensive herding styles in the years before World War II. They bragged about their herd-dogs. Later, I sat down to chat with my host, Jaakko, to talk about the "old days" and said, "You must have had some really great herding dogs in those days." Jaakko replied quickly: "No! We did not use any herding dogs. In those days, we had small herds…in the forested areas… we didn't use herd-dogs…."

I was mystified. Later in the discussion he commented: "Those Fofanoff men…their herds were out in the open tundra area…and they had many reindeer. They had to use dogs…." Then I realized that in pre-war days there had been two very different reindeer herding situations, based on two factors: the size of family herds and the nature of the terrain they controlled. Those factors called for two very different styles of management of the reindeer, and for the extensive, big-herd management, dogs were essential for keeping the herds under control. Jaakko proceeded to describe for me the "semi-domestic" herding style that he and his neighbors had practiced in those pre-war times.

My opening the interview with a comment (implied question) about herd-dogs was an attempt at what has been labeled "phased assertion." My attempt at phased assertion appeared to be a failure, but my informant, Jaakko, was a friendly man, and he set the matter right when he described the extensive herding of the Fofanoff men. One lesson in that exchange is that sometimes we can assert some information that is incorrect, and it still has the effect of opening up the informant's willingness to give information.

Peter Collings has described this technique as particularly useful and necessary as a strategy among Inuit people in the Canadian arctic. He defines the idea as follows:

> Phased assertion is…one mechanism by which the anthropologist demonstrates the kind of competence necessary to become regarded at some level as an in-the-know insider. Successful use of phased assertion necessarily requires possession of some prior insider knowledge, a demonstration to the informant that the researcher is ready for more detailed knowledge about a particular topic. (Collings 2009: 146–147)

Collings described that he developed the habit of visiting with the Inuit hunters informally, for tea and chatting, during which he learned a great deal of important information because hunting activities are usually the main topics of conversation. Based on the fairly extensive knowledge gained in this manner, he was equipped to use the technique of phased assertion.

> My interviews would therefore begin with statements about where my informant had traveled, what he had caught, and how long he was out on the land. (Collings, 2009: 148)

With that preamble, he could then ask for more detailed information about the topics he was particularly focused on.

There are many communities in which the interview style of direct questioning is seen as awkward and intrusive. Researchers should always try for a conversational style of interviewing with key informants. The strategy of phased assertion is part of that general approach to interviewing. Another part is quite the opposite: asking "dumb questions."

DeWalt and DeWalt (2010) have recounted their successes in asking "dumb" questions, or naïve questions, concerning issues for which they already knew the answers. They give the example of Bill DeWalt's interviewing people about shrimp farms in Mexico, when he asked "What happens to the water that is in the ponds?" He already knew the answer to the question, but his aim was to find out more about people's responses concerning the pollution effects of the shrimp farming industry. The DeWalts' discussion makes a good case for interviewers asking naïve questions to open up a broader discussion. Their example underscores the central fact that interviewing is a complex art, and researchers need to continue their training and practicing in order to get more effective, in-depth interviews (DeWalt and DeWalt 2010: 150–151).

FOCUS GROUP DISCUSSIONS

Focus group discussions (FGDs) became fashionable during the 1980s and 1990s, at the same time that ethnographic studies were becoming widely popular in many types of applied social science studies and in market research. Because of this, some people came to regard FGDs as the core data-gathering method in ethnography. For example, a few studies concerning people's attitudes about family planning consisted entirely of group discussions, with no other types of either qualitative or quantitative data.

By the 1990s, however, people were finding that, on sensitive matters such as sexual behaviors and alcohol use, group discussions resulted in serious distortions, as the participants presented "socially acceptable" attitudes and reported behaviors. Helitzer-Allen and colleagues carried out a comparison of FGDs and individual interviews among adolescent girls in Malawi concerning sexual knowledge and behaviors. Their study found that in the group discussions the girls gave "socially acceptable answers," which amounted to denying having knowledge about contraception and other sexual matters. In individual interviews, however, the informants were more open and forthcoming about both behaviors and knowledge relating to sexual practices (Helitzer-Allen et al. 1994).

Patton has referred to a more recent study by Kaplowitz, in 2000, comparing focus groups and individual one-on-one interviews concerning the respondents' willingness to discuss sensitive matters. The experiment was carried out in a rural region of the Yucatan Peninsula in Mexico. The researchers conducted 12 focus groups and 19 in-depth individual interviews. A professionally trained facilitator carried out both the group discussions and the individual interviews, using the same interview schedule. Patton summarized that "the findings showed that the individual interviews were 18 times more likely to address socially sensitive discussion topics than the focus groups" (Patton 2001: 289).

Jordan and Dalal have described growing disillusionment with FGDs as a data-gathering tool in market research. Noting the widespread popularity of focus groups at the end of the 20th century, they commented:

> Recently, however, market researchers themselves have become increasingly disillusioned with focus groups. In business journals, you now find articles entitled "Shoot the Focus Group" (Kiley 2005), the chief marketing officer at Yahoo says "I'm killing all our focus groups," and the Marketing Science Institute itself recognizes that the focus group is no longer the preeminent methodological tool for qualitative inquiry.... (Jordan and Dalal 2006: 365)

Jordan and Dalal go on to note that focus group data are a good source of information on what people say about products and perhaps behavioral intentions, but they also note the big lesson: "Do not equate attitudes with actions" (p. 365).

At the opposite side of the globe, a recent article mentions a similar disillusionment with focus groups in Australia. The article "Rise of Ethnography" in Australian marketing research quotes a market research specialist, Cochrane, who said, "Around 2003, I felt the whole area of focus groups in viewing facility goldfish bowls wasn't all that good at bringing consumers to life and showing marketers what consumers are really like.... So I started to experiment with ways of trying to capture more authentic slices of consumers' lives. I hadn't gone that far when I realized that what I was doing was ethnography" (Australian School of Business 2011).

It is interesting to find, in that quote and the accompanying discussion, that the Australian market researchers were making a clear separation between focus group research and "real ethnography." Cochrane and others were shifting to more direct contacts with consumers in their homes and other locations where commercial products were used, reflecting disillusionment with focus groups—hence the negative comment about "goldfish bowls." Apparently many places still have focus group facilities, where the market research people can view the FGD discussions from behind one-way mirror arrangements.

There are a number of problems with FGDs. In some groups, one or two local opinion leaders dominate the discussions and other participants appear to agree, though they may actually have views that differ from those of the dominant individuals. In many cases, FGDs are conducted by persons who are inexperienced in managing the complexities of group discussions. I have read the transcripts of many FGDs that were very poorly done.

The Positive Side of Focus Groups and PRA-Style Group Tasks

The idea of focus group discussions arose in World War II as a method for getting people's reactions to propaganda broadcasts and related materials. That was the reason for the term "focus" in the terminology.

Group discussions that are sharply focused on a task, a specific topic such as a radio broadcast or a film, or comparisons of two commercial products can be useful as sources of peoples' opinions, provided the group discussions are directed by experienced researchers. A. Vasan held a dozen FGDs with college students in southern Karnataka (India) in which the participants viewed selected clips from movies. She reported, "Participants watched the selected clips and discussed their interpretations and opinions...in terms of what they felt was appropriate/inappropriate, who they felt was right or not right, how realistic/unrealistic the situation was....These discussions...helped to understand how young people interpret situations in the films" (Vasan 2010: 8).

Based on the ideas and attitudes expressed in those focus groups, Vasan prepared a survey interview in which some of the same clips from films were shown to groups and each individual filled out a questionnaire. Thus the FGDs were an effective intermediate step in the research concerning the ways in which the south Indian college students react to and interpret situations in films. Group discussions are not useful as a source of quantitative data, however, so Vasan followed up the FGDs with a quantitative survey.

Another good example of using group discussions is in special tasks such as social mapping, which is described in Chapter 4. Some other PRA-style group work, such as asking villagers to construct bar charts to represent crop yields, rainfall per month, or other agricultural data, has produced excellent results, often more accurate than data produced by "expert outsiders" (Chambers 1997: esp. 141–150).

One important feature stands out in the students' discussions of films and the community groups doing social-mapping, rainfall estimates and other tasks: the data are not focused on the participants' own behaviors. Another characteristic of these "group discussions" is that, particularly in PRA methods, the focus on a specific topic is aided by the use of visual materials—mapping on paper or on the ground, or using physical objects such as sticks, stones, seeds, and other materials to indicate houses, locations, amounts, and other concrete information (see Figure 5.3).

Box 5.3 Basic Guidelines for Focus Group Discussions

1. Participants in focus group discussions (FGDs) should be a homogeneous group, for example, young unmarried men in their twenties, unmarried adolescent girls, middle-aged male farmers with at least three acres of their own cultivated land, male first-year students at the local college, or another such group.

2. The team for managing and recording the group discussion should include at least two or three resource persons: an experienced moderator and preferably two note-takers.

3. Recording is permitted, provided consent is obtained from the participants. Nonetheless, note-takers should try to get full written notes.

4. The moderator should have a carefully prepared checklist of topics and objectives for the discussion.

Another type of focus group discussion, again mainly used in the early phases of research, is to develop lists of the contents of specific top-

Figure 5.3. Group discussions are often a good way to get local vocabulary about key issues. © Dunja Pelto 2013.

ical domains and the local language usage in relation to the lists. Thus, lists of "women's health problems" can be created in group discussions, along with the terminology for symptoms, remedies, and other related information. Similarly, listings of "edible wild foods," changes in food use patterns, cooking vessels, and related information can be accumulated very handily in focus group discussions.

These types of FGD-produced inventories of topical domains, plus the explorations of local terminology, can quickly result in useful information, often linked to some social mapping. In a few days your research team can have an informative rough draft of materials for exploring with more in-depth methods.

Conclusions

Key informant interviewing and social mapping are the most useful data-gathering activities at the beginning of an ethnographic study. Group discussions can also be useful, especially in the form of social mapping, and also some listing and vocabulary tasks. I have detailed some of the negative issues concerning focus groups because there are still some research groups that have inflated expectations about that type of data-gathering.

Although I have emphasized the usefulness of key informant interviewing in the early phases of research, any research team that has sufficient funding and personnel should consider regular use of key informants throughout the entire period of research. In some cases, it may be useful to pay one or two key informants some kind of honorarium, if they are available to devote considerable time to your project.

One excellent approach to finding good Type Two and Type Three key informants is to do several sessions of social mapping in different parts of the study area, with varied groups of local informants doing the mapping. In each such group you are likely to find one or two individuals who are outspoken and appear to have good information about the local area and special sub-populations in the communities. Of course, if you are working with one or more NGOs, some of their outreach workers are likely to be good key informants, and they will also be able to introduce you to potential informants in their working areas in the communities.

Note Taking and Other Recording: Capturing and Managing the Data

Capturing the data is the most difficult task of ethnographic field work. Unless researchers are able to record, write down, and otherwise manage the raw data, the efforts of data gathering can be seriously undermined. Data gathering becomes even more complicated when the ethnographic work is a multi-site project with an interdisciplinary team of researchers. Here are the main types of data collection that field researchers undertake.

- Written notes of interviews and field notes of observations, with or without use of some audio-recording. The central core of ethnographic data consists of written notes and perhaps some audio recording of individual interviews, plus field notes from observations of events, actions, and related descriptive information. (Later in this chapter I will mention some cautions about the use of audio recording.)

- Daily log of activities. Some field workers (and research teams) keep two kinds of daily records: (i) a daily activities log that contains the amount of time spent on activities such as interviews and direct observations and other brief notes about "what I (we) did today"; and (ii) a personal diary/ of actions and thoughts related to the field work, including bits of planning, reviews of "mistakes," emotional reactions to sensitive interviews, hunches and hypotheses about the field situation and the state of the data thus far, and other personal thoughts. Based on the daily log, the field workers will be able to describe how many days were spent in actual case interviews and how many were spent in expanding and entering field notes and in other data management activities, and will have related descriptions of these field work processes.

- Collection of secondary materials, including newspaper accounts, newsletters, local writings, and organization records. In most types of

Pertti Pelto, "Note Taking and Other Recording: Capturing and Managing the Data," in *Applied Ethnography: Guidelines for Field Research*, pp. 103-126. © 2013 Left Coast Press, Inc. All rights reserved.

research, researchers should collect any brochures, information sheets, notices of immunization days, and other written materials circulated by governmental and private health facilities, schools, NGOs, and other organizations. During research in schools, for example, ethnographers will try to obtain copies of key teaching materials, messages circulated in the school system, and various other formal and informal documents that can be valuable resource materials in relation to ongoing activities in the school context. Whether in school-based research or other community-based ethnography, there are likely to be newspaper items that reflect local events, local community conflicts, and other information relevant to the study community. In some cases, in a multi-ethnic research setting, the researcher may need to hire someone to look for significant items in local news sources of a different language. In many areas in the United States, for example, there are likely to be some news sources in Spanish that relate to local events.

- Structured survey forms. Another type of data collection is the collection of structured survey forms, often a basic house-listing and demographic data set for describing the study communities.

- Photographs, videos, and other visual documentation. Photography is an intrinsic part of almost all ethnographic research, although very little has been written about "routine photographic activities." Instead, specialized uses of photography and video as major tools have been featured in some classic works. Field researchers should be careful to get permissions for photographing people, and there will of course be some sensitive situations in which you should avoid doing photography. On the other hand, many public events, family gatherings, ritual actions, meetings, and other scenes should be photographed if possible, as there will be situations in which you will only be able to describe certain features, including the types of people attending, by examining the photos and/or videos.

- Other miscellaneous data collections, particularly any available government or non-government statistics about the demographics and statistics in the local region. Letters that field workers write to families, colleagues, and friends often have valuable syntheses of field information. Many collections of letters from the field contain insights that are extremely useful "secondary data." The letters written from the field by Franz Boas, Margaret Mead, and many other ethnographers have proved to be valuable sources for the field workers themselves, as well as for other researchers (see also Mead 1977).

In the past decade, a whole new inventory of electronic data-management devices has become widely available. A variety of hand-held cell phones and hand-held computers have become ethnographic data-capture devices. Gravlee and colleagues have described the use of hand-held computers for "direct observation of the social and physical environment" (Gravlee et al. 2007). Although I don't advocate turning to "high-tech" for most ethnographic work, there are some situations in which your research team could explore certain specialized uses of these devices.

Taking Notes and Converting Raw Notes (Jottings) into Useful Data

In all the data-gathering methods discussed here, whether PRA, mapping, in-depth interviewing, or observing activities, field researchers should write down as much detail as time allows in the form of "jottings," or rough notes. Those notes are often just key words and phrases, although sometimes you should write complete sentences. In some cases it is useful and efficient to use audio recorders (see comments below), but even if a recording device is used, you should continue to take thorough notes.

Jottings into Data: Expanding the Pieces into the Full Story

Sanjek (1990) called them "scratch notes"; Bernard (2011) says "field jottings"; Spradley (1979) referred to them as "condensed notes."

> The terminology refers to the notes that you jot down during an in-depth interview, while watching a religious ritual, while observing people's interactions at a meeting, as well as things that just strike you as you are walking along. Jottings will provide you with the trigger you need to recall a lot of details that you don't have time to write down while you're observing events or listening to an informant. Even a few key words will jog your memory later. Remember: *If you don't write it down, it's gone.* (Bernard, 2011: 292. Emphasis in original)

When you are training field researchers in interviewing, they will need careful coaching about the following seemingly simple rules.

1. Note the time of starting the interview and the ending time.
2. Write down as many key words and phrases as you can while the informant is speaking, but don't try to write full sentences.

3. Try to retain that informant's exact words as much as possible. Sometimes you can ask the informant to pause a moment: "Just a minute—I want to be sure I got it exactly the way you said it." Then, read back the sentence from your notes, and ask the informant if it is correct.

4. Immediately after the interview, or as soon as possible, go over the notes to see that you are able to read and understand your own writing.

5. That same day, when you and your field team get back to your quarters, expand the "jotted notes" into fully expanded notes—full sentences, keeping the original sequence of topics and statements.

6. As a general rule, allow at least two hours of writing expanded notes for each hour of interviewing. (Of course, this depends somewhat on how fast you are at typing.)

7. Save each interview as a separate file in the computer.

EXAMPLE

EXPANDING JOTTED NOTES INTO A FULLY EXPANDED EXCERPT

Here is an example of jotted notes as given in *Community Assessment of Natural Food Sources of Vitamin A* (Blum et al. 1997).

JOTTED NOTES DURING AN INTERVIEW

> Earlier...all people collected them (calchan) [wild greens, stalks, leaves] had time. Children. Especially older women. Now. Too far. All summer. Cooked with meat. Poor people potatoes. Lazy. "Young women won't cook 'em. Edge of fields...river...people...Weaker now... Poor food..."

FULLY EXPANDED EXCERPT FROM THOSE JOTTINGS (MOSTLY FROM MEMORY)

The following is from the middle of the much longer, expanded interview and reflects the jotted notes above:

> The old grandmother in the _____ household told me that when she was a child and even as a young married woman, people gathered the wild greens called calchan which were available throughout the summer. "All people collected them...." The main locations were at the edges of the cornfields and also along the riverbank. They gathered the stalks and leaves. Sometimes they sent the children to gather them, but mainly it was older women who did not have small children to care for. The wealthier families cooked the greens with meat, but most families were poor and cooked them with their potatoes.
>
> When I asked why people do not gather those wild greens nowadays, she said that "people are lazy" and then she added that "...the

Figure 6.1. The interviewer and note-taker work together to write fully expanded notes. © Dunja Pelto 2013.

younger women won't cook 'em, because they view the greens as being inferior food and 'poor food'" (that is, food for the poor people). She also said that she believes people today are weaker now and less healthy because they do not eat the healthy foods 'from nature.' Like they did when she was young." (Blum et al. 1997: 113–114)

The preceding example is from Lauren Blum's field notes in Niger. The fully expanded notes have approximately four times as many words as the jottings during the interview. It is easily evident that only the person who wrote the jotted notes would be able to write out the full story.

Using a Dedicated Note Taker

When local people have been hired to be part of the research team, it is often useful to have them operate as two-person research teams. In that case, one person does the interviewing and the second person, sitting slightly aside, takes down notes (see Figure 6.1). I recommend that the interviewer also takes down some jotted notes, especially key words and phrases, in order to be able to review the notes in detail with the note taker afterwards. When you have a second person as the "dedicated note taker," the jotted notes will be much more fully developed than the example above, where the interviewer herself was jotting the notes.

Other Details in Expanded Interview Notes

The following are guidelines for developing the fully expanded interview notes.

1. Each interview file should have a heading giving the date, time, location, identity of the informant, interviewer, and other standard details.

2. The beginning of the interview file should have a description—at least one or two paragraphs—of how the informant was contacted, who introduced the researchers, the statement about the informed consent procedure, the location of the interview (in the house, outside under a tree, at the schoolyard, in a separate room in a clinic, etc.), and perhaps other people, interruptions, etc.

3. At some point in the interview there may be statements concerning some cultural, social, or perhaps political features, about which the researchers can write an observation or explanation, such as, "This statement about the local politician is very different from what our informants told us last Monday. We need to check on the family connections, or other 'political networking' that might account for this very different interpretation."

4. At the end of the interview, describe the dress style, the appearance of the informant, and her or his personal style, for example, "very open and friendly" or "At first the informant was very suspicious and a bit unfriendly, but she gradually opened up, and by the end of the interview she was fully cooperating, and talking very openly. She offered to give us coffee, but we were late for our next appointment, so we agreed that we would come back within the next two weeks and chat with her again."

5. Mention any interruptions, such as the informant stopping to do child care or other tasks, or interruptions by other persons.

Table 6.1 shows a step-by-step procedure, as outlined in one of the researchers' reports at the Center for Research on Environment, Health and Population Activities (CREHPA), a research organization in Kathmandu,

Nepal. The hardest part of this process is Step 3, "expanding the 'kachcha notes' into full text." As mentioned earlier, you should expect to spend at least two hours to expand the notes from one good hour of interviewing. Field work supervisors should spend a lot of time on this step when training field researchers, and then review their expanded notes to be sure they have done a thorough job, including giving some local language quotes in their expanded notes.

TABLE 6.1. Steps in Interview Note Taking and Processing

Location	Data Management
1. Face-to-face interview situation and observations in field sites	Researchers took down rough notes (jottings) such as key words, phrases, and sometimes entire sentences both during the interviews and while observing some activities (e.g., a meeting). [We call them "kachcha notes" (kachcha = raw)]
2. At or near the site, immediately after interviews and observations	Researchers reviewed their notes, checked they were legible, and filled in some additional observations and other "remembered materials."
3. Back at the workplace or home of the researcher	Researchers expanded the "kachcha notes" into full sentences and descriptive details, including descriptions of the interview situation, the informant and the sequence of information in the interview as fully as possible. Often the expanded notes were in the local language used in the interview. The core team members read the expanded notes and provided feedback to the researchers.
4. At the workplace (researcher)	Expanded notes were translated into English (or other working language of the research team) and entered as text files in the computer.
5. At the workplace (data entry person)	The data-entry person entered the appropriate codes into the interview file, using the ATLAS/ti[a] software program and the agreed-on code list.

[a] The ATLAS/ti software program (also mentioned in Chapter 12) is designed for coding and managing text data and other qualitative material. With a fully coded data set, a researcher can search for, and retrieve, all blocks of data that are labeled with a specific code, thus enhancing the researcher's data analysis capacities.
Source: Adapted with permission, CREHPA 2002b:15

Inexperienced interviewers always have difficulty in writing out their notes fully. Here are some common mistakes.

■ The interviewer presents only the main highlights or "most interesting points" from the interview, and fails to give any details.

■ The expanded notes do not include verbatim quotations, and no local language words and no explanations for vague or strange comments are included in the notes.

■ The field worker fails to present the step-by-step "flow" of the interview, following the sequence of the actual interview.

■ The notes are all written in the third person, so the "voice of the informant" is missing.

In the field work situation, supervisors or team leaders should read each interviewer's notes every day, and should ask the interviewers to explain points that are unclear. The interviewers should fill in more information at points where necessary details are lacking.

The following is an excerpt from notes of an interview with a Nepali drug-user, illustrating the kinds of detail that should be captured in effective documentation of interviews:

Q. Did you ever try to quit the drug use?

A. I did go to the rehabilitation center for four months when I was only into phensydyle and not into Tidigesic.

Q. When was it?

A. It was around 2052 [Vikram calendar] at Maharajgunj. I stayed there for 4 months at the end of 2052. [Note: The Vikram calendar is commonly used in Nepal. That date translates to around 1995–96]

Q. What did they have you do daily?

A. They made us do some exercise in the morning at 5 o'clock. They took us for running in the grounds and made us do some light exercises. We then cleaned our rooms. We had our breakfast at 8 o'clock, 4 breads, cup of tea and one egg. We then had class about drugs. Teachers would come from Rajyog and teach us so that we don't think about drugs. We then had lunch for one and a half hours. We rested for half an hour and then an inspector or someone trained in drugs would again teach us about drugs. We had tea at around 2 o'clock and then went for another class at 3 o'clock, which was conducted by a teacher from Baneshwor. We played football from 4 o'clock. We were back to our rooms by 5:30. (notes from a CREHPA interview with an injection drug user)

The Notebook: The Ethnographer's Professional Symbol

The writing of detailed notes is certainly one of the most important activities in the daily life of ethnographic research. Each field researcher should have the habit of always carrying a notebook for jottings, "scratch notes" and extended interview notes. Actually it is a good idea to always carry two notebooks—a small notebook can be used in situations where note-taking needs to be unobtrusive. Some researchers have reported that they developed skills in writing in a small notebook inside a large purse or bag.

Many researchers carry a mid-sized notebook as a visible mark of their dedicated research activity. That notebook should be large enough so that you can draw diagrams (or ask a key informant to draw a diagram), a timeline of some activity, or a quick bar chart.

DeWalt and DeWalt wrote:

> Kathleen used to use one that was approximately 2" by 3" and now uses a notebook the size of a 3" by 5" note card. Bill increasingly uses a legal pad. (DeWalt and DeWalt 2010: 161)

In my first field work in Finnish Lapland, I had a bunch of small notebooks, approximately 3" by 5", that fit into my pocket. That was partly because much of the year I traveled on skis from one household to another, or out to reindeer herding activities. My notebook was always handy—anything larger would have had to be in my backpack. At the end of my 15 months of field work I had about 25 or 30 of those little notebooks full of jotted notes. Each evening I wrote out expanded notes with my trusty little portable typewriter.

Lakshmi Ramachandar almost always carries a mid-sized notebook (6" by 9"), which is a good size for making diagrams or asking an informant to do a sketch map.

When to Take Notes

In most cases your biggest bunch of notes is from your in-depth interviews with key informants and case interviews. Usually you will want to start off the interview with some light conversation, about the weather, "How are your children doing?" "How are the crops doing?" and other topics. Also, you should spend some time explaining your project and reaffirming the person's informed consent. During these preliminaries, you don't immediately take out your notebook. After you have established a relaxed, positive interaction with the informant, then you say to the informant:

The information that we want to talk about is very important, and I want to be sure that I don't forget parts of it. I want to get it right. So, do you mind if I take some notes while you are telling me things?

If you make it clear that you consider the informant's words and descriptions important, very rarely will you get a refusal.

In a very few situations you might sense that the informant is somewhat tense and suspicious. You can then extend the attempts at light conversation and even get into some of your intended interview materials, and only take out your notebook after another few minutes, asking permission to write down some of the important things she is telling you.

Some field workers have reported that they felt awkward and "unnatural" taking notes during conversation or interviews. I believe that this is generally the researcher's problem, and not due to reactions of the informants. If the field researcher has clearly established her or his research role and explains to the informant that "I want to be able to 'get it right,'" the note-taking usually becomes a positive feature, encouraging the informant to narrate events and explain things.

Field Notes and Observations

Sometimes it's a bit difficult, or inappropriate, to take notes. M. Freilich has described difficult note-taking situations in his research among Mohawk people in Brooklyn and at their upstate reservation, including participant observation in a bar. Particularly in the bar environment there were negative reactions to any note-taking. He described that he did most of his note taking during periodic trips to the men's room, where he quickly jotted down important points (Freilich 1970).

Understanding the Importance of Note Taking

Even illiterate rural people understand the importance of note taking (see Figure 6.2). Some students and hired research assistants object to taking notes during interviews, saying that it interferes with eye contact, slows the pace of interviews, and interferes with building rapport. In India my team and I have heard those objections in almost every training session, so we take special pains to coach the research trainees concerning the importance of, and strategies for, effective note taking.

We suggest that the interviewers say to each informant something like the following: "The information that you know, and that I would like to talk about with you, is very useful, and your ideas are very important for me. If I don't take careful notes, I won't remember all the things you

Figure 6.2. Careful note-taking shows the informant that the researcher is serious about understanding the information. © Dunja Pelto 2013.

told me, and I might even remember some things the wrong way."

Lakshmi Ramachandar reported experiences in field research in rural India (2010) that are useful examples to pass on to your researchers, if they have any doubts about taking detailed notes.

Excerpt from the field notes of Lakshmi Ramachandar

I went to a village by the name of Kudligi on Thursday, February 18th. The objective of my visit was to interact with a group of sex workers and learn from their experiences. Two staff members from Vimukthi [the local community-based organization] accompanied me to the site. The sex workers had gathered even before we had arrived and we all got introduced. They described to me their routine weekly timetable as well as other highlights of their activities. There were twelve women and two male workers in the meeting.

I had taken their informed consent for writing down notes and they appreciated my interest in note-taking. On two occasions when I raised the issue about the formation of savings groups and housing loans they all started talking together. I was unable to take any notes and therefore I put down my note book on the floor.

I discussed my difficulties about taking notes with the programme coordinator and the local leader of the support groups. I told them all the information that they are narrating is of great value to me. But I am unable to store all the information in my brains and by the time I return to Bellary I may have forgotten half of the problems that they narrated to me.

The women realized the importance of my note-taking. One of the members took control of the situation and silenced all the others. In a way, she acted like a moderator. She told the women they should talk one at a time. If everybody talked at the same time it might not be possible to do any note-taking.

All the women obeyed her orders and started describing to me their grievances one at a time. Before I could lay my hands on my notebook and pen, one of the members who was sitting beside me handed me my note book and pens that were lying on the floor mat. (We were all seated, as usual, on the floor.)

The first woman described her complaints about her parent organization, and waited for me to write down her caste and her problems clearly. She said, "My name is Chitra [name changed] and I am a Devadasi." She was waiting for me to show the gesture that I had noted down the information.

One other person remarked looking at my notes, "See this madam said that she will forget if she does not take any notes. But our superiors from the offices in Bangalore and Bellary never carry even a piece of paper with them. We go around the village and we describe to them about housing conditions. There are three Chitras in our village. All those three Chitras have different problems. How would they remember if they do not take any notes? If madam can forget, even those official people also would forget all that we shared by the time they reach Bangalore." The women started discussing amongst themselves the importance of note-taking.

I was very pleased with the group that I interacted with, and they were very cooperative and they realized the importance of note-taking. Sometimes I ignored even their eye contacts and they did not care about my eye contact. They were observing my concentration while I was jotting down the notes. (Ramachandar 2010: 23–24)

The principle here is that the note writing should be publicly visible and accessible to the informants, even though it is unusual that we actually show the notes. (In the preceding case, the notes were written partly in Kannada script and partly in English and so very few informants could possibly make sense of them, but they would feel reassured if the researcher allowed them to look at the writing.)

The lessons from this event are as follows:

- People in the rural communities (and everywhere) can understand the concept of writing notes and keeping some sort of written memory record. The preceding example shows that even illiterate people can easily understand the importance of written documentation.

- The primary message the researcher needs to convey is that she is regarding as valuable (and thus writing down) the voices and feelings of the community people. If the community people listed their main problems, the note-taker/researcher will have that information accurately recorded in her notes.

Some participatory research advocates have suggested the systematic sharing and mutual revising of field notes, but here I am only suggesting an openness with the interview notes and a willingness to share and consider some corrections. That process of sharing is most likely to lead to further important details and perhaps even significant case examples.

The field situation just described shows that the actions of note taking have important political and social implications, and field researchers can use the note-taking actions to strengthen the effectiveness of local people's oral statements. One of these days, we may well hear of somebody in an eastern Karnataka community telling visiting officials, "If you are not taking notes on what we told you, we don't trust your promises. Write it all down, or we will not tell you anything."

USING AUDIO-RECORDING DEVICES

Voice recorders and the other electronic recording devices can be an important aid to effective documentation. Many ethnographers take the view that practically all structured and semi-structured interviews should be recorded with audio equipment (Bernard 2011; DeWalt and DeWalt 2010). The following is an overview of things that any research group should consider carefully if they are planning to use audio recording.

1. Researchers should always ask the informants' permission at the start of the interview, if they intend to do audio recording of interviews. When interviewing about sensitive topics, researchers should watch carefully for any sign that people are hesitant about the audio recording. Even if informants grant permission, they may be less open in discussing the more sensitive topics. It is not always clear as to which topics are likely to intrude on people's sensitivities.

2. As a "golden rule," there should be careful note taking, even if you are using a recording device. Note taking while using a recording device is extremely important a) as a backup in case of system failure; and b) to record nonverbal events, actions, impressions about the informant's honesty and attitudes, and other observations that are part of the record of the interview situation.

3. The note taker should describe the interview situation, details of interruptions by other persons, the dress, manner and personality of the informant, and other details.

4. In many applied ethnographic projects it has become usual to hire local persons (familiar with the local dialects and cultural patterns) as research assistants. Often those locally hired persons are the main interviewers. Some of these research assistants may not be fully familiar with recording devices—especially the newer types of equipment.

5. In some settings, a few people may object to the use of recording equipment. Even if it is only a few individuals, it raises problems about the comparability of the data among the informants.

6. Transcribing and "capturing everything" from the recorded materials is a time-consuming and expensive process. Often transcribers need several hours to listen to and transcribe one audio file. In some projects, the transcribing may lead to delays in needed data analysis.

7. Some interviewers are themselves nervous about the audio-recorder, and their interviews may be interrupted or complicated if they must spend time checking and adjusting the recording equipment. Even worse are those situations where the field researchers come to rely totally on the equipment and, despite their training, fail to take notes, assuming that "everything is there in the recording."

Nowadays well-funded research projects will always have up-to-date electronic recording equipment. My concern, however, is the many less-well-funded projects, especially in developing countries, where the new audio equipment is still quite costly and some researchers have had little opportunity to become acquainted with the new technology.

In some projects we have recommended that audio recording not be used in the first interview, but that it can be introduced in a follow-up second interview, once both the interviewer and informant are more comfortable with the interview situation.

There is considerable variation in the extent to which various researchers use voice recording of interviews. Bernard is strongly in favor of extensive audio recording. He wrote, "Don't rely on your memory in interviewing; use a voice recorder in all structured and semi-structured interviews, except where people specifically ask you not to" (Bernard 2011: 170).

The DeWalts are also positive about audio recording, yet some ambivalence is evident in their recommendations. They note the versatility and excellent recording quality of the newer, smaller digital voice recorders, saying that "people feel more comfortable with the smaller devices—they forget they are there...." However, their ambivalence is evident on the same page: "The use of recording is limited by its effect on situations. In our experience recording can be more threatening than note-taking..." (DeWalt and DeWalt 2010: 164). But they go on to mention an Ecuadorian colleague who "...always kept a tape-recorder in view and running, with little impact on the field work" (p. 164).

Susan Eliot, a professional evaluation researcher, described how she converted from use of audio-recording to intensive note-taking. She uses a shorthand writing method, and tries to write down nearly everything the informant tells her. She also uses the technique of halting the interaction for brief periods to check with the informant about the correctness of her notes and to give the informant a chance to think about the details covered up to that point. Eliot listed a number of benefits from this dedication to note writing. One of the important improvements she highlighted is that she pays more careful attention to the details of what the respondent is saying. She noted, "I'm more likely to identify ambiguous comments that need clarifying" and also, "The respondent feels I take them seriously when I write down everything they tell me" (Eliot 2010).

Decisions about Using Recording Equipment

Four main questions come into the decision-making about whether, or how much, to use technical recording equipment, namely:

- Who are the informants you will be interviewing?
- How sensitive are the topics you will be raising in the interviews?
- What are the levels of technical skills and interviewing capabilities of your interviewers?
- Do you have good quality modern audio-recording equipment, and do you have personnel for timely transcription of the recorded interviews?

In the current era of the HIV/AIDS pandemic, a great many studies probe into sensitive areas of sexual behaviors, the lives of sex workers, injection drug use, and other topics that were taboo subjects until 20 years ago. Recently I was reviewing a study about "condom breakage" in the experiences of sex workers. The paper included verbatim quotes from the sex workers about their experiences of negotiating condom use with clients and about instances of condom breakage. The data-gathering had included tape-recorded sessions. My reaction to the study was that the data were rather weak and superficial. Yes, the sex workers discussed some very intimate details, but my immediate impression was that much better in-depth information would have resulted if the interviewers hadn't used the recording equipment.

The third question encountered in decision making concerning the use of voice recording equipment centers on the nature of your research team. Much of the writing in books and articles concerning ethnographic field research has been addressed to academic professionals and their advanced students. If your research team is made up of skilled, experienced professionals, then use of audio-recording and audio-visual equipment may be a practical choice. Of course, your team will also need to have individuals for transcribing voice recordings into computerized text files. If, however, your team, or multi-site teams, don't have the skills and equipment for effective, time-efficient management of voice recording, then your choice should be to invest more time in training for effective, hand-written note taking, perhaps utilizing two-person interview teams.

In some research situations, if the data include materials concerning illegal activities, researchers must be wary of the risk that audio-recorded data and written notes might fall into the wrong hands, posing serious dangers for the informants.

An experienced Australian ethnographer, S. Belton, reported that much of her field research was on illegal abortion, in countries where there was the possibility of arrests by the police. "Therefore, I never recorded women's voices, as I was worried that the police may become overly interested and seize my fieldwork. I never wrote real names or locations in my field notes either, for the same reason. For me as the ethical researcher, it depended on what was being discussed and in what context. If I felt that I could not guarantee my participant's safety, then I avoided writing any identifying information and avoided recording their voices..." (Belton, 2012: 1). She went on to describe recent research in which she used audio recording extensively, because the topics of the research were much less sensitive.

Figure 6.3. Dictating field notes while walking through the community.
© Dunja Pelto 2013.

Dictating Interview Notes and Field Notes Using Audio Equipment

In situations when researchers do not use audio recording during interviews or when it has not been possible to take detailed field notes of a meeting or other event, it may be useful to dictate detailed notes using an audio recorder. The researcher can usually find a quiet location and, referring to the jotted notes from an interview, dictate at least a rough draft of expanded notes for later transcription and revision at the computer. The DeWalts noted that audio-recording of field-notes is much faster than typing at the computer. Furthermore, the dictating of field notes with a hand-held device can be done while walking (see Figure 6.3) or while riding in a vehicle, if someone else is driving. They noted, however, that dictating notes works out much better if there is funding to pay for the transcription of the recordings. Otherwise, busy field workers are unlikely to have enough time for the cumbersome process of writing out the audio-recorded materials (DeWalt and DeWalt 2010: 175–176).

USING PHOTOGRAPHY AND PHOTOGRAPHS IN FIELD WORK

Practically every field researcher does some photography during field work, at least to send photos back home to family and friends and to have a visual record of the unique experience of being immersed in a different cultural setting. However, photography can and should be much more than just casual snapshots for family and friends. At the very least, every field worker should consider photography as a tool for visual recording of "typical scenes": buildings, gatherings, the local market, street scenes, interview situations, group discussions, and other settings. These visual images will be useful later when writing descriptions of the study area, the people, typical activities, and a wide range of other things that otherwise can become hazy and distant just a few weeks after one leaves the research area.

Several decades ago John Collier wrote a book entitled *Visual Anthropology: Photography as a Research Method* (1967) that goes much further than our usual, casual photography. Of course, the book reflects the days before digital cameras, "smartphones" with photographic capabilities, and the entire technology of sending, sharing, and other manipulation of photographic materials. His field research took place in a small sample of Native American households in the San Francisco Bay area. Working with an ethnographic researcher, Collier photographed the kitchen, living room and bedrooms—the main locations in the households. The aim of the photography was to document the arrangements of furnishings and certain material goods, large and small, thus documenting what we might call the household "material style of life." The objects and conditions he documented were analyzed in terms of their varying expressions of ethnic identity by linking them to interviews and other data about the families (Collier 1967).

With today's technology, photos can be shared immediately with people in your research site. Lakshmi Ramachandar told me that, in her field work in eastern Karnataka (India), she often takes photos of the women's groups and individuals in rural villages and then passes the camera to the women, who can see themselves in the photographs. That process can be a way of developing rapport with the local people.

Participatory Photography

Gotschi and associates (2009) have described experimental field work in Mozambique, in which they gave cameras to small farmer groups and asked them to decide among themselves what they would photograph about themselves. The purpose of the exploration was "...to stimulate farmers in discussing their group membership, and to assess what it meant to them as individuals, families, groups, or community" (Gotschi, Delve, and Freyer 2009: 292). These researchers reported that the group dynamics were different in the three groups. It appears that participatory photography holds considerable promise as a method for getting people's individual and group expressions concerning how to visualize important aspects of their daily life. This report from Mozambique includes little detail about systematic "capturing" of the data, but the overall impression is that, for certain types of programs, the technique of "giving the cameras to the people" can yield important new insights if integrated with other data gathering.

Photovoice for Participatory Needs Assessment

C. Wang and colleagues introduced the term photovoice as a label for their style of participatory photography (Wang, Burris, and Ping 1996; Wang and Burris 1997). Wang and her team conducted an extensive photovoice participatory project in Yunnan Province, which is one of the poorer rural areas of China. They had extensive cooperation from the county government people, and the Women's Federation in the province provided support in the form of speeding up the developing and handling of films produced by the project.

> "In June 1992...53 women from Chengjiang and Luliang counties received intensive training in the techniques and process of "photovoice." Six months later, another 9 women were added to the project. The women were selected to represent a range of age, education, and marital status. During that first training session, after the women had been taught the fundamentals of using a camera (including flash), the trainees were asked to go out and photograph "the spirit of village women's everyday lives." (Wang and Burris 1997: 377)

The next stage of the project (after the developed photos were returned) consisted of group sessions in which photos were sorted and selections were made of the most important and useful visualizations of community needs. Storytelling from the selected photographs was the next step in the process, as the individual photographers explained the meaning and importance of specific images. Here's an example.

> The old woman is over sixty. She is carrying food to feed the pigs. I wanted to capture the industriousness of the women in the countryside. (p. 381)

The final crucial stage of the project was what they called "codification"—identifying main issues, themes, and theories. This process, carried out by the women, identified the following three main problem areas: (a) lack of access to clean water, (b) lack of transportation, and (c) lack of child care.

Wang and Burris pointed out that many needs-assessment programs assume, or claim to find, that women are lacking in information and understanding. However, their research showed that, to the contrary, the women have plenty of understanding and information about local needs and problems, but they lack channels for expressing these issues to the political authorities and policy makers.

In the past decade, the widespread use of cell phones for photography, together with the ease of sending digital photos to friends, Facebook, and other social network systems, has greatly expanded the use of photography as part of people's communications repertoires. It has also become increasingly easy to insert photos into letters, email messages, and written manuscripts. For many types of ethnographic studies it is the "new norm" to include plenty of photographs. At the same time, people in many communities are now more accustomed to being photographed, particularly during various public events.

Ethnographers involved in field work should consider the use of photography as a multipurpose tool for many types of projects. The low cost makes it possible for field researchers to take many photographs simply to be able to remember details of public scenes, meetings, and other features. To paraphrase an old saying: "One photo can be worth a score of jotted notes."

Be aware, however, that any research situations can be "socially sensitive," and photography may be highly inappropriate, particularly in research concerning socially stigmatized people such as sex workers, drug users, criminal gangs, and others. Also, certain scenes and situations in institutional settings—schools, hospitals, and others—may be considered sensitive and "off limits" to photography.

You should always ask people's permission if you want to photograph individuals or groups. In clinics, schools, and other settings you should ask the persons in charge concerning permissions for photographing activities and scenes. Even if the director or principal gives general permission, you should still ask individuals if it is OK to photograph them in their activities.

If you expect to show your photos to people immediately, we recommend that you use a digital camera with a good viewing screen. It can be problematic to be passing your smart phone around in a group of people.

VIDEO RECORDING OF REPEATED EVENTS: SCHOOL-BASED RESEARCH WITH THE VIDEO CAMERA

F. Erickson and G. Mohatt carried out research on teachers' classroom styles in a Native American school in Northern Ontario, in which a major data-gathering component was the use of video recording. The aim of the study was to examine certain hypotheses about "cultural congruence" in teacher-student interactions. The researchers videotaped classroom behaviors of one Native American and one non-indigenous teacher.

> Both first grade teachers were videotaped across one school year—in the early fall, in the late fall, in the winter, and in the late spring. The videotaping was done by a member of the reservation community. He knew the community culture intimately as a member of it, and knew the individual children and their families and the teachers. (Erickson and Mohatt 1982: 141)

Video-camera cassettes in those days were usually good for one hour of continuous recording, so the cameraman was instructed to do continuous recording, without interruption whenever possible. He was also instructed to record in the same style in the two classrooms, without much zooming in and out. Microphones were another technological component, giving the researchers relatively full transcriptions of the teachers' use of language. The total data collection on videotapes was 18 hours—10 hours with the Native American teacher, and 8 hours with the non-native teacher. Other data gathering included in-depth interviewing of the teachers and some participant observation, but in this type of research the videotapes were the primary raw data.

Data Analysis of Videotaped Behaviors

The analysis of continuous videotaping can be structured and quantitative. Erickson and Mohatt identified a small series of behavior/actions for systematic coding. The key activity then consisted of counting the frequency of each event and calculating the total minutes for each category of action. The behavioral events in their analysis include "entering and settling," "teacher at blackboard," "teacher passing out paper," "teacher circulating, giving individual attention," "teacher sitting, giving individual attention," and "small group work." There were also several other, less frequent categories. There were very few differences between the two teachers in the frequencies and total minutes allotted to the various categories of activities. The differences in teaching style were in more subtle qualities.

The categories for analysis predominantly focused on the teachers' actions, because of the specific theoretical concepts guiding the research. A secondary type of analysis of the videotapes was in the form of diagramming the teachers' movements relating to certain key actions, for example, setting up small groups to work together. The diagrams for "setting up group work" showed marked differences between the Native and non-Native teacher in patterns of movement. The researchers noted that the Native American teacher moved more slowly, and did not move to as many locations as the non-indigenous teacher. "Teacher I's [Native American teacher] strategies involved proceeding fairly slowly and deliberately....Teacher II moved more rapidly and moved around the whole room" (p. 151).

The researchers found considerable evidence of differences in "cultural congruence" in classroom styles between the two teachers. The Native American teacher's pace of teaching was slower and, in some sense, more evenly paced. Another difference in style was that the Native American teacher did not call out to individual students from a distance. Instead, communications with individual students were carried out at close range, in a more "one-on-one" manner.

A major area of difference in cultural style was in the delivering of directives (commands). In the segment of behavior labeled "leaving the room," the non-indigenous teacher had five times as many directives as the indigenous teacher (7 vs. 36 directives) (p. 153). The manner of giving directives was also different. In their description of the study, the researchers presented a section of transcript from the Native American teacher and commented:

> Notice that the directives issued by the teacher to the children...during the initial "off the record" phase are "privatized" by the close proximity and low voice volume of the teacher. This avoids putting the recipient of the directive in the spotlight of public attention.... (p. 159)

> The teacher also avoids explicit evaluation of the correctness of student answers, in the classic "lesson discourse" sequence characteristic of culturally mainstream teachers in Canada and the United States. (p.160)

Erickson and Mohatt pointed to a key feature that is widely reported in studies of Native American cultures, including studies of school-based behaviors:

> [that there is]...avoidance of direct and overt social control in situations where such exercise of control over others would be regarded as

entirely appropriate and "natural" by non-Indians. This feature of etiquette is mentioned frequently in the general ethnographic literature.
(p. 165)

Erickson has referred to this type of research as "microethnography," in which the researcher focuses on a "situation-specific" aspect of
peoples' cultural behaviors, often with the use of videotaping and other
systematic documentation. Microethnography contrasts with "standard
ethnography," which generally takes a much broader sweep of cultural
behaviors in order to understand and describe a more general system of
social relations.

It appears that schools and classroom behaviors are ideal for this
kind of intensive video recording, because the actions take place in a
clearly defined location and they follow much the same schedule and
format, day after day. That consistency of action makes it feasible to
quantify categories of behavior, following the model set by Erickson and
Mohatt, and also allows for the repeated cross checking and framing of
new research questions as the data gathering progresses.

A wide range of situations and activities is suitable for this form of
microethnography, with or without video recording. Harvesting crops
on large farms, activities in factories and commercial establishments,
location-specific recreational pursuits, and many other fixed-site, continuing actions are suitable for this methodological strategy.

Many school-based studies, such as the classroom observations by
M. LeCompte (1975) (see Chapter 13), are conceptually similar to Erickson and Mohatt's study, although video recording was not used. Thus,
we can refer to LeCompte's study as "microethnography," because of the
focus on a specific, small unit within a larger institutional system. Using
direct observation with extensive note taking, comparing two or more
teachers and classrooms is a fairly common and effective research strategy in the ethnographic study of schools and education situations.

Some of the descriptions of ethnographic marketing research
indicate widespread use of video recording and other photography,
particularly to get data about people's use of specific products in their
homes. In an article entitled "The rise of Ethnography: How Market Research Has Gone Gonzo," the authors note that "A key tool for the ethnographer is the video camera, along with diaries which the researchers
ask consumers to fill in. We video record 80% of our ethnographic work,
and often leave consumers with cameras to use themselves.... Clients receive a PowerPoint deck with recommendations and edited video which

show consumers talking about their lives, using a product and engaging with it. 'It brings the consumer into the boardroom.'" These quoted statements are attributed to C. Cochrane, a director of the research company Ethnography Australia (Australian School of Business 2011).

CONCLUSION

The capturing and organizing of raw data is the central, most important process in ethnographic field work. Although there are now many new gadgets and instruments for recording, photographing, and entering data into computers, much of the hard work must still be done "by hand." Also, the process of data capture—especially writing notes and then elaborating the notes—requires repeated informed and careful decision making in order to get as much as possible of the relevant, important information. At the same time, researchers must be assessing and exploring constantly to decide on "next steps," based on insights concerning emerging patterns.

Ethnographic research is largely an inductive process. Even studies with predetermined categories and hypotheses almost always encounter unexpected new features and processes that call for modifications in research plans. In the midst of data gathering, researchers are constantly engaging in preliminary analysis and understanding of the emerging data. Thus, even when writing up field notes, ethnographers should be making notes and comments about possible new questions and lines of inquiry, as well as noting issues that were inadequately probed in interviews.

Participant Observation

In the preface to this book I commented that applied ethnography in the 21st century has less space for participant observation, even though that method was, until recently, considered to be the foundation of ethnographic research. Of course, there is still plenty of informal observation in some ethnographers' data gathering. However, in many applied projects the time limitations have reduced the kind of participant observation that had traditionally been most closely identified with ethnography. Other changes in the strategies of conducting applied projects have also led to less reliance on participant observation, which is especially evident in the various manuals and guidelines relating to Rapid Appraisal Procedures (RAP), Participatory Rural Appraisal (PRA), and Focused Ethnographic Studies (FES) (see Chapter 16).

What is Participant Observation?

According to K. and B. DeWalt,

> …participant observation is a method in which a researcher takes part in the daily activities, rituals, interactions, and events of a group of people as one of the means of learning the explicit and tacit aspects of their life routines and their culture. (DeWalt and DeWalt 2010: 1)

The authors noted that for many writers "…participant observation subsumes the bulk of what we call field research…." There is a tendency for some anthropologists to regard practically all field work as "participant observation." However, I agree with the DeWalts that it is much better to regard participant observation as only one of many data-gathering tools in ethnography. Various interviewing techniques, as I describe in

Pertti Pelto, "Participant Observation," in *Applied Ethnography: Guidelines for Field Research*, pp. 127-140 © 2013 Left Coast Press, Inc. All rights reserved.

this book, are not participant observation. Similarly, some of the techniques for direct, quantifiable observation of people's behaviors should not be subsumed under that general label.

Bronislaw Malinowski is generally credited with developing the field work style that emphasizes participation in the daily life of the research community, and considers that participation to be an intrinsic part of the data-gathering strategy. Malinowski's description of his field work is a useful reminder:

> Soon after I had established myself in Omarkana Trobriand Islands, I began to take part, in a way, in the village life, to look forward to the important or festive events, to take personal interest in the gossip and the developments of the village occurrences, to wake up every morning to a new day, presenting itself to me more or less as it does to the natives. (Malinowski [1922] 1961: 7)

He went on to talk about his morning walk though the village, observing people at various tasks, and how the villagers came to be totally accustomed to his presence, so the people didn't alter their behaviors or ways of doing things, as they would if a "stranger" came to the village.

Many writers have emphasized the importance of living in the community that one is studying. On the other hand, what do you do if you have decided to study a set of three different communities? Or, suppose your task is to study the operations of a school district or a multi-site public health system. Then, how do you do "participant observation?" Many years ago, we surveyed a sample of anthropologists about their mode of residence during their field work. Some of them (a minority) described that they commuted daily to their research site but did not live there. Even then, many were doing a lot of participant observation—but not fully immersed in village life for 24 hours a day.

How Much Active Participation is Involved in Participant Observation?

Johnson and colleagues have presented three case examples of roles that ethnographers have adopted in order to have an active role in daily life of the study community. Johnson himself provides an example of "fully active participation," as his study in a fishing camp in Alaska (Bristol Bay) was made possible by his employment in several different roles—as a boat carpenter, a bookkeeper, and for a time, a member of a fishing crew (Johnson, Avenarius, and Weatherford 2006: 119).

The authors point out that in most field studies there are different roles available, including taking employment in some activity connected with the study community. They cite the example of C. B. Avenarius (one of the authors), who studied Chinese and Taiwanese immigrants in the Los Angeles area. Her participation included taking employment in a shop run by Taiwanese people and joining some of the local Chinese social groups. However, her study population was scattered across many neighborhoods in southern California. That was a quite different level of participation and different structure of observations, compared to Johnson's research in the fishing camp.

Johnson and coauthors pointed out that different participant roles (e.g., employment in the study site) may lead to greater or lesser access to information, and some types of participation may involve restrictions concerning freedom of social movement, different kinds of dependence on key informants, and different types of ethical issues. These authors also noted that positions such as Johnson's job as boat carpenter brought both high respect and excellent social mobility for getting information. On the other hand, a lowly position as "gofer" in the fish camp would also have good access to information, with good social mobility in the local community.

To my knowledge, the "active participant" examples described by Johnson and his colleagues represent a small minority of participant observation roles. Most ethnographic studies, if they include participant observation, take the form of residing in or near the research community and then visiting in people's homes and worksites, mainly as an observer. Thus, although I don't have a "census of ethnographers," my estimate is that at least three-quarters of the participant observers have limited themselves mainly to "being there," moving about the community in order to become known to many people in the study population, and getting the chance to observe a variety of different activities (see Figure 7.1). The "being there" facilitates informal and formal interviews to fully describe the most important aspects of people's cultural behaviors.

In my field research many years ago in Lapland, I spent a great deal of time visiting Laplanders in their homes and visiting reindeer roundups and other outdoor activities. I also joined a small group of Skolt Saami men in an expedition to Norway, to sell reindeer meat and buy various food and other household supplies. In all of those situations I lacked the skills for carrying out any actual reindeer handling, but took part in gofer activities such as fetching water or firewood.

The following excerpt from my field notes illustrates the kind of "being there" that greatly aided my understanding of the reindeer herders' activities, although I did very little active participation in the work and daily tasks.

Figure 7.1. Participant observation is often unstructured "hanging out" and getting to know people. © Dunja Pelto 2013.

Hunting Reindeer Calves Among Skolt Saami in the Sevettijarvi Area

FIELD NOTES, FRIDAY AUG 29 TO SEPT 6 SATURDAY [1958]

IN THE COMPANY OF JAAKKO K, JAAKKO G. AND SAVELI F.

[*Note added in 2012:* I accompanied the herders throughout this hunting expedition. Sometimes we returned to one of their houses, but we slept out in the backlands on at least two nights. It was tiring, but a very good opportunity for participant observation. I took notes in my little notebooks whenever we stopped, and in the evening. There were evening discussions—informal conversations. Practically all conversations were in Finnish (which I speak), but I was also able to follow some of the Skolt Saami language on those few occasions when the men spoke to one another in their local language. Below is what I wrote out from my jotted notes when I got back to my quarters on September 7th or 8th. At that time of year there was daylight in Lapland until about 10:00 pm or longer, so I was able to take plenty of notes even though there was no artificial light. When I returned to my quarters, I wrote out several pages of single-spaced notes on my little portable Olivetti typewriter.]

Field notes written out (September 1958)

The purpose of this hunting was to get enough hides of young calves to provide dressy winter coats for all three of the boys. These are admittedly not the warmest possible reindeer hide coats (peski), though warm as hell, but they are very dressy, for they are made of calves just in prime coat condition, and only the darkest calves are selected.

The boys said that Skolts do not make such coats, so they will have one of the "natives" of the area, the old Supru woman or a woman from Kessivuono, probably Inari Lapp make the coats. Each coat requires 5 hides.

[*Note added in 2012:* The Skolt Saami were "newcomers" in the area after World War II, having lost their homeland to the Soviet Union. The Sevetti area was very sparsely populated, due to the effects of the war. The few scattered families who had been there before the Skolt Saami came to the area were the Inari Saami and three or four Finnish families. The "old Supru woman" was an Inari Saami widow.]

Since all reindeer calves naturally belong to somebody, they can kill only a) their own reindeer calves, b) calves of close friends or relatives, or c) calves of people they have asked permission of (they only ask apparently of friends and relatives, however).

During the time I was with them the boys killed nine calves, as follows:

1. Jaakko G. killed Piera Porsanger calf [Piera is Inari Saami neighbor]
2. Jaakko K. killed Killanen calf
3. J. G. killed Aapo Aikio calf [Aapo Aikio is Inari Saami neighbor]
4. Jaakko G. killed Timo G (brother's) calf
5. Saveli F. killed Olli Gau calf [Olli is old man, near neighbor]
6. Jaakko (for Saveli) killed Simo Feodoroff calf [They must have asked Simo for permission to shoot one of his calves.]
7. Jaakko G. killed Jussi Gau calf [a Gauriloff relative]
8. Jaakko and Saveli (for Saveli) killed RV calf [Riikon Vasko is a Fofanoff, but they must have asked his permission.]
9. Jaakko Gau killed calf of Veikko Paltto's mo. calf [Veikko Paltto is Inari Saami, in the neighborhood...probably friends with Jaakko G.]

Saveli said they would shoot any Fofanoff calf...(quite a large bunch of animals).

Calves they did not shoot:

1. Jeffim Feodoroff calf...since they had not asked him and they said he is hard to get along with sometimes [although he is a neighbor]

2. Jakkima Feodoroff...same reason [also a near neighbor, but difficult]

3. Pimen Semenoff...not asked [Pimen S is at the other end of the settlement.... No close ties]

4. "Suonikylä descendant calf" belonging to Timo (Jaakko's brother). It is a lahjaporo (gift calf) [2012 note: A calf of a "gift reindeer" should never be killed.]

5. Any other gift calf

The calf shooting is very precise business because:

- The calf must be dark enough for the [good looking] coat.
- The earmark of it or its mother must be ascertained before shooting.
- Only those calves are shot as outlined above...can't shoot just anybody's.

Most of the calves we saw during the nine days were either not proper, or else got out of range after recognition of earmark, before the boys could shoot. Thus the main requirement in the business was not marksmanship, but quick recognition of earmarks. Both the Jaakkos very probably know all the earmarks in the Skolt territory (at least 300–400)...and also know a good many outside the Skolt territory, particularly those of the Partakko people to the SW. Saveli Fofanoff, on the other hand, is an incompetent, and does not recognize marks very well....

[*Notes added in 2012:* The "earmarks" of the reindeer are notches of two or three different configurations cut in the reindeer's ears. Ideally, the calves are earmarked in the summer calf-marking roundups, but some are only identified and marked in the fall round-up. In the time of my field research (1958–59), many of the calves remained unmarked until the fall and winter roundups.

Each household had its own earmark, but the practice had spread that even some of the children had their own distinctive earmarks, often with one distinctive additional mark added to the household earmark. That is the background for my notes referring to hundreds of earmarks. There are, of course, great differences among the reindeer men in their ability to remember hundreds of unique marks. Even the small number of examples in this set of notes shows that both Jaakko G. and Jaakko K. were indeed superior in recognizing the range of earmarks in the area.

Partakko people, mentioned above, are a mixture of Finns and (mostly) Inari Saami.]

The best shooting day was the [first day] when they got 3 calves; several days (3) they got no calves; Jaakko Gauriloff got the most. No calves were sighted for which the boys established the earmark but could not decide the owner of the earmark, even though dozens of different earmarks were seen.

Procedure in hunting:

1. A bell is used as lure and to hide our own identity [??]. We tramped for miles with the bell, occasionally finding stray animals in the woods and tundra. Usually the mother and calf were alone, but we sighted several partiot [bunches] of 6 to 20 reindeer in a group.

2. More often, however, we listened for the bells of the kellovaatimet [bell reindeer] and often found them in the woods, thus at least half of the calves shot were those of the kellovaatimet. The advantages of the reindeer bells in this case are that a) the animals can be found and b) when it runs off into the brush it can be followed...sometimes for miles.... Several times we ran from 1 to 5 km in chasing a bell reindeer in woods and tundra. No calf that was shot ever got away from us, though one shot on top of Kuosnapää ran for about 4 or 5 km before it was dropped with another shot. Shooting was with a .22 (pienoiskivaari) except for one that Jaakko Killanen shot with a larger caliber gun.

When a calf was found that was separated from its mother, it could be lured with the bell and with imitating the sound of the mother reindeer—a coarse snorting sound. Jaakko Killanen was the best at this imitating.

Many of the calves and reindeer were able to keep out of range of recognition, even though the boys used binoculars. Without binoculars it would, it seems to me, be impossible to carry out this hunting, for the earmarks are so difficult to see in the outdoors, especially when it is not snowtime. In winter the boys can see the earmarks much better [against a white background].

The animals that they shot belonging to other people must be paid back, generally at the winter erotus [roundup] rates (about 2000 Fmarks per head).

More probably, the boys will give a like sexed and developed calf in place of the one shot. If they killed the calf of a brother (e.g., when Jaakko shot Timo's calf), he will probably not give anything. "It's in the family."

> [The field notes continue for several more pages, concerning what we ate and drank during the day, the disposal of the meat (including sale of reindeer meat to households), and some notes on conversations.]

TRANSFORMING PARTICIPANT OBSERVATIONS THROUGH SYSTEMATIC INTERVIEWS AND ANALYSIS

Reading these notes a half century later, I can see theoretical issues that I could have pursued further in my research. As you may have noticed, Jaakko G. and Jaakko K. gave me glimpses of a clearly developed system of network relations. The decisions about which calves they could shoot began to look like a social map of a widespread network of households, reaching into the territory of a different ethnic group (Inari Saami).

Another line of interviewing that I could have pursued was the difficult question, "How do you guys learn all those earmarks?" I already knew some pieces of the complex answer. I had heard and watched the Saami schoolboys doing the game of quizzing each other to see who could recite the most earmarks. Also, I had seen the books listing earmarks in the local area. I did not pursue any such leads during the days of the calf hunting, however, as I perceived that the hunters were concentrating on their hunting strategies and were not interested in submitting themselves to complex interviewing.

In this kind of participant observation, that is, in an intensive activity, ethnographers should keep their mouths shut most of the time, take good notes, and think of some future interviewing situations. Part of my ethnographer's field notes from those days of calf hunting should have included planning for more detailed interviewing based on the valuable lessons I learned during that activity.

I was young and inexperienced. I didn't plan any follow-up to that promising opportunity. The lesson in this example is that the ethnographer is likely to have a wide range of participant observation adventures, and should always be carefully assessing which of these theoretical doors of opportunity should be used for follow-up interviewing. Many times the ethnographer refers back to some previous activity or event (shared with the informant), about which one can then probe for more details.

PARTICIPANT OBSERVATION: FORMALITY AND STRUCTURE

Most participant observation is very informal and unstructured.

> But as most practitioners know, ethnography is actually a grab bag
> of structured, semi-structured, and unstructured methods, both
> qualitative and quantitative, employed to understand bits and pieces
> of any social or cultural system. (Johnson, Avenarius, and Weather-
> ford 2006: 113)

In many descriptions of participant observation, as in Malinowski's
ethnographic works ([1922] 1961) and in his diary, which was (published
after his death) ([1967] 1981), there is a great deal of informality, lack of
structure, and reliance on serendipity to discover new information. In
fact, we don't label most of the carefully structured observations that
ethnographers plan as participant observation. Chapter 13 describes
examples of more structured observations, representing a different category of data gathering.

The main characteristics found in ethnographies with plenty of "good,
ol'fashioned participant observation," are the following:

- Much of the participant observation is a strategy for getting to know
  the local people and gaining their trust and willingness to give honest
  answers when we interview them about various topics in which we
  are interested.

- This kind of ethnographic activity allows us to see the actions and
  behaviors of people firsthand, so we can understand what people are
  talking about in conversations and interviews and so we can ask in-
  telligent questions about those observed activities.

- In many cases, only a small percent of observed activities are intended to be documented fully for later write-ups and reports. Many
  ethnographic reports include mention of participating in dances,
  drinking and other recreational activities—ball games, card games
  and other pastimes—which are mentioned as activities where one
  meets people, but without any intention of giving a full description
  of the activities. For example, in my field research among the Skolt
  reindeer herders there were many sessions of card games, but I never
  described those games in detail in my field notes.

- Many situations of participant observation occur accidentally, as unplanned happenings. The reindeer calf hunting described above came
  about accidentally, as I happened to visit those individuals when they

were planning the hunt. From my batch of field notes from 1958–59, it is evident that my primary concerns during the research were to observe all the main reindeer roundup activities, the calf-birthing activities in May, and the routine maintenance of herds in the backlands; but I also observed fishing activities and other significant aspects of the local economy, including expeditions to Norway to sell reindeer meat and buy provisions.

Going back to Malinowski's field research, particularly as given in his diary, the descriptions of the daily activities seem remarkably helter-skelter, and (at least in the personal diary format) there is only occasional evidence of systematically planning observations. The following pieces from his personal diary show some of the "accidental happenings" in his daily data-gathering.

Excerpts from Malinowski's Diary

Thursday, 12.20 I got up at 6 (awake at 5:30) I didn't feel very buoyant. Made the rounds of the village. Tomakapu gave me explanations concerning the sacred grove near his house. It had been raining all night: mud. Everybody was in the village. The policeman joined me at 9, I set to work with him. At 10:30 they decided to go for a poulo [fishing expedition] and I set out with them. Megwa [magic] in the house of Yosala Gawa. I felt again the joy of being with real Naturmenschen. Rode in a boat. Many observations. I learn a great deal. General Stimmung [atmosphere], style, in which I observe tabu. Technology of the hunt, which would have required weeks of research. Opened-up horizons; filled me with joy (Malinowski [1967] 1989: 158; italics in published original).

Monday 24 Got up at 7, walked around the village. Kumaidona tomuota bilousi wapoulo [everyone has gone fishing]. This annoyed me a little. Kilesi Imkuba ivita vatusi saipwana. I decided to take pictures. I blundered with the camera, at about 10 – spoiled everything, spoiled one roll of film. Rage and mortification.... Photographed females. Returned in a state of irritation (p. 163).

Malinowski's unplanned, sudden opportunity to join a fishing "expedition" is a typical instance of the serendipity on which much participant observation is dependent.

PARTICIPANT OBSERVATION AND GETTING THE TRUE PICTURE

One of the obstacles to "getting the true picture" in field work is what we refer to as "reactivity." Malinowski referred to reactivity in a paragraph quoted near the start of this chapter. He said that after he had been present in the daily activities of the villagers for some time, "...they ceased to be interested or alarmed, or made self-conscious by my presence...." He went on to comment that the villagers would not alter their behavior in his presence, as "always happens with a newcomer...." One could say, following Malinowski, that a centrally important reason for doing participant observation is to gain the acceptance and trust of the study population, to reduce the likelihood of reactivity.

Closely related to issues of reactivity is the fact that the people in any population will not tell a researcher about, or even talk about, sensitive matters until the ethnographer has gained their trust and has excellent rapport with the informants. In one of the very first systematic studies of possible biases in ethnographic reporting, R. Naroll did a statistical analysis of a series of ethnographic studies in which, among other variables, he compared the findings of studies of a long duration with those that involved less than a year of field work. His analysis showed that studies in which the ethnographers' fieldwork was of longer duration were more likely to include reports of witchcraft and magic (Naroll 1962). Matters of witchcraft and magical beliefs are sensitive topics, which are not freely discussed with researchers unless a good deal of mutual respect has been established.

Kathleen and Billie DeWalt reported their personal experience from research in Mexico, in which their informants regularly denied any knowledge of witchcraft and magic during their early field work. After six months of field research they took a three-week break away from the study community. "Almost the very day of our return, however, one of our key informants began regaling us with a recounting of a conflict that had occurred during our absence. The conflict included accusations by one of the parties that witchcraft was being used against them" (De Walt and DeWalt 2010: 95). During the remainder of their field work, some of the informants talked openly about those previously hidden topics.

Although the DeWalts framed their discussion of this ethnographic experience in terms of length of time in the field, I would suggest an additional factor. Several times, in informal discussions with other researchers, we have heard stories of "a noticeable shift in fieldwork relations" when the ethnographer(s) return after an absence. Sometimes we get the impression (hypothesis) that the local people are somehow impressed with the field worker's return: "Oh, she/he really is serious about studying our way of life." It may be that both factors are involved in that experience of opening up previously hidden information.

PARTICIPANT OBSERVATION AND
INFORMAL CONVERSATIONAL INTERVIEWING

Whenever field researchers have the opportunity to directly observe particular activities, there are greatly increased possibilities for participating in conversations, as much of the verbal discussion in connection with meetings, religious ritual events, family celebrations, work activities (such as in Figure 7.2), games, clinic routines, and other activities revolves around the immediate happenings. Conversations are likely to be about why certain things are happening, what is going right or going wrong, how this compares with last year's ceremony, and many other comparative comments as well as disagreements.

Much of participant observation includes listening to the conversations at an event or an unusual situation. In those situations, researchers can sometimes carry out "mini-interviews" using, for example, questions like the following:

- How does this (ongoing activity) compare with last month's (same meeting)?
- Can you explain to me why that man interrupted the chairperson just then?
- Who are the people in that group over there, the ones who came in late?
- I didn't understand the part about the "fines" or "penalties" for certain infractions? What infractions are they talking about? Is there a list somewhere of those infractions?
- Who in that group from the "other side" do you think I can talk with, to find out about their objections and ideas?
- In that part of the ritual that they just did, what different foods are offered, and what are the reasons for the different foods?

As mentioned in my discussion of the calf hunting expedition, notes from such conversations should include a review of possible plans for later interviews concerning points in the observations. Of course, there will be many events or observations that don't warrant any kind of follow-

Figure 7.2. Activities such as tailoring provide good opportunities for direct observation. © Dunja Pelto 2013.

up. However, some important events or situations may be repeated periodically, such as meetings, fishing trips, weekly markets, and classroom teaching, to name just a few examples. Those repeated events can offer possibilities for more detailed analysis of variations over time, filling in gaps from earlier observations, and other "special data gathering."

Comments and Summary

The concept of participant observation is a very general and unstructured approach to ethnographic field research. The most successful and impressive examples are those in which the researcher(s) have plenty of time, and their mission is to describe and analyze cultural activities that are limited to a specific community or small set of communities or institutional facilities. It would be difficult to use this method effectively, for example, in 15 different communities, 12 different schools, or 18 different branches of a commercial enterprise, unless researchers had a great deal of time to carry out the study.

Even in small-scale studies with relatively comfortable time frames, ethnographers should plan carefully structured observations for key aspects of cultural activities about which they need accurate and relatively full details. Many study "populations" are organizations that have a variety of meetings: some are regular weekly or monthly gatherings for planning activities, problem-solving, hearing reports from different work sectors, and other business; others may be for staff training, orientations concerning policy changes, and other regular, periodic communication. These are often particularly important opportunities to understand program operations and to identify the key persons whose activities you need to study in detail. As in all situations of participant observation, meetings are events from which one can develop various forms of semi-structured interviews with key individuals.

In recent times, there have been a number of criticisms of participant observation, often pointing to the loose and subjective nature of many ethnographic statements that appear to be based on only a few unstructured, poorly described observations. These criticisms have led to increased numbers of explorations concerning structured direct observations. Some of these more structured forms of observation are examined in Chapter 13. At the same time, there is ample evidence that relatively unstructured participant observation can help to introduce the researchers to the study community, and thus improve the levels of cooperation, including giving information in interviews.

FULFILLMENT CENTER

251 Mt. Olive Church Road
Commerce, GA 30599

RENA LEDERMAN
94 LINDEN LN

SHIP TO:
PRINCETON
NJ 08540
US

ORDER NO.	PAGE NO.
4451982452910	1 of 1

SHIPMENT NO.	SHIP VIA	DATE
ETZ01452660	USPS	06/22/16

Item Number	SHIP	Line	Item Description	Ord	Purchase Order No.
9781611322088	1	21898940	Applied Ethnography	1	4451982452910

Your satisfaction is our #1 priority, so we make it simple for you: 30 Day, from shipping date, money back guarantee-100% refund on the item purchased. To be eligible for a refund, you must return the item in the same condition you received it - Videos, DVD's, audio, and computer software purchases, returned in the original packaging will receive a 100% item refund. Video, DVD's, audio, and computer software purchases, returned opened and not in the original packaging are non-refundable. Shipping fees are non-refundable.

In order to receive your refund, please use the return label below and enclose this packing slip stating the reason for your return with the items that you are returning. Send the item(s) back to us so we receive them undamaged within 30 days of shipping. We do not accept packages marked return to sender. Postage fees incurred due to packages sent return to sender, refused, undeliverable or deemed to have an insufficient address by the carrier will be deducted from the buyers refund. Shipping and handling charges, for returning the item, are the responsibility of the buyer. A 20% restocking fee will be assessed to all items received returned after 30 days of ship date.

Please ship all returns to:

Fulfillment Center
Ref:[transaction or order number]
251 Mt. Olive Church Road
Commerce, GA 30599

** Tips for returning: Be sure to purchase tracking and/or insure when shipping your package! That way if it is lost or damaged you will still get money back from the shipping company. Also, please allow your return enough mail delivery time to reach us within the 30 day period.

Return Label

ORDER #   4451982452910

VIA: TLBM

SHIPPER NO.

PKG. ID#   92490999842288l300114

Fulfillment Center
Dept R
251 Mt. Olive Church Road
Commerce, GA 30599

Sampling and Counting
in Ethnographic Research

In the first half of the 20th century there was very little discussion of sampling in ethnographic research. As long as ethnographers confined themselves mainly to qualitative descriptive research, most ethnographic reporting had little or no statistical analysis. Even in cases where the field researcher talked with many informants, perhaps using a semistructured instrument, there was usually no felt need for any kind of "representative sampling," random or otherwise. This lack of concern about sampling was partly a reflection of researchers' assumptions concerning general cultural homogeneity.

In the past two or three decades, with the strong development of quantitative methods in ethnographic research and the increased use of the qualitative-quantitative mix in field work, discussion about sampling strategies has greatly increased. This trend also benefitted from the adoption of ethnographic methods in many disciplines. It is common now for researchers to comment on the importance of random sampling (whenever feasible), particularly if they intend to use standard probability statistics. In many studies, the intent to generalize research findings to the larger population from which a sample was taken adds to the importance of careful sampling. At the same time, there are many other sampling strategies, in addition to random methods, that are used for various purposes. The most prominent of these are the numerous opinion polls, which are usually based on forms of "quota sampling."

The social science literature contains many detailed discussions of methods and issues in sample design in ethnographic research. Among anthropological works, H. R. Bernard's *Research Methods in Anthropology* (various editions) is a very useful source, with thorough discussion of many sampling strategies. Patton's *Qualitative Research and Evaluation*

Pertti Pelto, "Sampling and Counting in Ethnographic Research," in *Applied Ethnography: Guidelines for Field Research*, pp 141-156. © 2013 Left Coast Press, Inc. All rights reserved.

Methods (2002) provides an excellent inventory of sampling strategies. Many other sources are available from the various fields and disciplines of the social sciences. This chapter only deals with some of the highlights of a complex domain with which every field researcher should become familiar.

RANDOM SAMPLING IN QUANTITATIVE STUDIES

Random sampling is the default choice for most quantitative studies. The central purpose of random sampling is to allow the researcher to assert credibly that the respondents or informants interviewed or observed in the study are representative of the general population of the research site. Suppose, for example, that your study population has about 1000 households, living in two separate villages. If your aim is to provide social and cultural descriptions and generalizations about that population, the ideal sample should somehow ensure that all of the individuals in your designated study population have a known probability of being included in your sample. One solution would be doing a "house-listing" separately in the two communities, and then drawing random samples separately in each of them, for example, 50 or 60 households in each community. Of course, your ethnographic study would include many other kinds of information, beyond some sort of survey with a random sample.

If your research plan includes a small, or not so small, structured survey, or if you have decided to include in-depth interviews with 30 or 40 "cases," or if you want to observe the selling behavior of a sample of vendors in a large market with over a hundred sellers, you should use a random sampling technique to select the persons or "vendor points" for your data collection. Selecting random samples is easy. Many books on statistics have tables of random numbers that you can use if you have some sort of a list of persons or cases to which you can assign numbers.

Suppose your research assistants have made a list of all the shops and sellers in a town, and you want to do interviews with a sample of these entrepreneurs. The list has 134 shops and sellers, and you plan to interview 50 individuals. Number each shop/seller, from 1 to 134. Go to a table of random numbers—it will probably have numbers from 1 to 999. (Bernard (2002) has a table of random numbers in Appendix A, starting on page 701.) Select a random starting point in the list and start reading the numbers. Each time you come to a number between 1 and 134, select that number.

Here is a short batch of numbers from a table of random numbers: 383 570 <u>45</u> <u>110</u> 896 549 672 340 264 <u>51</u> 777 942 327 176 <u>12</u> 348 585 639 874. The underlined numbers are the ones you are selecting and assigning. From this batch, thus far you have selected 45, 110, 51, and 12, so you have to keep going. Continue until you have selected 50 numbers. Then select a few extra to allow for refusals.

If that seems too cumbersome, write out the numbers from 1 to 134, each on a separate little piece of paper (you don't need to write down the names—just the numbers). Put all 134 slips into a plastic bag and shake. Now, have your eight-year-old daughter select pieces of paper out of the bag. She continues to select the slips of paper until you have 50, plus 10 extra for good measure. That's your random sample.

Sampling Frame

The "sampling frame" is a list of all of the units from which you will select the sample. For example, the list just mentioned of "all the shops and sellers in town" is a sampling frame. In field work, the most usual sampling frame is produced when the ethnographer does a complete listing of all the households in the study communities. In some situations the local telephone book could be the sampling frame. Others might be specialized study populations such as associations, religious groups, or other organizations that have up-to-date membership lists.

Unfortunately, in many cases, out there in field work, you don't have a list to work with. Maybe the community is too big, so you don't have the time and personnel to do a house-listing. However, you intend to choose your sample from the universe of households with a random process. Here's an example of a sampling process, described by Adam Kis (2007) in his field work in Malawi:

> I used a variant of the space sampling method.... Starting at the center of the village, I randomly selected streets and walked in a straight line toward the edge of the village. Using a random number generator, I initially visited every nth house on that straight line, interviewing the first adult I came in contact with at each house. However, this resulted in a disproportionate number of women being interviewed. My research assistant explained to me that men tend to be away from home often, wandering the streets or drinking in bars in the afternoon, after attending to their dimbas (wet gardens). To balance the gender representation without introducing bias, I altered my strategy to interview every nth person I encountered on the street. This captured the wandering men.... (Kis 2007: 132)

If you are out in a village or a town, and you estimate that there are about 180 households, and you want to select a sample of about 60, you would probably decide to contact every third household, having selected a random starting point and randomly selected directions for walking along the lanes, paths, or streets.

Stratified Random Sampling (Cluster Sampling)

Many quantitative studies make use of a two-stage procedure in which sub-groups, neighborhoods, or small-scale local sampling points are selected first and then random sampling is carried out among the people within the local sampling units. Chakravarthy and associates have described a two-stage sampling process for the random sampling of sex workers in several districts in Andhra Pradesh, India. Their HIV/AIDS intervention program had identified local clusters of female sex workers in so-called "hot spots." After a random selection of hotspots, individual female sex workers were selected at the hot spots using a random time-allocation procedure, in order to be sure that the local selection of sex workers adequately represented the variations in the availability of the sex workers at different hours of the day (Chakravarthy et al. 2012).

Bill Dressler and his Brazilian colleagues have described their testing of several measuring tools, including a "family life scale" and a "lifestyle scale," in a Brazilian community. "The survey sample [271 individuals] was selected using stratified random sampling in which the strata were four neighborhoods ranked by socioeconomic status. Households were randomly selected from complete enumerations within each neighborhood, and adult members of selected households were invited to participate in the research (response rate = 72.3%)" (Dressler, 2007: 5). At each selected household, both male and female heads of household, plus one child over 18 years of age, were asked to participate in the study. The measurements (scales) constructed by Dressler and his Brazilian colleagues were used to test theoretical propositions about "cultural consonance" and psychological symptoms of stress and depression (Dressler et al. 2005).

A stratified sampling strategy similar to that described by Dressler and colleagues would be useful if a research group found itself with three or four ethnic groups, each in their separate neighborhoods or hamlets. On the other hand, if a research team had literally dozens or even hundreds, of small clusters (as in the sex worker sample of Chakravarthy et al. 2012), then there must be a systematic, or random, sampling of the small clusters followed by a randomizing process in each selected cluster.

Non-Random Sampling Strategies

In many situations, there is no way to achieve a truly credible random sample of a specific population. The problem is likely to occur in research on injection drug users, illegal immigrants, and other hard-to-reach or partially hidden categories of persons.

Michael Q. Patton has written a thorough review of different non-random sampling strategies often utilized in ethnographic research. His discussion includes descriptions of the logic and usefulness of strategies such as "extreme deviant case sampling," "intensity sampling," "criterion sampling," "maximum variation sampling," and "snowball (chain) sampling." Several other, lesser-known types of non-random sampling are included in his discussion (Patton 2002).

Tamang and colleagues at the Center for Research on Environment, Health and Population Activities (CREHPA), a research organization in Kathmandu, Nepal, carried out interviews concerning "sexual risk behavior and risk perception" among men in border towns of Nepal, drawing samples from both resident and non-resident men. They were able to do a random sampling of the young male residents in the towns, but could not devise a way to do random sampling of the non-resident, transient men. Concerning the sample of 300 non-resident men in the five border towns, they wrote:

> The sample of non-resident men (60 per town) was obtained through purposive sampling to represent different occupational categories. The occupational categories considered for the study were drivers; conductors/helpers of public and private vehicles; rickshaw pullers; businessmen; students; and personnel engaged either in construction activities or execution of development projects requiring frequent visits to the towns. These respondents were approached at meeting places such as bus parks, public places, places of work, restaurants and lodges. (Tamang et al. 2001: 197)

Tamang and his colleagues spread their purposive sample across the different occupational groups to be sure they were getting something like a "maximum variation sample," and could claim that the sample was generally representative of the range of different kinds of non-resident men in those border towns. Although the main part of the study consisted of a quantitative survey, they also conducted 22 in-depth interviews to explore the young men's reasons for engaging in risky sexual behaviors. The researchers found no significant differences between residents and non-residents in overall rates of "non-regular sexual encounters." However, the non-residents reported much higher rates of contacts with sex workers, while the young male residents reported more sexual contacts with "friends." The data showed that condom use was more frequent among the non-resident men because of their resort to sex workers.

Lauren Blum, in her study of natural food sources of Vitamin A in Niger, appears to have used something like a "maximum variation sampling." She reported that "A sample of respondents was chosen in five neighborhoods representing a range of ethnic backgrounds and socio-economic levels....Twenty-seven compounds were visited over five weeks where structured interviews were carried out with mother-respondents" (Blum 1997: 77–78). Each of her informants was contacted four times, to cover the several components of the focused ethnographic instruments.

Although researchers in applied research projects have not generally used labels such as "maximum variation sampling" and "criterion sampling," it appears that something like those strategies may be a common feature in the sampling patterns, for example, in studies related to health problems. A study by Archana Joshi and colleagues in Gujarat is an example in which "criterion sampling" was a primary strategy but an element of "maximum variation sampling" was also included. The first phase of the research was a house-listing in eight villages (total N = 1067) and the collection of data on the women's current reproductive health problems. From the house-listing the researchers then selected a sample of 100 women in which the reports of current symptoms were in proportion to the incidence of those health problems in the overall sample. For example, of the women reporting symptoms, approximately half of them complained of vaginal discharge. "Subsequently community mapping was done in order to select women from different clusters to represent the different sectors of the local population. A group of 69 women who were successfully contacted at least five times during the study period form the study sample..." (Joshi, Dhapola, and Pelto 2008: 137). The main selection criterion was the presence of reported reproductive tract illness, but the mapping to select women from the different clusters (hamlets) represents a partial exercise of "maximum variation sampling," in this case mainly focused on social and economic diversity of the different hamlets.

Many studies of sex workers have involved opportunistic samples that depended on the help of gatekeepers, key informants, and others to recruit individuals into the sample. For example, in the study reported by Bhattacharya and Senpati of sex workers in Kolkata, "One hundred sex workers were identified with the help of volunteers of the local clubs and elderly sex workers..." (Bhattacharya and Senapati 1994: 552). In that study (described in Chapter 3), the sex workers were in brothels, and the men in the "local clubs" constitute, in effect, a special category of gatekeepers who volunteered to assist in the data gathering.

Extreme or Deviant Case Sampling: Sampling the Best and the Worst

Patton has noted that "In many instances more can be learned from intensively studying exemplary (information rich) cases than can be learned from statistical depictions of what the average case is like" (Patton 2002: 234). He describes the situation in which an evaluator is assessing a large program with 100 or more sites. "With limited resources and limited time, an evaluator might learn more by intensively studying one or more examples of especially poor programs and one or more examples of really excellent programs" (p. 232).

A study by Cynthia Myntti in Yemen, which focused on the healthiness and unhealthiness of small children, gives a clear example of this sampling strategy. Myntti's study is also an excellent example of interrelating qualitative and quantitative data gathering.

She reported that: "We began by conducting a household survey of children's health...[after eliminating households not resident year-round] from the remaining households resident year-round, we selected a systematic one-half sample" (Myntti 1993: 234). The survey included detailed reproductive histories of the women, with information about infant deaths, breast-feeding histories, child care, sanitation, and the mothers' knowledge of prevention and cure of childhood illnesses.

After the survey, Myntti and her team selected a sub-sample for more intensive study. That sub-sample consisted of all the women aged 25 to 39 who had at least one child aged 5 or under. "Each of these women was then scored on two measures: retrospective, the number of her children who died; and current, the weight-for-age of her children aged 5 years and under.... The resulting aggregate 'child health score' allowed the women to be ranked from lowest to highest, that is, the worst 'child health' to the best 'child health'" (Myntti 1993: 234). Although she referred to the scale as "child health score," the score is actually a characteristic of the woman and does not apply to individual children.

Based on the rank ordering of the women on the child health score, she then chose the eight "most healthy" and the eight "least healthy" for extreme case analysis. She found that the eight women with the worst scores had experienced all of the child deaths and that the ten most malnourished children also belonged to those same eight women. In her analysis of the women with the most healthy child scores, she found that, although several were suffering economic hardships, these mothers generally had strong social support networks, very good coping abilities, and ability to interact effectively with their children.

Myntti's analysis of the "very healthy" compared with the "very un-healthy" cases shows that poverty, all by itself, is a predisposing factor but the mothers' managerial capabilities, including maintaining good social networks of support, are crucial elements in maintaining the health of their children in the face of economic adversity. She found that the women with the "most unhealthy" scores had rather disorganized households, weak social networks, and were lacking in coping skills. She stated, "....my data suggest that it is the interaction of chronic economic problems, social isolation and a mother's inability to cope—the psychological dimension—that has the negative effect on child health. Each negative factor is surmountable if it is the sole constraint. Disorganized mothers may be saved by strong social support and sufficient financial resources..." (p. 239).

Opportunistic Sampling

Whatever the scope of your applied ethnographic research, you hope to have some basic ideas of the variables you might include in purposeful sampling or in a stratified random sampling design. However, you are likely to encounter situations in your field work for which you have no advance information, and therefore you have to take whatever individuals or events (or other units) come along.

Many clinic-based samples, particularly of relatively unusual health problems, are likely to end up in this category. Markovic has described research with recently diagnosed cancer patients:

> The study involved immigrant (N = 17) and Australian (N = 13) women newly diagnosed with gynecological cancer and receiving care at a tertiary hospital in Melbourne, Australia. None of the women in the study had any prior history of a malignancy. The women were approached during their visits to the outpatients department or while they were receiving treatment as inpatients, given a participant-information statement about the study, and asked to participate. All interviews took place at the woman's home. (Markovic 2006: 413)

Markovic used an entirely inductive approach to look for "themes," including "delay in seeking treatment," "interpretations of the symptoms," and various patterns of encounters with the doctors.

Snowball Sampling Strategy

"Snowball sampling" is often used as a kind of opportunistic strategy with difficult-to-find hidden populations. A study by V. Kulkarni gives a good example of the process used to get a sample of men who have sex with men (MSM):

> Our study sample was selected through "opportunistic sampling," starting with individuals with whom we had had contact in our medical practice. Our first informants assisted us in contacting and recruiting other persons. In this manner we collected a total of 30 MSM informants. (Kulkarni, Kulkarni, and Spaeth 2004: 204)

The snowball effect comes as some of the newly contacted informants help contact other individuals and those in the "second wave" of informants help contact more informants, so the sample expands through those intermediaries. As mentioned in Chapter 3, in some studies researchers who are new to an area may seek out key informants through that same snowball process, perhaps starting with an initial small group suggested by NGO outreach workers.

In a study of hospital-based childbirth experiences of Arabic-speaking immigrant women in Australia, Abboud and Liamputtong (2007) used snowball sampling to get their cohort of 25 informants. The researchers stated that:

> Snowball sampling is when a researcher identifies one respondent and asks whether the respondent knows any other people who might meet the sampling requirements (p. 179).

Quota Sampling

Quota sampling is a special, widely used strategy for the non-random selection of cases. In its simplest form, the strategy is to designate specified numbers or percentages of cases to represent key categories of persons, such as male/female, specified age categories, or racial/ethnic groups. Suppose, for example, the population of interest is composed of about equal numbers of Latinos, non-Latino (White), and Black, and the hypothetical research team wants to learn about women's feelings of empowerment, comparing younger and older women. A quota sampling might specify that interviewers are to get a total of 40 interviews of females in each of the three racial/ethnic categories, equally divided (20 and 20) between young women (18 to 30 years of age) and older women (31 to 50 years of age). Interviewers would go out into the designated community with instructions to try to hit all the main parts of the community but end up with approximately equal numbers—40 each of Latino, White, and Black and approximately equal numbers of the younger and older (female) informants.

Quota sampling, although it is a non-random strategy, is widely used in opinion polls. The experts in polling organizations have developed elaborate systems for specifying the quotas for different kinds of variables (characteristics of individuals), based on decades of past experience with polls, for example, in trying to predict election outcomes. Quota sampling is also widely used in marketing research, partly because it is extremely difficult to identify specific populations that would be useful sampling frames, as the "public" they wish to reach is usually widely scattered.

Here is an example of quota sampling involving cars, seeking information about potential car buyers in the Ukraine. The study of 500 car owners was based on a quota sampling of people who had bought their cars in 2005 to 2007. The quota sampling criteria were based on the different types and models of vehicles (Action Data Group 2008). Quota sampling is attractive to people in marketing, because they frequently focus on specific target groups such as owners of cars, TVs, other appliances, or consumer items such as packaged foods, cosmetics, or specialized clothing.

Researchers in Sydney, Australia, reported a comparison between a quota sample survey and a randomized sample survey concerning health care attitudes and behaviors (Cumming 1990):

> Two surveys in the same defined population in Sydney's western suburbs in 1986 and 1987 provided the opportunity to compare results obtained from a quota and a probability sample survey. These surveys were designed to provide information for the planning of local health promotion programs. The quota sample survey was conducted in shopping centres and used quota sampling to select 1727 respondents. In the second survey, area probability sampling was used to select 484 respondents. This survey had a response rate of 65%. There were 15 questions common to both surveys; results of only three differed significantly ($p < 0.05$) between surveys. None of these differences was important from a public health perspective. (Cumming 1990: abstract)

Discussions about quota sampling generally point out the negative side—that, since the sampling is not random, there are large possibilities for biases. On the other hand, the handbooks and methodological statements point out that quota sampling is much easier to administer, that it is practically always less expensive in terms of personnel and time, and there is no need for great effort in establishing a sampling frame. Thus, it can be argued that carefully designed quota sampling is a useful alternative approach for many applied studies, particularly where it is difficult to define and find the study population.

Given the fact that many applied social science studies end up using non-random sampling strategies, using quota sampling may be the best alternative in some cases.

AN UNUSUAL SAMPLING STRATEGY

Char and colleagues used a rather complex sampling strategy for selecting 60 sets of informants for their study of the "influence of mothers-in-law on young couples' family planning decisions in rural India." The study was carried out in the state of Madhya Pradesh, where marriage and family patterns conform largely to the north Indian cultural norms.

> For this study, 12 villages were purposively selected from among the villages involved in the social marketing intervention. The aim was to choose…households where young married couples and the parents of the young husband were in regular day-to-day interaction. Information on the number of eligible couples residing together within the same household was gathered, and all households in the 12 villages where the mother-in-law, son and daughter-in-law were all living in the same house, or where the mother-in-law lived close by in the neighborhood, were listed. Based on this listing, five families per village were randomly selected, one from the centre and four from the four corners of the village, to ensure that the sample was representative. (Char Säävälä, and Kulmala 2010: 155–156)

The most innovative feature of the research design was that the mother-in-law, daughter-in-law and the son (husband) were all interviewed simultaneously, separately, in order to assess the degree of influence of the mother-in-law on the family planning decisions of the young couple. "Short, open-ended interview guides were used." The researchers reported that mothers-in-law had strong influence in the decisions about when the daughter-in-law goes for sterilization to end child-bearing, but decisions about temporary contraceptive methods were much more in the control of the son and daughter-in-law. The authors noted that the study area was unusual in that a major family planning intervention had made temporary methods of contraception widely known and widely available, in contrast to most other areas of India. Thus, any generalizations of the results to a broader population would be limited to communities affected by the family planning intervention.

SAMPLING NON-PERSON PHENOMENA

There are many other kinds of units for which researchers need to develop sampling strategies, either as a main focus or as an adjunct to the primary ethnographic study. In some areas researchers may find written advertising of medical remedies—in the newspapers, billboards, and various one- or two-page flyers, or leaflets. Hossain et al. n.d.) carried out a study of "street-based and newspaper advertising by 'sexologist' practitioners in Bangladesh." The collection of materials was an opportunistic sample that consisted of 36 advertisements in newspapers and 20 leaflets/brochures in Dhaka city. The authors noted that the various advertisements contribute to misinformation about men's sexual health problems and unnecessarily raise young men's anxieties about sexual matters.

Movies and videos are another informational medium that may be sampled for particular types of contents. Akhila Vasan's literature review of the contents and effects of TV and movie media noted that "... analysis of nine Hindi films randomly selected from 1997–99 box office hits found that 'moderate' sexual violence is depicted as fun, enjoyable, and a normal expression of romantic love. Vasan also found that "In an analysis of films released in 2004–2005, the Burning Brain Society...a Chandigarh-based non-governmental organization, found smoking depicted in 89% of the films released since the [Indian] government banned direct and indirect forms of tobacco advertisement in 2004..." (Vasan 2010: 5).

BEYOND SAMPLING: LOOKING FOR EXCEPTIONS AND POSITIVE DEVIANTS

Most ethnographic samples are opportunistic or purposive samples. Most are also relatively small. We know that, generally, the sample does not do justice to the varieties of exceptional cases out there in the study community. Very early in the analysis of the case data you have collected, start thinking about what is missing from your sample. This is where you go back to your good key informants. "Here is what we are getting. What are we missing?"

I was working with a research group that had collected interviews about early marriage in two states in India. Their case interviews presented a uniform picture: "Girls should get married early; they don't need to go to very much schooling, because they will be just doing household work and raising babies."

What about the exceptions? The research team didn't have any examples. We sent the researchers back to the communities, and they soon found that there are interesting "deviant cases." Instead of early marriage, a daughter was sent to a residential school for additional education. Other exceptions were also discovered. Those exceptions (positive deviants) were powerful indicators for program managers about possible directions of interventions.

Every generalization from a collection of qualitative interviews should show the variations, even if the positive deviants are a very small fraction of the sample.

INFORMAL COUNTING

Field researchers should generally adopt the habit of "informal counting" as part of daily life in field work. Ethnographers should keep in mind that all ethnographic reports frequently include language such as "very few of the young boys were," "most of the people in the meeting were," "the women were more active than the men" and other quasi-quantitative statements. When attending meetings (e.g., a village meeting, political gathering, teachers' meeting, health workers' monthly review meeting) or other group events, you should maintain habits of counting and tabulating, in order to be able to justify those quantitative generalizations. In many situations, you will want to compare males and females concerning participation, assertiveness, and other characteristics. You should also keep an eye out for differences in ethnic groups—in dress style, use of language, and other characteristics. How many different kinds of vendors/sellers are there on this street—compared to that other street?

Sometimes you will become aware of cultural patterns because you counted something, for example, the number of women who were formally dressed at some particular occasion. Perhaps a similar occasion arises and something has changed—dress style, ratio of young to old, numbers of males and females present, or other countable characteristics.

Another general principle is to use counting to explore the local variations (intra-community variations) in dress, in patterns of informal groups, or in language use. Many situations that you observe in the field include multiple languages. Researchers in the United States frequently encounter mixed groups that include Latinos (of different origins), African-Americans, and Whites. In some mixed groups there is frequent language switching.

From counting various observable phenomena, you will often get new ideas about patterns of behavior, which then become topics to bring up with key informants or which lead to new topics for your in-depth interviewing of cases. You should also look for changes over time, as well as recurring, time-dependent patterns such as those reported in the mapping of the "high risk scene" in Harlem (mentioned in Chapter 15), in which there were special recurring times such as "Mothers' Day" and "Fed Days."

TRIANGULATION: MULTIPLE METHOD STRATEGY TO STRENGTHEN CREDIBILITY

Triangulation is a concept that is particularly associated with ethnography, although the idea can be applied to any kind of assembled information. In the social sciences, triangulation means that you use more than one source or type of data to arrive at any generalized statement or conclusion. Suppose that a small survey in your study community finds that families of higher socio-economic status tend to be more protective and restrictive toward unmarried daughters, compared to lower socio-economic status families. Your next step in triangulation could be to do in-depth interviews with small numbers of parents from the higher and lower socio-economic status families, to get detailed information about their acts of restrictiveness of daughters and explanations of why they are more or less restrictive.

The cross-checking using quantitative survey data and small-scale, in-depth ethnographic data is probably the most common form of triangulation. On the other hand, in some of the small-scale, FES-type studies, terminology regarding children's illnesses and symptoms from a small number of informants is cross-checked with statements from people who bring their children to a health facility for treatment of actual illnesses. In the clinical situations, you can confirm whether parents are using the terminology and explanations given to you in the home-based interviews with informants.

A common form of triangulation occurs when you hear a piece of information from one key informant and go to other key informants to cross-check the information. Cross-checking also occurs when you get a generalization from an informant about some physical place, or a repeated event such as "In the weekly market you will see many people from the tribal village—you can recognize them by their unusual decorated dress style." Then you go and see for yourself. Such direct observation to check on informant accuracy is also a form of triangulation.

We use the word and the concept of triangulation frequently in ethnographic field work, because our data-gathering is generally a multimethod approach.

Box 8.1 The Power of Myth

Always watch out for certain kinds of stereotyped "mythology" in your data. Suppose you find that two or three key informants all said that "ethnic group X is engaged in all kinds of criminal activities." Even with triangulation—going to other informants—you can continue to get the same statement, simply because the myth is widespread in the local community.

Discussion

In applied research projects, the main purposes are often descriptive in nature in order to understand "what is going on here...," and the resulting descriptive ethnographic data are useful for introducing a new intervention program or developing policy changes. Perhaps a new school is to be built, or agricultural specialists are intent on introducing a new food crop. For such research aims and targets, the task of research is to provide valuable new information; the process is not intended to be generalized to a wider population and, accordingly, the sampling processes need not include random sampling.

Consequently many applied ethnographic studies use some variant form of purposive or opportunistic sampling as a basic research strategy. It should be kept in mind, however, that in many projects the objective is to generate sufficient descriptive information about a specific target population so that a credible intervention program can be designed. For example, the various focused ethnographic studies described in Chapter 16 are intended to provide information about the health beliefs, or "explanatory models of illness," and the patterns of treatment-seeking behaviors in specific ethnic populations, so that public health measures can be initiated, or modified, to more effectively treat designated illnesses.

Now, to turn the argument in the other direction, I suggest that ethnographers doing applied research should pay close attention to issues of effective sampling strategies for at least three reasons:

- In many modern, complex programmatic situations, failure to pay attention to sampling challenges can lead to biased results or to ignoring parts of the key target populations in the program area. In complex changes in educational programs, if some of the most marginalized, low income sub-groups are left out of the descriptive materials, there can be serious gaps in the effectiveness of proposed changes.

- Quite often the program administrators and, even more likely, funding agencies want the applied research to be solid enough to be "publishable," or at least "transferable" to other program sites. That means that at least some of the "lessons learned" are supported with quantitative information that is a credible product of systematic data-gathering. Careful triangulation adds to the potential usefulness of the data.

- Whatever might be the base of operations and disciplinary backgrounds of applied social science researchers, we should keep in mind that the people we need to impress with our main substantial findings are likely to be persons who expect to see some numbers, statistics, and other signs of systematic data-gathering and analysis.

In-Depth Interviewing:
Case Interviews

In the past two or three decades there has been a substantial increase of studies in which the main core of data consists of a sample of "cases" (qualitative interviews) that have some common characteristic or identity. In education research the cases may be a sample of students with reading difficulties or perhaps individuals of an ethnic minority. In HIV/AIDS studies, samples of truckers, female sex workers, injection drug-users, and other "high risk" persons are common. In studies of domestic violence, samples are sometimes selected from a large survey population—perhaps some 30 or 40 women reporting physical violence and a matched sample of the same age and socio-economic status but reporting no physical violence. For some topics such as nutrition and food use, sampling of households is a common strategy, and the female head of household is the most usual informant. Many other types of cases are found in current ethnographic studies.

In earlier decades, many studies that had samples of cases were presented in the form of a small number of "case descriptions," with very little attention to any quantitative information. The earlier studies often concentrated on the most typical cases, with some secondary attention to the unusual cases. More recently, however, this type of study has involved some quantitative analysis, including comparisons of two groups, sometimes with statistical hypothesis testing.

CASE INTERVIEW DATA

Case interviews are different from key informant interviews. The main ways they differ are the following:

Pertti Pelto, "In-Depth Interviewing: Case Interviews," in *Applied Ethnography: Guidelines for Field Research*, pp. 157-167. © 2013 Left Coast Press, Inc. All rights reserved.

- Case interviews are intended to focus on information about the informant herself or himself concerning treatment seeking, dealing with children's schooling, experiences of working mothers, farmers who have adopted a particular innovation, and/or other specific individual characteristics.

- Unlike key informant interviewing, in which (ideally) each interview is different, case interviews have a core of semi-structured topics that are the same for all the cases. It is not necessary that the interviews are all the same, as there can be unstructured portions allowing for individual characteristics and personal stories.

- There needs to be a good set of individual demographic variables, including age, education, socio-economic status, marital status, and others. All of these "background variables" can result in "confounding effects," unless they are systematically controlled in statistical comparisons.

- The sample of cases should always be described in terms of main background (demographic variables), usually in a table showing the numbers in each category of information, for example, how many are married, how many single or divorced, and how many in each age category.

- Case interviews should constitute a sample that is large enough for at least some sort of simple numerical processing. Samples of first-time mothers, vendors in a marketplace, buyers of a specific product, persons with a specific illness, recent abortions, drug users, school drop-outs, or other cases are often 50 or 60, or up to 100 informants, depending on the time frame, difficulties in finding cases, and resources available for the interviewing. Some quite special types of cases may be very difficult to find, so that samples may be limited to only 15 or 20 cases. Even in such small samples, however, it is useful to present some numerical information.

- Case interviews often involve the use of words from the local language. Interviewers should have spent sufficient time in the research setting to have a general grasp of terms pertinent to the subject of the study (see Figure 9.1).

- Whereas key informant interviews (with a few exceptions) are generally not sources of quantitative data, and key informant interviews are not generally compared and contrasted, the sets of case interviews, regardless of sample size, are always in some sense representative of the variations in the study population.

- Key variables, representing the objectives of the applied research, need to be operationalized in some structured way, so that variations among the informants can be at least tentatively related to background variables and other "discovered factors."

Figure 9.1. In case interviews with sex workers, interviewer pays careful attention to special local vocabulary. © Dunja Pelto 2013.

Here are a few examples.

- In HIV/AIDS research, samples of individuals in high risk groups are sources of quantitative estimates of a) specific high risk behaviors, b) contributing factors such as alcohol use, c) contacts with prevention programs, d) testing and treatment-seeking for sexually transmitted infections (STIs), and iv) other factors.

- Studies of domestic violence generally pay attention to a) husband's alcohol use, b) husband's occupation, c) main "triggers" of violent behaviors, d) age disparity between husband and wife, e) social support networks, f) education, and g) many other possible variables.

- Projects that deal with students' school performance pay attention to a) parental occupations and relations to the student, b) peer group relations, c) ethnicity and language use in family, d) alcohol and drug use, e) membership in organizations, f) socio-economic status of students' families, and g) other potential factors.

Examples of Studies

CAMBODIAN STUDENTS: ETHNIC IDENTITY IN AMERICAN SCHOOLS

A study by Chhuon and Hudley (2010) in a California high school included a mix of participant observation, case interviews, and key informant interviews to explore aspects of ethnic identity in relation to school performance. Within the complexities of ethnic identities, Cambodian students are sometimes identified as "Asian Americans" and sometimes as Cambodians. The two different identities have important implications. Chhuon carried out eight months of participant observation in a large, ethnically mixed high school, where he became well acquainted with the students, teachers, and the routines of the school system.

In-depth interviews were conducted with 52 Cambodian students (28 females and 24 males). The interviews were designed to explore each individual's well-being and academic performance.

> ...purposeful sampling techniques were used to recruit the appropriate range of participants. For instance, teachers and students often nominated other individuals whom they thought would be helpful for this research. Those individuals who fit the study's criteria (e.g., ethnicity, grade level, gender, academy assignment) were contacted by phone, e-mail, or in person to participate in the study.... In addition to student interviews, individual interviews were carried out with 15 teachers, 5 counselors, 4 administrators, 2 school psychologists, 1 librarian, and 2 teachers' aides. (Chhuon and Hudley 2010: 345)

The tape-recorded interviews were mainly conducted in classrooms, cafeteria, and other settings at the high school.

The "ethnic identity question" was of particular interest because the school is divided into a series of "academies," or learning clusters, some of which were identified as high prestige, "higher achievement" academies while others were considered to be for "lower school performance." Most "Asians" were in the "higher achievement" academies, but Cambodians, Latinos and African Americans were mainly in the "lower" academies. The researchers' purposeful sampling included nearly equal representation from the two levels—23 from the "higher achievement" academies and 29 from the "lower achievement" groups.

For Cambodian students, ethnic identity was found to be particularly ambiguous because of the prevalence of a general, positive stereotype of "Asians as high achievers." Whenever Cambodian students were seen as "Asians," that gave a positive image, whereas the label, "Cambodian," turned out to have much more negative connotations—poor school performance, dropping out, and "involved in crime." The researchers found that many of their informants wished to identify as "Asians." In their sample of Cambodians in the higher achievement academies, 18 of the 23 informants "explicitly described a preference for panethnicity" [meaning "Asian"]. These students were not comfortable with the Cambodian ethnic identity. According to one informant:

> Well people always ask me, "What are you?" I say I'm Asian and they say, "No, but what are you?" I think it's funny to go on and on. I identify myself as being Asian just because it's easier to say that I'm part of this group. Because obviously I'm Asian. I look that way. But like within the Asian community they ask me what are you? And I say I'm Chinese because I guess I think it like just looks better sometimes. I mean, I'm half anyways. (Chhuon and Hudley 2010:349)

Whereas a majority of the Cambodian students in the "higher achievement academies" preferred the general (positive) "Asian" ethnic identity, the researchers found the opposite to be true in the "lower achievement academies." Of the 29 informants in this category, 23 expressed preference for Cambodian/Khmer ethnic identity.

In this study the combination of participant observation, key informant interviews, and in-depth case interviews was effective in exploring issues in a complex institutional setting. The sample of "cases" gave the researchers possibilities for quantitative statements, which could have been elaborated further. On the other hand, ethnographic studies like this one generally rely mainly on quoting from the verbal contents of in-depth interviews. The study illustrates the ways in which having a sample of cases make it possible to assess the importance of variations and "deviations" within the study population.

Nigerian Rural Women's Views of Hospital-Based Childbirth

This is a contrasting case, as the study has a "sample," but no quantitative information is included in the report.

Izugbara and Ukwayi (2007) interviewed a sample of women in a remote area of Abia State in Nigeria concerning childbirth issues, including people's views about hospital deliveries. Most of the population in the research area is Christian, living from subsistence farming. "Respondents in the original study include 13 TBAs [traditional birth attendants], 23 women intercepted while presenting at the home of TBAs for pregnancy and birth-related matters, and 42 local women comprising mothers, grandmothers, and some local authoritative women" (Izugbara and Ukwayi 2007: 149).

The general tone of the interviews showed that women consider pregnancy and childbirth to be risky and hospital-based childbirth not risk-free. The dangers during childbirth included "supernatural, natural, hereditary, biological, and situational factors." One informant talked about the dangers of "curses" as follows:

> If her father or mother or an elder curse a young girl, it may work against her during pregnancy or child-birthing. If my daughter offends me and I say, you bad girl, you will die during childbirth or you bad girl you will suffer in this world.... It will certainly work. Curses are bad. That's why good parents don't curse their children.... (p. 149)

It appeared that there was a good deal of fear of supernatural sources of harm in the population, as informants also told the researchers that "Evil children (umu ojoo or ogbanje) can also sometimes find their way into women's womb to cause them problems. Such children, often from the spirit world (ala mmuo), may be on a special mission to kill, torture, or cause complications for these women" (p. 149).

Some of the informants told negative stories of complications in hospital childbirths; nonetheless, the researchers found that hospitals were "one of the more popular birth sites," even though the use of hospitals for deliveries had only developed quite recently. The researchers also commented that "Hospitals were seen as only good at dealing with natural risk factors.... When women were sure they would not suffer complications resulting from supernatural causes, they reportedly preferred to use hospital services" (p. 155).

DEALING WITH REPRODUCTIVE TRACT INFECTIONS: WOMEN IN RURAL GUJARAT, INDIA

Archana Joshi and colleagues (Joshi, Dhapola, and Pelto 2008) carried out an ambitious study of women's reproductive tract infections, treatment seeking, marital life, and related information in a sample of 69 married women in eight villages in rural Gujarat. Over a period of several weeks, they visited each of the women five times to gather in-depth data about their perceptions of their health problems, histories of treatment seeking, and sexual relationships with their husbands. The study report contains many quotes from individual interviews concerning perceptions of causes of reproductive health problems and treatment seeking experiences. Contrary to some stereotyped reporting concerning rural women failing to seek treatment, Joshi and colleagues found that most of the women with reproductive health problems (54 of 69) had sought treatment, and many of the women had gone to more than one kind of health provider or facility.

As in many such ethnographic descriptive papers, no formal statistical analysis was included, but numbers were reported for a variety of points in their article. For example, the concept of "garmi" (heat, "heatiness") was found to be a very common explanation for their reproductive tract infections, particularly vaginal discharge. The causal explanations for garmi included intake of "hot foods" (20); sexual intercourse (11); exposure to hot days (10); "hot body constitution" (5) and "hot medicines" (4). One informant, for example, described her "hot constitution" but also mentioned dietary factors:

> My body has a tendency to heat (garmi no kotho). I never feel cold in winters also. People shiver after getting wet in the rain; I don't get affected. My body constitution is hot (garmi no kotho che). White discharge is also because of that. And if I eat brinjal [eggplant] or jaggery [unrefined sugar], then the white discharge increases. (Joshi, Dhapola, and Pelto 2008: 146)

This study illustrates unusually thorough, in-depth case interviews (five visits to each informant), and combines extensive quoting from the informants with information about numbers (frequencies) of main patterns in the data. The pattern of multiple sessions with each informant insured that strong feelings of rapport and trust were established, so that sensitive topics, including discussions about sexual relationships with husbands, could be discussed with confidence in the later sessions. Participant observation was not a possibility, partly because of the nature of the research topic and partly because the sample was recruited from eight different villages.

STRATEGIES IN IN-DEPTH INTERVIEWS

Whenever possible, you should have more than one interview session with each "case" in your sample. In some situations, having multiple interview sessions to some extent substitutes for participant observation, and allows for greater in-depth exploration of the main research topics.

In-depth case interviews should be designed to give the informant ample opportunity to narrate events and ideas at length. Interviews are generally semi-structured, but interviewers should try for a flexible, conversational style. It is a good idea to ask the demographic, background questions later in the interview—not at the very beginning. At the start of the interview, try to develop an informal, relaxed relationship with the informant, through friendly discussion about the weather, recent events, and explaining the intent of the interview. Then try to get the informant to "tell stories" about key events and behaviors.

Concerning treatment seeking for any health problems, a good start can be the following:

"Please tell me about the most recent time you went to some facility or provider for treatment of a health problem. Please give me the full story—when you first had the problem, what you did, who you went to—the whole story."

If the informant does launch into a full narration, it is best to avoid interrupting, if possible. You should hear the whole story first, and then ask questions to fill in details and clarify points that you didn't catch in your notes. On the other hand, if the storytelling is sparse and vague, you will probably need to interrupt early and ask for details about specific points.

A Day in the Usual Routine: A Useful Form of Questioning

For many types of case interviews it is possible to get extremely good information if you ask informants to "Please tell me everything you did yesterday—from the time you got up—so I can understand your regular daily routine." This kind of questioning is especially effective when your research is mainly concerned with regular, daily behaviors. Mothers taking care of small babies, sellers in the marketplace, school-going students, and many other types of "cases" are likely to give a great deal of information in describing what they did "yesterday." The approach is also effective with drug users, as you can be almost sure that there was drug use yesterday, in the usual patterned sequence. You ask: "Please tell me all the things you did yesterday. Please start when you got up: what you did first, step by step, so I can get a good picture of your daily routine." The same form of questioning is productive for asking about a sex worker's "yesterday," or asking a school student about what happens in school. Focusing on "yesterday" generally is productive of more specific behavioral information, instead of vague generalizations.

Getting Good Interviews: Advice from an Expert Ethnographer

James Spradley's *The Ethnographic Interview* is an excellent source of advice, and should be consulted when you are training field interviewers for a project. Spradley begins by emphasizing that the ethnographic interviewer should try to make the interview as much as possible like a friendly conversation. He notes that it is, of course, necessary to insert some "ethnographic elements" during the interview but that should be done cautiously. "At any time during an interview it is possible to shift back to a friendly conversation. A few minutes of easygoing talk interspersed here and there throughout the interview will pay enormous dividends in rapport" (Spradley 1979: 59).

His list of the main contents of a good interview focuses on (a) having an explicit purpose and strategy; (b) explanations of the purposes, so the informant understands what the interviewer is trying to learn; and (c) ethnographic questions. Spradley includes more than thirty kinds of ethnographic questions in the appendix to his book. The example above, asking the informant to tell "all about your yesterday," is an example of what Spradley labeled a "grand tour question."

Spradley pointed out that if you do a "grand tour question," the informant's answer produces a complex field of "points along the way." For those, you will need to go back and get more detailed information about some particular actions or settings. The grand tour question is just the first step. Then you follow up to get more depth and specific contents.

Do not bypass the significance of the "grand tour question" as a strategy in ethnographic work. Such large questions strongly emphasize the concept of the informant having large amounts of useful information, of which we (the ethnographers) are ignorant.

Probing with Follow-up after a "Grand Tour Narrative"

"Probing" refers to the wide range of ways to get further information within the framework of what the informant has told you up to this point in the interview. Everyone—whether ethnographer, teacher, or just an ordinary person—does probing to some extent in many ordinary conversations. Probably the first probing you remember from childhood was your mother asking something like, "What do you mean—they made you be late in getting home from school?"

Experienced ethnographers, like experienced police interrogators, teachers, and TV interviewers, have a wide range of "probing techniques." Here are some common forms.

- "So, there was conflict in the meeting. Could you tell me what sort of conflict—what actually happened? Please give me the details."
- "Hmmmm. That's very interesting. Tell me more...."
- "You say he was drinking at that time?" In this probe, you simply repeat what the informant said, but with a questioning tone.
- "You just used the Hindi word, 'garmi.' What symptoms were you actually experiencing?" (In some parts of India people use the word 'garmi' to refer to a probable sexually transmitted infection.)
- (Referring to part of the student's narrative about "yesterday") "You said those guys were Asians. What kind of Asians, specifically? Tell me more about them."

- "It seems that for several hours, in the middle of the day, your two-year old Rafael is cared for by your seven-year old daughter. What do you suppose they do during all that time? What are all the preparations you do? Do you have food prepared for them? Do they go visiting? I'd like to get a clearer idea about how that works…. Who do you think your daughter would contact if she had some sort of problem?" This is an example of the "long probe." Often, if you ask a long question, you will get a long answer.

- Sometimes you do a blatant leading statement/question. In this example, the informant has just mentioned an unpleasant encounter with a government official. Interviewer (emphatically): "I'll bet underneath you were really flamin' angry when that happened!" If you have good rapport with the informant, that kind of blatant statement may open up considerable expression of emotions and new information.

A Useful Probe: "Can you give me an example of that?"

This question demonstrates one of the most useful types of probing for more information, particularly because informants often give their first answers in generalizations. For example, informants often make statements like this: "When we [ethnic minority] go to the school to ask about our child's problems, they don't treat us right." The interviewer then responds: "Can you give me an example, like a recent situation that you experienced, or one of your friends?"

The "Please give me an example" question should be one of the most frequent occurrences in good ethnographic interviews. (See Chapter 14 for examples of "hypothetical scenarios" in interviewing.)

SUMMARY AND CONCLUSIONS

The collection of interviews from a set of 50, 60, or more cases is one of the most powerful ethnographic research designs in use today. Of course, it should be carried out with a carefully planned interview strategy that you develop from a combination of some participant observation and sufficient key informant interviewing, so that you get the right local language, realistic questions, and realistic probes and your interviewers understand the language, the issues, and people's answers.

Thus, your research plan should ideally adhere to the following guidelines:

1. Before your "case sample" is selected, you should ideally have a period of social mapping, participant observation, and key informant interviewing—hopefully at least a two-weeks "exploratory phase" to get clear ideas of the local population(s) and some of the locally relevant issues that you will incorporate into your interviewing. Very often, that preliminary data gathering will reveal critically important features (e.g., a big difference in the two ethnic groups in your sample) that you must be aware of in planning the interviewing formats.

2. The selection of the sample should be carefully planned. If there is an available sampling frame (e.g., a house listing or a list of students in an ethnic group), then selection of a random sample may be the best choice. On the other hand, often random sampling is not feasible. Carefully designed purposive sampling is another option.

3. Ideally, each individual should be interviewed more than once, in order to "break the ice," develop rapport and trust, and get "deeper" into detailed key information. Two or three sessions with each individual can produce credible, in-depth data.

4. In most studies interviews should deal mainly with actual behavior, unless the research topic is intentionally narrowed down to a focus on "cultural beliefs."

5. While the interviewing is mainly about behaviors, events, and actions, answers to questions like "Why did that happen?" or "Why did you do that?" will practically always result in a good deal of information about cultural beliefs, motives for behaviors, and other concepts.

6. Interviews should always include key "background variables," and parts of the interviews should be structured in a standardized manner for all the informants, in order to allow for quantifiable variables and some statistical analysis. At the same time, other parts of the interviews should be open-ended with good depth of detail.

7. Although qualitative analysis will reveal some general themes and characteristics of particular groups (e.g., ethnic groups, different socio-economic levels, castes, occupations), good research with effective sampling should always find interesting variations in practically all categories of behaviors.

Free Lists: Getting an Inventory of Things in a Cultural Domain

Free listing is the easiest, quickest, and most productive interview technique for getting a good "start list" of the contents of a specific cultural domain, or topic, that you are interested in. Of course, "cultural domain that you are interested in" covers a wide range, and there is an endless number of possible free lists. In some cases you might feel comfortable with getting full lists from just 10 or 12 key informants. However, you can do much more analysis of the data if you have lists from 30 or more persons. It all depends on your research objectives and the complexities of the specific cultural topic(s) you want to explore. Of course, if you want to understand the differences between two or three different ethnic groups (or compare rural and urban groups) then you need to have more informants. The results of free listing are so robust that it is usually unnecessary to worry about getting a random sample.

Ethnographers have used the technique of free listing for a long time, but this research tool became more prominent and better understood as a result of Weller and Romney's *Systematic Data Collection* (1988). They noted that one important use of free listing is to identify the inventory of items and, by inference, the boundaries of a particular cultural domain. "There are several things that can be observed and inferred from such lists. First, some items are more 'salient', 'better known', 'important', or 'familiar' than other items, and those items occur earlier or higher up in an individual's list than those that lack such characteristics. Second, there is usually a great range in the number of people that mentioned each item" (p. 10–11). This leads to two somewhat different measures of "salience": the relative placement of items in individual lists (earlier or later), and the total number of individuals who mentioned the item. In a great many free lists, a relatively small number of items are "very salient" and a large number of additional items are in the domain (belong in the topic), but are "less well known." That means that very few informants mentioned them.

When a research group collects even a relatively small number of lists from informants (15 to 20 or so) tabulation of the data quickly shows which items are "foremost in their minds," or "most common." In many research situations the most important objective is to get a rough draft of the inventory without worrying whether the list is complete. If you collect 25 lists of "all the animals you can think of," you might not care if nobody remembered to mention bandicoots and wombats.

FREE LISTS AS THE TRIGGER TO RE-THINKING A DOMAIN

Free lists of "male sexual health problems" led to re-thinking the entire domain in a study in South Asia. During the 1990s, researchers collected several batches of free lists of male sexual health problems in India and Bangladesh, which showed that men's health concerns included a number of high salience items that are not sexually transmitted infections (AIMS 1997; Collumbien and Hawkes 2000; Verma et al. 1999).

Table 10.1 presents the result of free lists of male sexual health problems collected from practitioners and sexually active males in a Mumbai (India) low-income community. This result from a series of free listings opened up an entirely new chapter in understanding men's sexual health issues in South Asia. Similar results have come from free lists in other parts of India and also in Bangladesh. It is strikingly important in these results that a number of the "problems" are not sexually transmitted infections. These data point to the importance of dealing with young men's psychosocial worries, in addition to the usual focus of medical attention on syphilis, gonorrhoea, and HIV/AIDS. In more recent years, medical doctors treating men's sexual problems have found that a large share of their clientele are presenting with concerns about "semen quality" and "semen loss," including nocturnal emissions and masturbation—all of which relate to deep-seated, traditional physiological concepts in the Ayurvedic medical system (Hawkes 1998; Hawkes and Hart 2003).

Doctors trained in modern allopathic medicine seldom paid attention to "semen anxiety problems," because they did not consider them within the domain of sexual health. However, now that the free-list data have been confirmed by other research, the medical definition of that health domain has been redefined. At a Male Health Clinic in the Matlab rural area (Bangladesh), Dr. Hawkes found that "over 40 percent of attendees reported psychosexual dysfunction as their main reason for coming to the clinic." (Hawkes 1998; quoted in Hawkes and Hart 2003:94)

TABLE 10.1 Free List of Male Sexual Health Problems in a Low-Income Area of Mumbai (N = 56 males and unqualified practitioners)

Illness or Problem[a]	Approximate Meaning	Frequency
Kamjori	"Sexual weakness"	35
Khujli	Itching	31
Peshab main jalan	Burning urination	30
Jaldigirna	Early ejaculation	28
Jakhamhona/fori, foda	Sores in genital area	28
Dhatgirna	Semen loss	27
Echchanahona	Lack of sexual desire	17
Tedhapan	Bent penis	17
Khadanahona	Erection failure	15
Hasthmaithun	Masturbation	15
Dane nikalna	Boils, sores	14
Dhatpatlahona	Semen becomes thin	13
Ling dard	Pain in penis	11
Swapnadosh	Nocturnal emissions	11
Garmi	"Heat" (sexual infection)	10
AIDS	AIDS	9

[a] To save space, the seven lowest items, including syphilis, gonorrhoea, chancroids and herpes, were removed from the list. Source: Adapted with permission from Verma et al. 1999.

THE MANY USES OF FREE LISTING

Free listing is such an easy (and usually pleasant) interviewing tool that it should be in every ethnographer's repertoire of frequent practices. The "ease of use" goes along with another important quality—the technique has a wide range of uses. The following list includes only the most salient uses; innovative researchers will develop additional, ingenious ways to use the results of free listing.

- To develop a preliminary inventory of the contents of any cultural (topical) domain of interest. This is the main use.
- To obtain measures of the "salience," "importance," and "commonness" of the various items and/or clusters of items in any given domain. In many applied programs, it is important to find out the most salient

(often the most common) health problems in a specific sub-population or community, or the most salient social problems in general. There are many different ways that knowing "the most salient" members/items in a domain can help to focus programmatic efforts.

- To identify individual informants who are particularly knowledgeable about the contents of the cultural domain and who therefore are likely to be good key informants.

- To relate individual knowledge/competence about the cultural domain to other key variables such as sex, education, and ethnicity.

- To examine the internal structure, organization, and/or other patterning within a domain.

- To compare groups (e.g., ethnic subpopulations or religious enclaves) in terms of what they consider salient and of their differences in their overall familiarity with and structuring of specific cultural topics (domains). For example, education researchers often need to find out about ethnic differences among parents with regard to math information, literacy habits, and other cultural elements that affect school students' interest levels and academic performance.

THE CONCEPT AND CALCULATION OF SALIENCE

The list of "men's sexual health problems" in Figure 10.1 provides the number of men (frequency) who mentioned each problem or condition. Kamjori ("sexual weakness") is listed by 35 respondents so that, in terms of simple frequency, it has the highest "salience," that is, it occurred widely in the men's consciousness. There is a second component for "salience," however. Psychologists have demonstrated that the items that are commonly known to most people tend to get mentioned early in the lists, while the less commonly known items are usually remembered later. These two components—frequency of mention and relative ranking in people's lists—are generally combined to give an overall measure of salience. That measure is known as Smith's S, based on the first journal publication of the statistical process (Smith 1993). Quinlan has given the detailed computational steps you can follow to compute salience for any set of free-list data (Quinlan 2005: 226–227). However, it will be much easier for you to get the software program ANTHROPAC (Borgatti 1993; Borgatti no date), which is handy for quickly analyzing free-list data, as well as many other kinds of qualitative and quantitative data.

COMPARING SALIENCE IN DIFFERENT GROUPS AND SUB-GROUPS

Thompson and Zhang (2006) have presented data in which they used free-list results to examine differences in the salience of different countries/nations from the point of view of students (informants) in several different Southeast Asian nations. University students in six different countries were asked to list countries in the world. Data were collected from samples in Thailand, Malaysia, Singapore, Indonesia, the Philippines, and China. Almost all the lists showed the highest salience for the students' own country, except for Singapore, where Malaysia had the highest salience. However, the lists showed wide differences in salience of the Southeast Asian nations. For example, Laos had very low salience in most lists, but ranked second among Thai students. In comparing only the salience of nations in the Association of Southeastern Nations (ASEAN), Singapore was fourth in salience among Indonesian students, but was a lowly 13th among Thai students (Thompson and Zhang 2006: 408). That study shows the usefulness of free listing in comparing different groups concerning a specific topical area.

STUDYING AMERICAN KINSHIP SYSTEMS

The American (English language) kinship system is often used as a handy example of the uses of free-listing techniques. Back in the 1960s, Romney and D'Andrade (1964) collected free lists of kinship terminology from high school students ("all the names for kinds of relatives...in English.") Their study showed that "mother" is the most salient, both in terms of number of mentions (93%) and is often listed first. Since the data were collected from school students, it is not surprising that kinship terms like granddaughter and grandson were quite low in salience for that population.

STUDYING CLUSTERS AND CATEGORIES IN FREE LISTS

In studies of patterning within free lists, a common measure of "clustering" has been to explore the "inter-item distances" in informants' lists to see which pairs are "close to each other" and which pairs are widely separated. For example, examine inter-item distances in the following list from one individual informant:

Apple banana orange guava watermelon honeydew cantaloupe blueberry

You will notice that (for this informant) apple and banana are "together," while apple and watermelon are separated by three intervening items, and that apple and blueberry are the most distant from each other, separated by six intervening items. Using this general idea of "inter-item distance," it is easy to show that, in many parts of Euro-American culture, dog and cat tend to group together. Similarly, we would expect some clustering of lion, tiger, and leopard. It is interesting that in a study by Henley (1969), the strongest "bond" among animals was found to be "sheep and goats." That appears to be a result of a common expression—"this will separate the sheep from the goats," as pointed out by Bernard (2011: 226).

Robbins and Nolan noted that the simple measure of "inter-item distance" has some mathematical problems, and so for certain types of free lists they have proposed a different formula, which is explained in detail in their paper entitled, "A measure of semantic category clustering in free listing tasks" (Robbins and Nolan 2000). To demonstrate the method, they collected lists of family and kin persons from an opportunistic sample of university students in Missouri. They tested and confirmed the hypothesis that "father's side relatives" and "mother's side relatives" tend to cluster separately, and they also confirmed the hypothesis that mother's side relatives tend to be of higher salience than father's side relatives in the American kinship system. That result confirmed an earlier study concerning "matrilateral asymmetry" reported by Poggie and Pelto (1969).

COLLECTING THE LIST OF "ALL THE TRADITIONAL MEDICINAL PLANTS"

The ethnography of plants (ethnobotany) is probably the topical area that has seen more use of free listing than any other cultural domain. A study by R. Trotter is often cited as an exemplar of thorough use of the free-listing methodology as part of a broad study of home remedies (*remedios caseros*) among Mexican Americans. He collected listings from 378 individuals of the home remedies that they knew, and the use of each remedy. The total list of *remedios caseros* came to slightly over 500 items (Trotter 1981). Lists of home remedies (and other lists of treatments and medicines) are useful for comparisons of male and female "health care knowledge," as well as for comparing urban and rural members of specific ethnic groups.

Quinlan (2006) reported that she carried out over 1000 free-listing interviews concerning medicinal plants in a rural area in Dominica, West Indies. First she did a pilot testing, asking people to list "all the bush medicines [herbal remedies] you use." She found that free-listing approach to be too broad, as people concentrated on some categories of illness and forgot others.

> After conducting the aforementioned unsatisfactory pilot interviews on all bush medicines, I conducted a series of free-lists focusing on illnesses Dominicans know how to treat with medicinal plants. I used a prompt in the local English Creole (developed with key informants to aid comprehension). "Here in BwaMawego [the village] what things they curing with bush medicine?" (Quinlan 2006: 225)

She reported that each session using that particular free-listing question took from two to ten minutes. That certainly is one of the advantages of the free-listing technique—once people get going with the listing, it is over rather quickly.

Based on that free listing of illnesses, she then selected 18 illness domains, so that she could ask people to list the bush medicines used for each of those domains separately. She then collected the 18 short listings from every adult in the village, giving her 126 full responses to the listing task. She reported that this approach gave her a much more complete listing for an inventory of bush medicines. It is important to note that, according to Quinlan, very few individuals got tired or bored with answering for all 18 illness categories, and many people said they enjoyed the task.

Thus, for a complex domain such as bush medicines in general, Quinlan recommends that researchers break the free-listing process down into a series of separate, short listings—in this example, of remedies for each specific sub-domain of health problems. Using that method, she was able to collect what she regarded as a relatively complete listing.

How Complete an Inventory?

Do you need to get all the individual items in a cultural domain? The answer to this question varies. In many applied ethnographic studies, free listing is carried out in the early phases of research in order to get a preliminary inventory of topics such as crops, health providers, types of interference with studies or foods. Often the researchers are interested in getting an initial view of the more salient sectors (most commonly mentioned items) of the cultural domain, as in the example of "male sexual health problems." Further research, in-depth interviews with key informants, and collections of cases will then fill in some gaps, perhaps leading to defining some of the secondary sectors of the cultural domain.

On the other hand, in some complex free listings, researchers may feel that some sectors are incomplete and the overall inventory of items needs to be strengthened. D. D. Brewer (2002) has been concerned about the problem of completeness and has explored ways to improve free lists through supplementary interviewing. He suggests the following additional methods:

- Additional probing. Actually, almost everyone includes additional probing, in the form of "Can you think of any other X [medicinal plants/health problems/children's games, etc.]?" Additional probing is something that all experienced ethnographic researchers learn to do in interviewing, using various strategies and styles of probing.

- Reading back the informant's free list. Brewer noted that "This technique can be used under the guise of checking the accuracy of the interviewer's written record...." (p. 111).

- Using free-listed items as semantic cues. Brewer notes that this is a more powerful and effective tool for improving the listing. The technique utilizes a well-known feature of human thought processes—the tendency to remember items that are similar or somehow associated with a particular word or phrase. The procedure is relatively simple: after an informant has completed their free listing, the interviewer introduces one item at a time from the list. In Brewer's example from his methodological exploration about "all kinds of fruit," the interviewer takes each item in the informant's list and asks whether any other fruits come to mind.

Overall in Brewer's research, the third method in the preceding list—using each item as a semantic cue—led to an increase of almost 50% in the case of listing of "all different fruits." On average, informants added nine fruits to their list during this "prompting from the list." However, Brewer suggests that researchers should use all three of these supplementary techniques, if the goal is to get a full listing.

FINDING OUT THE NICKNAMES OR "CODE NAMES"

The list in Table 10.2 was collected by the CREHPA research team in a number of different cities and towns in Nepal. It shows that, in most locations, the common pharmaceutical drugs tidegesic and nitrosun, along with the powerful cough syrup phensydyle, are the most salient and widely used drugs. In addition to learning the variations in salience among the different substances, the researchers were also interested in learning the various "nicknames," as they would be important in individual in-depth interviews concerning drug use patterns.

TABLE 10.2 Types of Drugs Mentioned by Injection Drug Users in a Nepalese Border Community (top 15 items) (N = 15)

Name of Drug	Local Terms	Number of Mentions
Tidigesic	Maal, T, Tata, Ampoule, TD, Snooker, Pool, Bullet, Dose, Masi, Bhala, Bhitti, Dot	15
Nitrosun	Bhatmas, N, Sun, Gedagudi, Makai, Taak, Button, Naatibabu, Ten, BP, Nitro	15
Phensydyle	P, Dyle, Pyachche, Jhol, Beer, Liquid, Kalo, Horlics, Bottle, Chadole, Sano Bhai, Maal, Black tea, Dose	15
Calmpose	—	14
Ganja	G, Butti, Shankarjikobuti, Makada, Join, Jharpat, Osi, Chir, Grass, Prasad Gansh	14
Spasmoproxibon/S.P.	Kala daiza	14
Rakshi (alcoholic drinks)	Buch, Tharra, Kho.Bi., Bam, Daru, Sarab, Ghachchu, Wangepani, Chisochiya	14
Avil	—	13
Corex	Jhol, Beer, C, Jholjhal, Dyle	13
Phenargon	—	11
Cyclofam	—	8
Chares	Black, Koila, Kaalo	7
Fortwin	—	7
Brown sugar (heroin)	BS	5
Valium-10	—	5

Source: Unpublished data from a CREHPA study in eastern Terai districts, Nepal; used with permission.

The actual list collected by the CREHPA researchers is much more extensive, but the other items are "less salient," as they are known and mentioned by very few individuals. As is evident in this list of the top 15 drugs, the researchers found a wide range of nicknames in use for most of the more widely known substances. The list also shows that ordinary alcoholic drinks are relatively less salient in the drug-using populations.

One item that is lower down on the list is of special importance in the research. "Brown sugar" (heroin) is considered quite special among drug users in Nepal, but it is relatively costly and less available in many parts of the country. In a few of the more affluent locations the CREHPA research team found "brown sugar" near the top of the list, a finding that immediately signaled important differences in the drug-using styles in those locations.

In this location the listings gathered by the CREHPA researchers actually resulted in a total of 51 different substances. Later data-gathering confirmed the preliminary picture that emerged from the free lists, namely, that in this region of Nepal tidigesic and nitrosun are the most commonly used drugs, along with phensydyle.

Conclusions

In this chapter I have emphasized the usefulness of the free-listing technique, along with the fact that it is extremely easy to collect a sufficient number of free lists for some interesting data analysis. Sometimes 15 or 20 lists are enough for a quick exploration depending, of course, on the complexity of the cultural topic you are interested in, and also depending on the relative homogeneity of your study population. Borgatti (1999) recommends 30 as a reasonable sample size for many serious research purposes.

If there are a number of literate people somewhere near (perhaps in a nearby school), it would be easy to collect a good set of free lists in half an hour or less, if your topic is a general cultural domain that "everybody knows." However, in most applied projects you will have a more special study population in mind. It is not difficult to get free lists from a sample of "married women in households," or "sexually active young men," but it's more work to get a good sample of "unqualified health practitioners," "school dropouts," or "active commercial fishermen."

Next Steps

It is useful to consider free listing as an early step in data gathering, often undertaken around the same time you are doing some social mapping. The social mapping is intended to get a good idea of your study community or the locations of specialized sub-groups—such as different ethnic groups, two or three special occupational categories, or other "target" populations. At the same time that you do some geographical mapping, your free listing will get some "mapping of cultural topics." Sometimes you can do both "mapping" tasks with the same individuals.

In most cases you will follow up the free listing with several different data-gathering procedures. For example, for lists of foods or health problems (and many other types of lists), the next step is to explore the ways in which your study population sorts those foods or health problems into groups. Very often, your next procedure can be pile sorting and ratings, using a set of cards with simple illustrations, if part of your study population is illiterate. With your lists of foods, your next set of interviews can include getting ratings of "How healthy are those different items?", "How costly?", and "How tasty?" These next steps are explored in detail in the next chapter.

In both free listing and social mapping you will discover some good key informants, and you can make arrangements for in-depth interviews with them. Depending on your time frame, you should be able to do some visiting for direct observations and to make new contacts at the key sites you learned about in the social mapping, for example, NGOs, marketplaces, health facilities, workplaces, recreational sites, or other scenes that you need to know about firsthand.

11

Pile Sorting and
Other Structured Interviews

As discussed in the previous chapter, analysis of the free lists by themselves can give many clues about the contents of the cultural domain or topical area that you are investigating. The results of free-listing interviews are the raw materials (inventory of the topical area) for exploring many practical questions. If your free-list interviews include background information on the informants, you can find out something concerning the effects that gender, socio-economic status, and other variables have on different qualities and quantities in the lists themselves (see also Quinlan and Quinlan 2007; Robbins and Nolan 2000). You can also identify some good key informants from your free-list interviews.

For the next data-gathering steps, such as pile sorting and ratings, you will need to decide which items from your free-listing results you want to include in the follow-up interviews. If your free listing resulted in 60 items, you should cut it down to 20 or 25 (or even fewer)—usually the most salient things in your list results, perhaps plus a few unusual, low-salience items about which you are curious.

PILE SORTING CARDS, PHOTOS, AND THINGS

Pile sorting, as the name implies, means that you ask informants to sort things into piles, or groups. The most usual format (with literate persons) is to have words (for foods, plants, illnesses or other things) written on small cards. You then say to the informant: "Please put these animals (or whatever the domain or topic) into groups of those that are similar. You can use as many groups as you want, and you can use whatever reasons or criteria you wish."

Figure 11.1. Woman doing pile sorting (categorizing) of women's illnesses.
© Dunja Pelto 2013.

In some cases, if people do not at first understand these instructions, you could do a small demonstration with an unrelated domain. Some of our friends have used "sorting out the laundry" as an example to explain what we want the informant to do.

Although words written on cards is a common form of pile sorting, the cards might instead have some sort of illustration, particularly if some of your informants are not literate. In the sorting of "women's illnesses" in rural Bangladesh, Ross and his associates drew pictures on the cards as memory aids (see Figure 11.1). "For example, *jauntis* (jaundice) was represented by a totally yellow figure of a person; red drops represented menstrual problems; and a slice of papaya with white drops coming from the slice represented 'white [vaginal] discharge', or *meho*. This illustration arose because village women referred to the drops from the papaya as similar to their own white discharge" (Ross et al. 1998: 96).

Sometimes it is possible to use actual objects in the sorting. One famous example is a study conducted by J. Boster, who paid Jivaro people in his study site (in Peru) to bring him examples of all the different kinds of birds in the area. The preserved, stuffed birds were then laid out on a very large table, on which he asked his informants to group the birds in terms of similarities. He found that the groupings of birds by the Jivaro tribal people were not much different from the biological (scientific) classification of birds (Boster 1987). In another example, C. Kendall and his research team were studying dengue fever in Honduras and wanted to find out people's concepts about insects. They mounted each of the insects in their sample in small boxes, which informants were asked to sort into groups (Kendall et al. 1990). Some researchers have used photographs of things for sorting, for example, photographs of animals. On the other hand, many topical domains are abstract, and would be very difficult to present as visual products. For example, pile sorting of various psychological moods would be difficult to portray as pictures.

Pile Sorting Women's Health Problems: Gujarat Tribal People, India

P. Patel, at the Center for Health Education, Training, and Nutrition Awareness (CHETNA), carried out a study of Bhil (tribal) women's concepts of illness in Panchamahal district of Gujarat state (India) (Patel 2011). She collected free lists of illnesses and health problems from 41 women, resulting in a list of 24 health problems (illnesses) that were mentioned by more than one individual. Table 11.1 on page 184 shows the 13 most salient items (mentioned by 9 or more informants).

Based on the data from the free listing, Patel then chose ten of the most salient health problems and asked informants to sort them (written on cards) into groups "that go together or are similar." Figure 11.2 shows the multi-dimensional scaling result from 26 informants' pile sorting. Items that are close to each other in this "picture" were frequently grouped together in the same pile by the informants, whereas items that are distant from each other were seldom or never placed in the same pile. For example, burning urination was not put in the pile (group) with heavy bleeding.

In sorting these conditions for "severity," the researcher found that the women considered fever and night-blindness to be relatively "not severe," and considered "white discharge" and "tiredness" to be the most serious. It appears that the dimension from left to right in Figure 11.2 represents "less severe" to "more severe." In the interviews, many of the Bhil women considered white discharge and burning urination to be the main causes of tiredness and backaches. Patel also found that many women believe that the *safed pani* (white discharge) is due to witchcraft. For that reason, they generally seek treatment first from a traditional healer (*badava*). "When any of these conditions are not cured by the traditional healers, only then do they go to the medical doctor, it was reported" (Patel 2011: 93).

TABLE 11.1 Free Listing of the Most Salient Women's Health Problems Among Tribal Women in Rural Gujarat, India (N = 41)

Local Terminology	Approximate Meaning	Number of Mentions
Safed Paani/dhat	White (vaginal) discharge	37
Hath pag tute	Hand and leg pains	26
Kamarma mar chale	Backache	25
Pakhado	Heavy bleeding during and after delivery	24
Mathuchale	Headache	23
Choru vachoti jay	Miscarriage	22
Tav	Fever	22
Kamshakti	Weakness	18
Swas chale	Breathlessness	17
Chadine/vahelu masik	Irregular menstruation	14
Ratondi	Night blindness (during pregnancy)	12
Peshab bek ave	Burning urination	12
Jhada	Diarrhoea	9

Source: Adapted with permission from Patel 2011, p. 90.

The study by Patel among tribal people in Gujarat is only one of many instances from South Asia in which the listing of women's health problems results in "white discharge" at the top of the list and the condition is considered serious, particularly because it is often extremely difficult to "cure" (Bang and Bang 1994; Ross et al. 1998; Patel and Ooman 1999; Patel, Andrew, and Pelto 2008; Rashid 2007). The studies by Patel and colleagues and by Rashid have particularly linked the problem(s) of white discharge to psychological tensions (*tenshun* in Indian colloquial speech) and *chinta* (anxiety, worry), as noted by Rashid in Bangladesh.

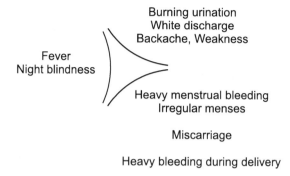

Figure 11.2. Multi-dimensional scaling result from pile sorting.

Pile Sorting of People

H. R. Bernard wrote, "I've used pile sorts to study the social structure of institutions such as prisons, ships at sea, and bureaucracies, and also to map the cognitively defined social organization of small communities. I simply hand people a deck of cards, each of which contains the name of one of the people in the institution, and ask the informants to sort the cards into piles, according to their own criteria" (Bernard 2011: 233). Undoubtedly, many researchers have done that kind of "sorting out" for exploring small group structures. Very often, such informal interviews result in learning new information about people's perceptions of qualities of persons, network relations, and sometimes "hidden patterns" (see Figure 11.3). Often the informants say that they enjoyed the sorting task—it's much more interesting than the usual forms of survey interviewing.

Pile Sorting to Establish a Scale for Measuring "Lifestyle"

Bill Dressler and his colleagues (2005) used free listing followed by pile sorting to establish the items (indicators) for a rather complex measurement of culturally patterned "desirable lifestyle" in a Brazilian community. They wanted to have a strong, culturally validated way of measuring what it takes for "having a successful life" or "being successful" in their Brazilian study communities. Based on initial interviewing and observations, they collected two types of free lists: (a) "material goods or possessions that people need to live a good life," and (b) "for leisure activities…list the activities in which people typically engage in their free time" (p. 337–338). That first step resulted in 80 items of material possessions and 66 leisure activities.

Figure 11.3. Woman rating local health practitioners into three groups: good/ excellent, intermediate, and not good. © Dunja Pelto 2013.

The next step in their strategy was to select 21 items from each of the two lists, concentrating mainly on "high salience" items from the "higher frequency" parts of the lists, but also including a few "low salience items." Those 21 items in each sub-domain (possessions and activities) were then written on index cards and used to obtain pile sorts from new samples of informants. During the pile sorting, the research team paid special attention to the language of choices in groupings, in order to get the underlying reasoning people used for grouping or separating the items.

Dressler and his Brazilian research colleagues carried out further statistical analysis and developed a "cultural consensus model" that consisted of 19 indicators (possessions and activities). These key items for having a successful lifestyle, in their order of importance, included:

1) house, 2) stove, 3) personal study, 4) money for school, 5) refrigerator, 6) time to rest, 7) talk with friends, 8) telephone, 9) time to read, 10) play sports, 11) sofa, 12) dining table, 13) church attendance, 14) money for extras, 15) car, 16) television, 17) computer, 18) washing machine, 19) web access.

The rank ordering of the 19 items for "importance for the model" was based on getting informants' ratings on a four point scale. All 19 items "hang together" in the sense that they are all validated by testing for cultural consensus. In the list of indicators (items), there are more material goods than activities (13 material goods vs. 6 activities). There appears to have been less agreement concerning the importance of specific activities compared with the consensus concerning material possessions. The analysis for "cultural consensus" was carried out using the computer program ANTHROPAC (Borgatti 1993), which utilizes the cultural consensus modeling mathematics developed by Romney and associates (Romney, Weller, and Batchelder 1986).

Dressler and colleagues used similar steps (free listing, pile sorting, rank ordering, consensus modeling) to develop scales for measuring "social support," "family life," and "national characteristics." Having developed those complex scales, they incorporated the sets of indicators into a quantitative survey. This interesting example illustrates the usefulness of techniques such as free listing, pile sorting, and ratings for developing more sophisticated quantitative and qualitative data-gathering tools. In many studies—especially short-term formative research—free listing and pile sorting are often used as basic data-gathering instruments, providing quick and useful ethnographic information. On the other hand, because they are usually easy and quick to administer, these tools can be used to lay the foundations for more complex research procedures.

Rating Items: A Specialized Form of Pile Sorting

The process of rating items refers to assigning relative values to each item in a set of objects, statements, or other contents. Rating is a common procedure in many kinds of studies, and is often done as a specialized pile sorting using cards. In fact, all research, whether qualitative, quantitative, or mixed methods, includes some form of overt or implied rating of people, actions, material goods, or other "things." In structured survey instruments it is common to ask persons to respond—on a scale from "high to low," "good to bad," or some other judgment—as the interviewer reads off each item from her or his interview protocol.

Usually the best method for asking for ratings is to present the informant with a set of cards on which the things to be rated are printed, one item per card. In some studies, researchers asked informants to do the ratings with the same cards they used in the free-pile sorting. For example, Ross and colleagues in rural Bangladesh asked female informants to pile sort "women's health problems" (as previously described), and then obtained ratings of the "severity of the problem" using the same cards (Ross et al. 1998).

Hypothetical Scenarios for Rating Items of Ethnic Identity

D. D. Caulkins and his colleagues used the technique of rating with cards in their study of various ethnic identities in the United Kingdom (Caulkins et al. 2000). The successive steps in the development of their "ethnic identity" instruments were similar to the steps described by Dressler and colleagues in Brazil (Dressler et al. 2005), but Caulkins and his team decided to construct "scenarios" of familiar behaviors that they had observed or heard about during field work. Scenarios for their "Welshness scale" included the following:

> A university professor has tea in his kitchen with the workers who are repairing his garden wall. (item represents "egalitarianism")
>
> A middle-aged farmer speaks in hushed tones about how moved he is by the words of a hymn. (emotionalism)
>
> A mother, who needs a new winter coat, goes without so that her not-very-talented daughter can continue her piano lessons. (self-sacrifice) (Caulkins et al. 2000: 274)
>
> We asked consultants [informants] to evaluate a set of cards, each card printed with a single scenario. We made the cards using 12-point type and heavy card stock.... The cards can be laminated in plastic for durability. Before each interview, we randomized the order of the cards to avoid introducing order bias. We asked consultants to read each card in turn and rate its "Welshness" according to a 5-point scale. (p. 269)

The "Welshness scale" contained twenty-one scenarios and was administered to 152 informants ("consultants"). Consensus analysis showed that there was indeed an acceptable level of agreement among the informants, so that the scale can be used as a culturally valid measure of ethnic identity in further research steps in Welsh populations. Caulkins and his colleagues, like the Dressler group, used ANTHRO-PAC for the testing of "cultural consensus." They noted that, at the time of their research, the ANTHROPAC program was particularly suited to older computers, using MS-DOS, and thus may be especially suited to low-budget research groups and field schools.

Ranking People: Wealth Ranking and Social Prestige Ranking

The exponents of PRA (participatory rural appraisal) have recommended the ranking of wealth and of well-being as important data-gathering tools, often utilizing small groups to do the ranking. As Robert Chambers pointed out (Chambers 1997: 142–143), wealth ranking, when done in terms of local criteria and by local informants, is usually more accurate and more informative than using a structured survey to ask about income and economic resources.

Wealth ranking or social status ranking, I suggest, should be carried out by informants in one-on-one interviews. According to Chambers, local ranking criteria may take into account a number of different locally-relevant criteria. "Proxy indicators have included quality of housing, tin roofs, numbers of rooms, occupation, number of items of clothing, furniture..." (p. 177). Many studies in South Asia, without using the PRA interviewing style, have used quality of housing and number of rooms as useful indicators of relative socio-economic status, though a number of studies have incorporated larger numbers of relevant indicators.

In some studies, researchers have found it useful to examine locally relevant assessments that focus more on the social status of households, instead of simply concentrating on wealth. Silverman, studying a rural community in Italy in the 1960s, found that local community people used the term *rispetto* (respect) in talking about relative positions in the local social hierarchy (Silverman 1966). She prepared a set of 175 cards (representing 175 families in and around her study community). She then asked the three key informants (separately) to sort the cards into groups in terms of their relative rispetto. Each informant took about two hours to complete the sorting, and there was overall strong agreement among the three informants. All of the informants placed the land owners, merchants, professionals and white collar workers in the "high rispetto" category.

Other kinds of ranking of individuals can be useful for specific research questions. For example, Bill DeWalt asked three key informants to describe the different levels of "drinking and drunkenness" among the men in a rural village in Central Mexico. He described his procedure as follows:

> For my measurements of alcohol use, I decided to rely more heavily on key informants who had spent all of their lives in participant-observation in the villages. I prepared cards containing the names of the sixty-two individuals in my random sample of the *ejidatarios* of Puerto de las Piedras. In separate sessions I presented these cards to three of

my best informants and asked them to compare each individual with every other individual as to their frequency of alcohol use. (DeWalt 1979: 516)

Although the three key informants used somewhat different categorizations in their ratings, DeWalt found a high level of agreement among the three raters (above .80 correlation). For example, one of the informants, "Pedro," gave the following categories: drunkards (*borrachines*) = 15, drunk once a week = 16, occasional drunk = 10, and abstainers = 20. DeWalt constructed an overall "alcohol use" score by simply treating the categorizations as numerical values and adding up the three ratings for each of the 62 individuals, giving a range from a low score of 3 (little or no alcohol) to a high score of 11.

This approach to rating and ranking is usually "credible," as long as the researcher has had sufficient time in the study area so that he or she can be confident in choosing good key informants. If you find that there are rather low levels of correlation among your key informants' ratings, you will need to contact more informants or else turn to something like paired comparisons (discussed later in this chapter), utilizing larger samples of informants.

Measuring Traditional Agro-Ecological Knowledge with Pile Sorting

Jorge Rocha used a series of steps involving pile sorting of photographs in order to develop an instrument for measuring Peruvian peasants' levels of "indigenous ecological knowledge" (Rocha 2005). He pointed out that there is increased interest in understanding marginal rural people's traditional environmental knowledge systems, particularly in projects attempting to improve agricultural production, including the introduction of new varieties of cultigens.

The basic data gathering was carried out in two stages. In the first stage, Rocha worked with four households of key informants. "I first conducted informal, in-depth interviews with four household heads (both men and women), two of them older couples and two of them younger ones. They talked about their crops, fields and soils, the weather, and fertilizers and pesticides..." (Rocha 2005: 362).

USING PHOTOGRAPHS TO COLLECT THE DATA

From the key informant data Rocha then put together sets of questions for his sample of cases by developing three different sets of photographs. The three parts of this more structured approach consisted of 34 photographs of different crops, 12 of different soils, and 7 of fertilizer types. With a randomly selected sample of 37 informants, he used the photographs for a "directed pile sorting." He directed the informants to sort the 34 photographs of crops into five separate piles, based on "difficulty of tending to the crops" (1 = not difficult at all to 5 = very difficult). He also asked the informants to sort the 34 photographs of crops into five categories based on the degree of need for fertilizer. The photographs of soils and fertilizers were smaller in number, so he asked each informant to sort them into three piles (high, medium and low) concerning which soil type was best for growing potatoes, the major crop in the area. The fertilizers were also sorted into three groups in terms of "best," "medium," and "least good" for growing potatoes.

TESTING THE RESULTING AGRO-ECOLOGICAL KNOWLEDGE SCALE

Rocha then constructed a scale of traditional agro-ecological knowledge by combining three components: the degree of difficulty in tending the crops, the quantity of fertilizer for the crops, and the suitability of soil types for growing potatoes. To test his newly constructed scale in terms of "degree of traditional-ness," he examined the correlations between scale scores with "modern schooling," "traditional views about development," and a "gender attitudes scale." As predicted, the correlation with "extent of Western-style schooling" was strongly negative (-.657), and the other two scales were strongly positively correlated with his "agro-ecological knowledge" scale.

This study is an important example of how systematic structured data can be used effectively for developing a theoretically important composite variable (a scale) using a relatively small sample of informants. The credibility of the constructed "agro-ecological knowledge scale" was made much stronger through the careful system of getting informants' ratings and testing for "cultural consensus" of the ratings. Rocha used the Romney-Weller-Batchelder cultural consensus modeling (Romney, Weller, and Batchelder 1986; Weller and Romney 1988) in the same manner that Dressler and associates developed their complex rating scales in Brazil (described earlier) (Rocha 2005).

One interesting feature of this example is that, although the product of the study is a culturally shared model of the local people's agricultural knowledge, the product nonetheless includes measurement of the differences in degree of that knowledge in individuals. The product does not assume that all the households in the study area are "the same" in their extent of traditional knowledge.

Box 11.1 Steps in Getting a Locally Meaningful (Culturally Relevant) Ranking of Individuals, Families, or Other Entities

1. Before asking informants to rank-order persons or anything else, find out through informal discussions, observations, and the like, what are the characteristics, qualities, and other markers that the local people use to assess or characterize persons.

2. Methods for that first exploration can include very open-ended discussion: "Please tell me about your neighbor over there. What sort of person is he?" Then, ask about other individuals and probe for details, all the while listening for key words.

3. Informal paired comparisons are another strategy: "What are the differences between Mr. Gomez and Mr. Chavez?" (two fairly well-known local persons).

4. Select a small number of well-known persons, and test out your ranking question(s) with three or four key informants (separately). It may be useful to try somewhat different language with each: "If I asked you to compare all of these same people in terms of their 'wealth,' what changes would you make in your answer?"

5. Now select your sample of individuals, families, or whatever it is that you want to rank order.

6. Prepare a set of cards (e.g., index cards, or other firm materials). Write each individual person or family on a separate card.

7. Check your language use with your key informants and research colleagues.

8. With each informant that you interview, shuffle the cards into a different order so that you don't accidentally introduce some "order bias" in your card set.

9. Explain the card-sorting task carefully to be sure that the informant understands.

10. Take careful notes of what the informant says during her or his sorting of the cards.

OTHER TECHNIQUES FOR RANKINGS AND RATINGS

There are many other useful techniques for getting rankings and ratings. In their book *Systematic Data Collection* (1988), Weller and Romney provide clear descriptions of how to do triad sorts, full-rank ordering, "sentence-frame formats," and other techniques.

Triad Sorting

Triadic comparison (triad sorting), like some of the other methods, is often done with sets of cards, although for literate informants the questions can be incorporated in a questionnaire. Some ethnographers would argue, however, that using cards is "more fun" for the informants, and gives a better opportunity for the researcher to observe the process and take notes concerning the verbal comments many informants utter in the triadic sorting process.

When using cards for triadic sorting, the basic question (instruction) to informants for triadic sorting is: "Among these three [items], which is most different—does not belong with the others?" or "Which two of these are more alike, and different from the third?"

In an interesting study of cognitive mapping of illness terminology, Lieberman and Dressler (1977) examined the effects of bilingualism on the ways in which individuals in St. Lucia (Caribbean) sort and distinguish illness terms. They used triadic sorting of nine illness terms for examining differences among individuals, focusing on comparisons of English-dominant versus Patois-dominant individuals. The triad-sorting task was done both in the local Patois and in English. Their research also included a measurement of individuals' bilingualism, ranging from English-dominant to Patois-dominant. One of their interesting findings was that bilingual individuals who were Patois-dominant displayed somewhat different results for their "illness model," depending on which language was used in presenting the triad sorting. When dealing in the English language, their responses resembled those of the English dominant informants. However, when doing the triad sorting in Patois, the Patois-dominant individuals shifted their responses to become similar to the monolingual Patois speakers' responses.

Paired Comparisons

The technique of "paired comparisons" is another type of structured, qualitative interviewing, and is a simple, highly useful way of getting valid data. Suppose you want to get some sort of ordering of the "dependability" of cars. You could start by getting free lists of cars, and then use the most salient ones for asking questions from informants. You would present every possible pair—for example, Saab/Citroen, Plymouth/Ford, Plymouth/Saab, Citroen/Plymouth, etc.—and ask each time: "Which of the two is more dependable?" Then you tally up the number of times each car "wins" in the comparisons. If you have 15 different cars in your free list data, you would have a total of 105 pairs to ask each informant. Twenty-one cars would require a set of 210 pairs—every car compared with every other car. That's a fairly long list to work with, but it's possible, since each pair represents a very simple question.

Ecological Data about Fish among Menominee and Majority Culture Fishermen

Ross and Medin (2005) reported an interesting small-scale experiment, in which they asked 15 Native American Menominee and 15 majority culture (White) expert fishermen to answer paired-comparison questions about 21 species of fish in the Wisconsin region. The paired comparison was in the form of "Does fish A affect fish B and/or does fish B affect fish A?" (Ross and Medin 2005: 145). The researchers constructed a questionnaire having a total of 210 pairs. If the fisherman (informant) reported that fish B affects fish A, he was then asked to explain how fish B affected fish A.

One of the objectives was to find out if the Menominee and majority culture fishermen have different "ecological models" about the fish. Ross and Medin found that the "cultural consensus analysis" (the same as mentioned earlier) showed that the two groups share the same overall cultural model about the fish. However, they also found that the Menominee have a model with some additional complexity. For example, "Menominee responses refer to the whole lifecycle of fish, whereas majority culture experts mainly answer in terms of adult fish" (p. 145).

This fish-comparison study demonstrates the practical feature that we can include more items in paired comparisons than in triadic sorting, which has severe limitations. If we were to include all the possible triads for 21 items, we would have an impossibly large number of questions. On the other hand, the 21 items (fish) in the Ross and Medin study are about the upper limit in the numbers we can deal with, unless there is some way of systematically limiting the numbers of comparisons.

Incomplete Cyclic Design

A problem remains, however. Twenty-one items generates a large number of pairs, and so what do we do if we want to find out about, say, 50

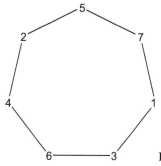

Figure 11.4. "Incomplete cyclical design."

animals or 50 persons? Michael Burton has described a system for "trimming" the total number of questions by limiting the number of paired comparisons, and has empirically tested the system, which he refers to as "incomplete cyclic design" (ICD) (Burton 2003).

The system sounds a bit complicated, but it is actually quite simple. Figure 11.4 illustrates the system using seven items. Let's say that this part of our study is about the prestige ranking of seven families. The first step is to randomize the order (the numbers in Figure 11.4 represent the seven families, randomized). Next, arrange the items in a circle. Now, following Burton, "the first ICD will consist of all the pairs of adjacent items.... [e.g. 5–7, 5–2, 2–4, 4–6, 6–3, 3–1, and 1–7]. The design has N [7] comparisons, and each item appears in two comparisons..." (Burton 2003: 117). We can design additional rules in order to put each item into four comparisons. For example, after constructing pairs from adjacent items, we can use the rule that comparisons are with each item two steps away. (In Figure 11.4 we get 5–4, 5–1, 4–3, 3–7, 2–6, 6–1, and 7–2.) If we put those pairs together with the first set, we have a total of four comparisons for each item.

Using the ICD system, Burton extracted a large number of different sub-samples using a set of 21 animals. He took some ICDs that had only two comparisons per animal, some containing four comparisons for each animal, and others that included six and eight comparisons for each animal. He found that an ICD with only two comparisons per animal produced rather poor results when compared to the full data set. However, for ICDs that had four comparisons per animal (about 20% of the full data matrix) the lowest correlation he got with the full matrix was a fairly respectable .58, and the average correlation was above .90. Thus, it appears that for many purposes, we don't need to do the full nine yards of paired comparisons. Often just four comparisons per item will do a fairly good job.

Going back to some basic numbers for a moment, we need to keep in mind the simple formula for the total number of pairs in any list of items. The formula is:

$$\frac{N \times (N - 1)}{2}$$

In the recently discussed example, 21 fish gave us 21 x 20 = 420 and 420/2 = 210 pairs. In Burton's explorations with the ICDs, if he used an ICD with four comparisons each, for 21 items he would have a batch of 42 pairs, instead of 210.

Burton, however, was much more impressed with the solutions he got with ICDs containing six comparisons for each animal. In those experiments, he got a minimum of .80 correlation with the original full data set. And with ICDs containing eight comparisons for each item (utilizing 40% of the raw data set), the correlations were all in the .90 to .99 range. Although these numbers apply to a particular size of data set and a particular type of data (animals), it appears, for most practical purposes, that the strategy of using ICDs containing six or eight comparisons for each item will be quite satisfactory. Some issues in applied projects might be handled well enough with an incomplete cycle design of only four comparisons per item.

These examples are important to understand, because the system of paired comparisons is basically very easy to develop and to explain to your research team and to the informants. In many cases, you might not need to have a large number of items in your paired comparisons. In the examples earlier in this chapter, P. Patel believed it was useful to work with just 10 of the most salient women's health problems, and Lieberman and Dressler did their triad sorting using nine main illnesses. Free listing will produce longer lists, but your focus of questioning can be on the more salient, better known items. For example, the total number of crops in an area may be a long list, but the most important, salient plants are usually a much smaller inventory.

Conclusions

All of the procedures in free listing, pile sorting, ratings, and the other data-gathering techniques discussed in this chapter are relatively easy to explain to your research assistants and to the informants. Also, almost all of the main types of tabulations and analysis that you will be doing can be carried out by hand—the only problem is that it may take you considerable time if, for example, you have 21 kinds of occupations and a total of 210 comparisons to tabulate.

Box 11.2 Guidelines for Pile Sorting, Triad Sorting, Paired Comparisons and Rating Tasks

1. Free listing is your usual best source of the items you want to use for these data-gathering methods. The free listing gives you a good idea of which plants, kinds of persons, foods, animals, illnesses, or other topical materials are common, well-known, and/or considered important in your study area(s).

2. Free listing is also your best source for getting the local terminology.

3. Select the most salient (most frequently mentioned) items, plus a few less frequent items that you especially want to know about. For pile sorting, twenty-five items is a good limit; for paired comparisons, fifteen to twenty.

4. About thirty informants is enough in all of these tasks, unless you have multiple different ethnic groups or sub-populations.

5. When presenting the cards or pairs to each informant, randomize or shuffle the cards or items first.

6. Remember, people all over the world can do listing, pile sorting, rating, and such tasks, as long as you explain the task simply and clearly, in their language.

7. In most cases, it is useful to ask additional questions, after individuals give their choices or selections (or pile sorts). Probe for explanations about choices, differences, judgments, and other qualities.

Here are some suggestions for using these structured qualitative tools.

- Often you will want to have an inventory of some topical area, such as "crops grown around here," and then specific knowledge about those crops and the local peoples' ideas about growing the crops, using them, and marketing them. When in doubt, start with free listing to get a starting inventory.

- You will often need to do some social mapping (usually a group activity), along with collecting some free lists from individuals.

- Always look for opportunities to ask additional questions—about the mapping, items in the list of usual crops, alternative ways of marketing, and other details.

- Always ask about recent changes and new developments.

- The same goes for asking about local variations: "Who are the people who grow those special crops?" or "Who are the innovators around here?"

- Pile sorting (free form) is a good way to find out about "similarities and differences." Often you get new information when you compare male and female lists or pile-sorting products. Ask about these differences.

- Another good way to get new information is to show some of the free-list, pile-sorting or paired-comparison data to your key informants and ask for their comments and explanations.

Analysis of Qualitative Text Data: Basic Steps

The main purpose of this chapter is to present some useful guidelines to follow in organizing and making sense of ethnographic field data. It is difficult to make all of this concrete and clear, partly because much of qualitative ethnographic research has been presented with only vague descriptions of the steps of data-gathering and the processes of making sense of those raw data from the field. That situation contrasts with the presentation of quantitative survey data, which is most often presented in ways that can be clearly understood and replicated by others.

INTRODUCTION

Before getting down to some steps of data analysis, we need to remind ourselves of certain features of applied ethnographic research. First of all, many writers want us to believe that ethnographic research is undertaken for "testing theoretical models" and "building theory." That language is partly connected to the increased requirements of some funding agencies, who want intervention programs to be "theory-driven." Sometimes those agencies suggest that intervention programs and associated research should "contribute to theory."

The fact is, however, that much applied ethnographic research, as well as the parallel quantitative-survey-data gathering, is basically descriptive and meant for practical use within the limited locations where the data gathering takes place. This formative research is intended to answer basic questions about "What's going on here in these sites?" Also, in the many studies that are intended as parts of an "evaluation" process, ethnographic data are intended to answer questions such as: "What happened during this intervention program?" and "Why did certain portions of the program 'succeed,' while other aspects seem to have fallen short of the program goals?" Those essentially descriptive goals rarely contribute directly to testing theoretical propositions.

Martyn Hammersley has written, "There is the fact that much of the interest of ethnographic research comes from descriptions of events in types of settings of which the reader has no experience. Sometimes the information provided concerns simply what happens; who does what, when and how" (Hammersley 1992: 22). He goes on to say, "There is an emphasis within ethnographic methodology on the importance of understanding events in context.... Indeed, it has been argued that placing events in context is a form of explanation that is particularly suited to ethnographic research.... From this point of view description is explanation" (p. 23).

The point I am getting at is that much of ethnography, especially applied ethnography, is intended to be explanatory description, rather than theory-building. Thus, as you struggle to make sense of your field data, your first thought should be something like: "What are the patterns of information in my data that can helpme to understand what is happening, and what may happen in the future, in the intervention program?"

In many studies concerning issues in health care, applied researchers are expected to identify specific factors (behaviors, beliefs, environmental features, etc.) that contribute, for example, to high infant mortality or avoidance of treatment-seeking, or to other social problems. So researchers are likely to be asking: "What specific information about local beliefs and behaviors can we present to the health care people to help them combat morbidity and mortality in this population?" Keeping in mind the remarks about "context" at the start of this introduction, a further question should be added: "In addition to the local people's beliefs and behaviors about illnesses, what other situational factors (economic, social, or cultural features) impinge on the management of health problems in this population?"

THEORY IN APPLIED ETHNOGRAPHY

Applied ethnography incorporates much implicit, and sometimes explicit, theory. This may sound like a contradiction, but researchers should be aware that considerable "theory," of various origins and shapes, is imbedded in the way we do much of our ethnographic work in the 21st century. The structured ethnographic methods described in Chapters 10 and 11, notably the free listing, pile sorting, and paired comparisons, borrow heavily from psychological methods and theory. For example, the concept of "salience" of free list items comes right out of psychological theory. Sociological and anthropological theory, including constructs about "cultural behaviors," has added to the implicit theoretical elements in ethnographic methods. Further, the mathematical construction and related analytic components for "cultural consensus" are important theoretical building blocks.

DATA ANALYSIS IN ETHNOGRAPHIC STUDIES

Analysis of ethnographic data should always start at the beginning of data gathering, not at the end. That primary lesson is difficult for some researchers, especially if they are used to the idea of quantitative survey research, in which it is usual that the data analysis is carried out after all the interviews have been collected, entered in the computer, and "cleaned."

So, what is the "analysis" that begins at the beginning of data-gathering? Mapping and general (preliminary) description of the study community and study population(s) usually come first. Of course, those descriptive materials will be revised and expanded as more data accumulate, but your first generalized impressions and descriptive materials are extremely useful, particularly for planning the next steps in the research design.

The collection of local language, special vocabulary related to your focused research topics, and narratives connected to your central areas of interest are often part of the initial steps of data gathering. As soon as you have some of these language materials, you should read through them carefully and start organizing the materials into tentative categories. In many formative research projects, early data gathering includes collections of lists of behaviors, types of people, reasons for certain actions, and other inventories that begin the categorization for organizing your data. You should also pay attention to recent developments, including current, ongoing changes (economic, political, technological developments) in the local area and region.

Of course, the kinds of "preliminary analysis" necessary in early phases of research are extremely varied, depending on the study populations and type of project. For example, a watershed (environmental) project has very different research needs than a school project for economically and culturally marginal students. The lists of items for initial preliminary analysis can go on and on, but a primary rule of thumb is that ethnographic research is an inductive discovery process in which researchers often change the directions and data-gathering strategies as a result of the new information found in the initial mapping, key informant interviews, and contacts with the study communities.

EARLY DATA ANALYSIS IN THE FIELD: KEY LANGUAGE AND CATEGORIES

Some ethnographic projects, or early phases of larger projects, are designed to collect the key words and phrases of the topical area, for example, local foods and eating patterns, and to get the inventory of categories in key domains.

Janice Morse has described a research project in which the main focus was identifying the categories of "gift-giving in the patient-nurse relationship" (Morse 1991). The research was carried out in a northern Canadian city, where the research team collected data from a total of 44 nurses working in eight different clinical settings. Thus, it appears that the sampling strategy was to maximize diversity among the informants. (Michael Patton (2002) calls this "maximum variation sampling.") Most of the informants were interviewed more than once, so a total of 82 interviews were conducted.

> ...the first interviews [were] unstructured. Participants...[were] asked to reflect on gifts they had received from patients and to "tell the story" concerning these patients. Interviewers were asked to obtain information on what kinds of gifts were given, who gave the gifts, when the gifts were given, and why they were chosen. Were the gifts given to the nurses personally, or were they given to the staff as a whole? What kinds of "speeches" were made by patients when they gave gifts? Had these nurses ever refused a gift? If so, how and why was the gift refused, and what were the consequences? What was the administration's attitude toward gift-giving? (Morse 1991: 598–599)

Box 12.1 Preparation for Follow-up Interviews

Whenever multiple interviews with individual informants are planned, always review the results from first interviews before planning follow-up sessions. Look carefully for key language features.

That first phase of Morse's research was clearly aimed at getting a preliminary inventory of language use, types of gifting situations, and other relevant information for the next, follow-up phase of research. The second phase consisted of a series of card-sorting tasks. Card sorting was introduced because the main aim of the research was to get an inventory of "types of gift-giving interactions," and to understand the functions of the gift-giving events, as perceived by the informants (nurses).

This example of ethnographic research shows how analysis of the very first one or two weeks of mapping, key informant interviewing, and first round of interviewing may require a "pause" to review the first batch of data and prepare the relatively structured second round of interviews.

The card set for the second phase of the research was constructed from the gift-giving events that had been described in the first interviews. The card set had approximately 40 items (different gift-giving events). Each informant was asked to do three different kinds of pile sorts: the triadic sort into three piles; another sort into just two piles; and, finally, a free-form sorting into as many different groups as the informant wished to use. Informants were asked to "think out loud" while they were sorting. "The participant was asked to name each pile, give the characteristics of each pile, and discuss how each pile differed from the other" (p. 599). Those data from the card-sorting interview formed the basis for the set of categories (taxonomy) developed in the research.

The analysis of the card-sorting data produced a set of five basic gift-giving categories: "gifts to reciprocate for the care given; gifts intended to manipulate or to change the quality of care yet to be given or to change the relationship between the nurse and the patient; gifts given as a perceived obligation by the patient; serendipitous gifts or perks and rewards...and gifts given to the institution by a patient as a benefactor recognizing excellence in care received" (Morse, 1991: 602).

The taxonomy has many sub-categories and explanatory notes. For example, the category of "gifts to reciprocate" has three sub-categories: "as atonement," "of gratitude" and "retaliation." The last sub-category, "retaliation," includes writing letters of complaint and also initiating a lawsuit!

DISCUSSION

In this research example the initial, unstructured, in-depth interviews provided the raw materials of different gift-giving events, including vocabulary and prototypes. As a result the analysis of those first interviews (the first phase of research) was the essential step for developing the second phase. Most ethnographic research involves this feature of data gathering in phases: data gathering ⟶ analysis ⟶ more data gathering ⟶ analysis ⟶ final data gathering, followed by comprehensive analysis and writing up the results.

Several of the research examples described in the preceding chapters had free listing as an early, preparatory step, for example, the studies of women's health problems by P. Patel (2011) and by Ross et al. (1998). The majority of the ethnographic studies that I refer to in this book have had at least two separate phases of data analysis in the course of the project. In addition to the relatively concentrated data analysis (e.g., of the free lists and paired comparisons) most ethnographic studies have an informal process of ongoing scrutiny, often through regular meetings of the research team, in which there is not only discussion of "problems," but also exploration of "new insights" that need to be incorporated into the next steps of research.

The Importance of Identifying Categories of Persons

A preliminary identification of "categories of persons" should be one of the early steps in most ethnographic field work. In many applied projects (e.g., agricultural change or community development) the researchers are looking for the "innovators," "good informants," "informal leaders," and many other categories of persons. At the same time, the researchers should be mentally sorting people's behaviors and beliefs into categories such as "traditional," "modern" and other possible "types." As the research progresses, these categories often become more complex and more numerous.

Some of the categories arise from the language and cultural beliefs of the people in the study communities. In fact, one major aim of ethnographic research is to understand the "emic" (local people's) categorizations and perspectives. On the other hand, based on the usual ethnographic inductive processes, researchers also construct systems of categories that are basically "etic" (resulting from the researchers' putting together new types of data). For example, in some studies researchers have identified "positive deviants," such as persons with unusually high scores on "gender equity" or "household management."

Strategies for Developing Categories of Persons

In some ethnographic research it may be useful to structure your data entirely in terms of one basic set of categories. For example, in research concerning female sex workers in India, it is common to find researchers referring to three basic categories: "brothel-based," "street-based," and "home-based" (Pelto 2006). Sometimes "highway-based" is added to the categories (see also Saggurti et al. 2008). Depending on the type of location, "lodge-based" may be included, as in the following news item: "The number of street and home-based sex workers was increasing considerably in several towns in the State [Andhra Pradesh], while the figure for those operating from brothels and lodges was coming down equally significantly, according to preliminary findings of mapping of high risk groups (HRGs)" (*The Hindu* 2010). Many research reports in India are organized to show comparisons among these basic categories of sex workers. Also, programmatic interventions often have different approaches for the different categories of sex workers. Many sectors of applied research are structured around a small number of basic categories of persons.

Categories Derived from Key Informant Interviews

The examples discussed in Chapter 11 using key informant ratings of alcohol use (DeWalt 1979) and using prestige ranking in an Italian community (Silverman 1966) illustrate a useful, widely applicable strategy, in which ratings on some particular quality (e.g., hierarchy of prestige in the community, alcohol use, degree of ethnicity) can be categorized as "high," "medium," and "low" or into other groupings. That form of categorizing can be used as an ordinal measurement to examine the relationship of the rank-ordered scale to other patterns in the data. If the main aim of your research happens, for example, to be focused on alcohol use or status hierarchy in the community, then that categorization strategy will be used throughout your data analysis. On the other hand, in many cases, this type of categorization is used as only one "chapter" of the research report.

Researching Domestic Violence: Concretizing your Categories

In the current climate of methodologically well-defined research, it is essential that we give clear and concrete information about the specific behaviors or language that we identify as the indicators for identifying themes or patterns. Let's take the following examples of domestic violence:

a. He abused me badly whenever I didn't have his dinner ready.

b. Once when he was angry he hit me with a stick, but not very hard.

c. Six weeks ago, he was angry about the food, and he yelled at me.

d. Many times he gets angry when I am late returning from the market.

e. Last week, when he was drunk and demanded sex and I refused, he hit me very hard. I still have the marks.

These "typical responses" are extremely difficult to classify into any clear "degree of domestic violence." In the first statement ("he abused me badly"), there is no indication of whether the abuse was only verbal or whether it involved physical violence. Item (e) can be rated as "severe violence" and item (b) looks like "moderate violence," but items (a), (c), and (d) are practically unclassifiable.

Those statements, all from case interviews, call for more probing to get clearer details of what actually happened. In many cases it is extremely difficult to get a clear picture of verbal and emotional violence, but with careful, thoughtful interviewing, we can get concrete data about actual physical violence.

In data sets I have examined concerning domestic violence in South Asia, it is possible to categorize cases into "serious physical violence," "minor physical violence," and "no physical violence." Any study concerning domestic violence in a given population should include the "no violence" cases when exploring the patterns and themes in the qualitative data. Certainly one part of the theme analysis should include careful documentation of the triggers, or "motives and situations" that result in physical violence. In any set of domestic violence cases it is essential that researchers categorize the different motives and situations carefully, and provide tabulations of the frequencies for the categories.

The next section examines a study from Bangladesh that gives a clearer picture of some main components of domestic violence, with some frequencies of the categories that are worth noting.

Domestic Violence: Mixed-Methods Study in Bangladesh

The following example illustrates the sets of categories commonly emerging from qualitative case interviewing. In the topical area of domestic violence, recent (21st century) research has produced prototypes of taxonomies (systems of categories), which are useful as initial frameworks. Nevertheless, each research project should look for ways that the categories should be modified and perhaps expanded as a result of new discoveries.

M. E. Khan and A. Aeron (2006) have described a study of domestic violence they conducted in four districts of Bangladesh. A large quantitative survey was carried out in the four locations, involving a total of

3,900 female respondents and a smaller number of male respondents. In addition, in-depth interviews were carried out with a random sample of 134 women. Interviewing the 134 women required, on average, three sessions, each lasting about an hour and a half, in order to complete all the parts of the semi-structured guidelines. Of interest here is the categorizing that emerged from analysis of the qualitative data.

The very thorough interviewing with the women explored the full range of mental and physical violence, including threats to send the woman back to her parents and/or threats to take a second wife. In the exhaustive list of various kinds of scolding, threats, and other hurtful actions, 54 women reported being slapped, and 24 described "severe beating," including kicking, punching, and being hit with sticks or other objects.

Using the descriptions of the data in the paper, we can, with careful attention to the details in each case, sort the cases into at least three categories, as suggested earlier: "no physical violence," "low level of physical violence," and "severe physical violence." Based on the data, at least 24 women would be in the "severe category." The three categories could then be the basic framework for more complex quantitative analysis.

WOMEN'S REPORTS OF "CAUSES" OF DOMESTIC VIOLENCE

Another set of categories that is important in this type of data analysis is the inventory of the "causes" or "situations and actions" that provoked the violence. Here again the researchers produced a detailed inventory. The lead item, with the largest frequency, is "wife does not meet husband's expectations in managing household." The two items with frequencies over 100 are "any issue related to cooking" (101 responses) and "children not properly cared for" (107). The sexual relationship is the next highest category, with "refusal of sex by wife" (82), and "wife suspects husband's infidelity" (74) (Khan and Aeron 2006: 41).

Other categories were "wife deviates from her expected role patterns," "poverty and other financial issues," "problems with in-laws," and "husband's bad habits" (interestingly, only 30 women mentioned drinking and gambling). "Dowry demands" came up in only 15 cases, and "other causes" included childlessness and having only girl children. The total list comes to 36 separate subcategories, but the main headings are eight categories.

MEN'S VIEWS OF "BAD ACTIONS" THAT "DESERVE A BEATING"

A closely related set of categories comes under the theme "behaviors that justify strong scolding and/or beating the wife." This theme has been explored in a number of studies in South Asia, and it shows the strong patriarchal, male-dominance pattern that is still pervasive in many parts of the region. The strongest (highest frequency) item is "wife does not obey the husband," which 59% of the male respondents said justified physical beating. The next highest item was "getting an abortion without telling the husband" (44% said it justified beating), which was closely followed by "argues with husband" (39% said it justified beating) (Khan and Aeron 2006: 45 Table 5).

Box 12.2 The Steps in Data Analysis, Using the Domestic Violence Example

1. The commonly used categories in the study of domestic violence provide a useful format for the set of codes you will use in that kind of study. At the same time, you must be prepared for new angles, new surprises, and new codes. Preparing the code list and then coding your interviews are among the first big steps of analysis.

2. We can easily see that "causes of violence" would be a very useful code category in an ethnographic study such as the Khan and Aeron research described in the preceding section.

3. The paper is basically descriptive, so the authors have given many quotes that illustrate the main categories. As I have mentioned in other chapters, all qualitative papers should include ample quotes from informants.

4. To go from description to first steps of theory, the next phase calls for cross-tabulations.

5. You need the "degree of physical violence" variable that I suggested earlier. Now, cross-tabulate "degree of violence" with a socioeconomic status variable: age, education, number of children.

6. Cross tabulate "degree of violence" with some of the different "causes."

7. Explore for other interesting variables in your interviews.

8. Develop a profile—a tentative model—of women who experience no violence.

Box 12.3 Notes on Managing Your Text Data

Basic ethnographic data are in the form of text materials—mainly interviews and field notes. For this discussion, I am assuming that you and your research team have access to computers, in which you are storing all your text data and photographs. Here are some main points regarding data management (also see Chapter 6).

1. Each interview and each field note should be a separate file. A system is needed for assigning labels to those files. It is useful to include the date in the file label.

2. If the field notes for a whole day are rather brief (as opposed to your interview notes), you may prefer to store one day's field notes in a single file. On the other hand, extensive notes from meetings or other special events should be in separate files.

3. Be sure to have clearly different labels for key informant interviews, case interviews, and field notes. Don't mix them up in the naming (labeling) process.

4. If you have several different field sites, label them clearly so you can always separate out Site A, Site B, Site C and Site D.

5. Always keep a system of back-up copies.

6. Be sure that your interviews and field notes are written in neat paragraphs of about two to four inches each. Those paragraphs are the "blocks" to which you attach codes for easy retrieval of information.

CODING TEXT DATA: IDENTIFYING CATEGORIES OF INFORMATION FOR LATER RETRIEVAL

Coding your text data is an essential early step in your data analysis. "Coding" means putting labels (codes) beside each block of text that refer to the information in that block (see Table 12.1). Each block is usually one paragraph, and may have several codes identifying the different kinds of information in the block.

TABLE 12.1 Example of Coding Text Data to Identify Categories

Expanded Interview Notes (Excerpt)	Coding[a]
[Interviewer has asked the traditional birth attendant about "most recent case" of childbirth she conducted.]	
Dai (informant): Past midnight it was around 02:15 am. I was sleeping and there was a knock at my door. I woke up washed my face and there was a call from a family. The mother was waiting at the doorstep. I suggested that she should go to the hospital but the mother refused and insisted that I should go to her house. I went and observed the position of the baby. Thalae patla odaedhu hoggithu (the sac had burst out draining the water content). I motivated the family to take her to the hospital. The family members said that it was late in the night and they had no transportation. Men refused to cooperate. That was her second delivery. Ten to fifteen minutes the members of the household were debating and discussing. At 03:45 am she delivered the baby at home.	Timing/duration Transportation Client actions Money/compensation Male participation Local language Decision-making
Interviewer: How many deliveries do you do in a month?	
Dai: Six to seven in a month.	
Interviewer: How much do they pay you?	
Dai: They pay 50 rupees and other items include dry turmeric root, betel leaves, nuts and dry cocoanut.	

[a] Suggested coding (for illustration). Note that other codes might be developed later.

The purpose of the coding is to allow you to easily retrieve relevant pieces later on when you are analyzing the data. For example, with the help of text management software, you will be able to retrieve all the pieces of data that have mention of illness, or you can find all the mentions of the different "providers." There are several software programs designed for that purpose; I generally recommend that people use ATLAS/ti.

In order to code all of your interview notes and field notes, you need to have a codebook with a list of the codes, along with instructions concerning the use of those codes. The code list in the following example has only 12 items (codes), so it is only the beginning of a longer, full list of key words (codes).

Box 12.4 Example of a Preliminary Code List

Natal family	Treatment	Spouse	Medicines
Illness	Money matters	In-laws	Social support
Providers	Transportation	Chores	

DEVELOPING A CODE LIST AND RELATED INSTRUCTIONS

Here are the steps for developing a code list, using examples in which health care is the research topic.

1. In your research plan you have mentioned a number of issues, types of data, and perhaps some theoretical concepts. From that, develop a start list of perhaps 12 to 15 codes that reflect your basic research plan.

2. Read through your first few interviews and field notes carefully. Insert codes from your start list. Wherever you find a useful piece of information not covered in your start list, add that topic to your list.

3. Try to limit your list to 35 or 40 items. For example, don't create separate codes for doctor, nurse, clinic, and hospital. Use just one code: "providers." And don't use separate codes for fees, costs, income, debt, and salary. Use "money matters." In other words, try to invent codes that are fairly broad—it will make your data analysis easier.

4. Continue reading and re-reading your interviews and field notes to see if there are complex interactions or unusual types of events that you have failed to code.

5. Don't include codes for usual words that can be found with a "word search." For example, you usually don't need a code for "alcohol" or "condoms," provided you instruct your team to be sure they use those words in the appropriate places in transcribing interviews and notes.

6. You can always add codes later, when you discover a need for a more complex code for a behavior or a situation not previously coded.

FAST TRACKING THE DEVELOPMENT OF A CODING LIST

Suppose you are pressed for time and don't have time for full coding. Many have had that experience: "The report from our one month of quick ethnography is supposed to be ready next week. They want to start the intervention program. What to do?" If you had planned perfectly, you would have been coding your data from the start. But it didn't turn out that way. "There were unforeseen delays in getting our interviews and field notes entered in the computer." Now you have to "code on the fly."

With ATLAS/ti (and other programs), you can do "autocoding," which is based on word-searching. For example, you ask the program to find doctor|clinic|hospital|nurse|. Each of the blocks with any of those words can be coded "providers." That will work in ATLAS/ti—the system may be different in other programs. If you need to get drinking behavior you will search on drink|alcohol|beer (if it is a beer-drinking popula-tion). Of course, you need to include local words for alcoholic drinks in that process. With a combination of autocoding and word-search opera-tions, you can combine some quick, makeshift coding and equally quick writing, that is, provided you are thoroughly familiar with your raw data in this unfortunately rushed piece of applied research. Next time, how-ever, you should work harder at writing up pieces of your data report, starting in the second week of data collection—or even earlier.

Box 12.5 Simple Descriptive Analysis

Suppose you have collected about 40 or 50 interviews from women who have recently had abortions. The data are from three different locations. Now you want to write a piece about the different types of practitioners and facilities that the women went to for terminating their pregnancies. Here's what you can do.

1. Using ATLAS/ti or other software, retrieve all the blocks of data that were coded for "providers" for Location A.

2. Print out the pages of data for Location A.

3. (Optional) Using scissors, cut all the individual data blocks into separate slips of paper.

4. Sort the data blocks into different groupings, for example, medical doctor, village nurse, unqualified male practitioner, NGO clinic, government health center.

5. Do the same process with the data for Location B and for Location C.

6. Examine the results to see if there are important differences, including different frequencies.

7. Write up the general picture: "Most of the women went to private practitioners. Only two women went to the govt. health center. Com-munity B is exceptional—they mostly go to the NGO clinic. Etc."

8. Now do the same process for other topics you want to cover in the report.

9. Perhaps you noticed in writing that you are missing some impor-tant descriptive information about those different practitioners. In this case you may need to do some follow-up.

Simple One-Variable Tables

Simple, one-variable tables can often give good summaries of important features in your data. For example, in the rapidly changing patterns of abortion-seeking behaviors among women in developing countries, it is important to identify what methods for inducing abortions are being used and to what extent newer methods, especially less intrusive and less dangerous methods, have been introduced. In most parts of the world, medical abortion, use of the relatively new "abortion pills," (especially misoprostol and mifepristone) is spreading among both trained, qualified practitioners and less qualified persons, including nurses, community health workers, and various practitioners of "traditional medicine." Table 12.2 is an example of a univariate table. The tabulated data, from a rural area in South India, show that by 2007 the use of tablets, especially misoprostol, had spread widely in the area, but medical doctors still preferred to do "old-fashioned" dilatation and curettage (D&C), for a variety of reasons (Ramachandar 2008).

Table 12.2 Abortion Procedures Reported in In-depth Interviews of Women who had had Abortions (2006–2007) in a South India district (N = 107)

Procedure/Methods[a]	Frequency[b]
Misoprostol (cytolog) tablets used, usually followed by D&C[c]	76
Manual vacuum aspiration used with misoprostol (estimated)	16
"Pure" D&C (no tablets or injections)	21
Medical abortion with mifepristone	3
"Some kind of injection" only	4
Traditional (some unknown substance)	3

[a] Data from qualitative in-depth interviews
[b] Multiple responses allowed
[c] Dilatation and curettage
Source: Adapted with permission from Ramachandar 2008

Grounded Description and Grounded Theory

A great deal has been written about "grounded theory" since the appearance of *The Discovery of Grounded Theory* by Glaser and Strauss (1967). In most discussions, the central theme is the primacy of inductive processes, although in actual practice the process is a mixture that we refer to as "abductive method." Abductive research is a mixture of inductive and deductive operations. The sequence of research is: (an interesting problem has been detected in a social program) ⟶ (collect data concerning the problem) ⟶ (look for the most likely "causes" of the problem) ⟶(collect more data, more cases) ⟶ (look for exceptions or negative results) ⟶ (revise your "causal hypothesis") ⟶ (repeat the process until you have a well-developed model that seems to account for the data in that program situation).

Two important tasks during this progression are (a) inductive coding, along the lines described above, and (b) "memoing." Memoing consists of writing notes to yourself while you are reading and re-reading your data. The notes are your ideas (hypotheses) about the patterns and connections you are discovering in the interviews and field notes. In software programs such as the ATLAS/ti there is a provision for inserting memos directly into your data set. That feature makes it possible for you to link your hunches and discoveries to the specific raw data (interview file) that sparked your new hypothesis. Weitzman and Miles (1995) have examined the range of computer programs designed for text analysis, and report that most of those software products include a system for doing memos.

Although a great many applied ethnographic projects are basically inductive processes, they don't necessarily follow all the principles and strictures of grounded theory. For example, some exponents of grounded theory write that you should not have any initial hypotheses and should not do a search of the literature before you start collecting data. In practice, that degree of "purely inductive process" is impractical, and most of the people you work with would criticize you for failing to explore some of the work relevant to your research topic.

CONCLUDING COMMENTS

The main point emphasized throughout this chapter, and in other chapters, is the need for concrete, clearly defined data language. The codes that you develop for analyzing text data need to be clearly defined, and you need to train your data gatherers to use clear, precise language in describing events and in interviewing informants.

Another important principal in various stages of data analysis is that counting and measurement are essential operations throughout ethnographic research. Measurement in its simplest form is identifying specific cases with feature X (e.g., cases of actual domestic physical violence in the past six months). It is a Yes–No (nominal) variable. With a little more measurement (and more careful definition) you get an ordinal variable, as mentioned above: "no physical violence," "low to moderate physical violence," and "severe physical violence." For numerical analysis you can convert these to 1, 2, and 3. For many cross-tabulations, that kind of ordinal measurement is very practical.

Many applied ethnographic studies and reports in today's international research world include some quantified operations, at the least to present frequencies of the various categories of persons, their behaviors, and cultural beliefs. In many studies, including the study of domestic violence in Bangladesh discussed in this chapter (Khan and Aeron 2006), the qualitative ethnographic research is linked to quantitative survey data, and the two bodies of information are integrated into a unified presentation.

In those ethnograpy-plus-survey designs, the role of the ethnographic component is to provide a detailed examination of the categories of persons, situations, and behaviors and other similar descriptive information. Quotes from informants provide glimpses of the raw data, the vocabulary and the "cultural color," along with exploring some of the patterns of inter-connectedness in the qualitative materials. Sometimes parallel statistical results from the quantitative survey and the ethnographic cases are compared in order to strengthen the credibility of the two separate data sets.

The study of gifts from patients to nurses discussed in this chapter (Morse 1991) illustrates the way in which card sorting and related interviewing are suitable techniques for getting informants in study populations to develop categories and sub-categories of key data. In effect, the use of free listing, pile sorting, paired comparisons, and other structured qualitative methods are ways to get the study populations to provide much of the basic data analysis. At the same time, those structured methods provide credible measurement of key variables, such as the relative severity of illnesses as perceived by the local women in rural Bangladesh, which was described in Chapter 11 (Ross et al. 1998).

Structured Observation of
Behaviors and Events

As discussed in a previous chapter, participant observation has been a core element of ethnographic field research in earlier decades, but its use has diminished in recent years because of time constraints and changes in the strategies of applied research. Increasing numbers of applied research programs in the 21st century are relying on in-depth interviews, including structured qualitative interviewing, in relatively short-term programs of data collection. Another trend is the increased use of structured direct observations, carried out with samples large enough to permit quantitative analysis of the data. It should be noted that nearly all participant observation had been non-quantitative, almost by definition. Also, many applied ethnographic studies are now carried out by non-anthropologists, who have had little or no exposure to the concept of participant observation.

QUALITY OF INTERVIEW DATA

Problems with interview data have motivated explorations in direct observation methods. There is ample evidence that data from interviews have a strong likelihood of containing faulty information. The longer the recall time, the more questionable are the data (Bernard 2011, Johnson and Sackett 1998). In some cases, the faulty information is intentional—for example, answers to questions about drinking alcoholic beverages or about church attendance often result in some people giving "socially acceptable" answers.

> The fact is that humans (including both trained field workers and untrained research subjects) are surprisingly incapable of accurately describing scenes they have observed with their own eyes (and ears and

Pertti Pelto, "Structured Observation of Behaviors and Events," in *Applied Ethnography: Guidelines for Field Research*, pp. 217-235. © 2013 Left Coast Press, Inc. All rights reserved.

other senses). Abundant evidence shows that, when research subjects are asked to report on their own behavior and these reports are compared to researchers' records of the subjects' behavior based on direct observation, the research subjects' accounts of their own behavior are substantially "wrong"—that is, they show errors of from 50%–80% when compared to the observational data. (Johnson and Sackett 1998: 302, citing Bernard et al. 1986)

Example: Remembering the Malaria Episode in Sri Lanka

A. de Silva and colleagues carried out a small survey to check on people's accuracy of recall concerning malarial episodes in a high malaria region (Kataragama) in the southern part of Sri Lanka. The research was part of a broader program of malaria control, conducted by the Malaria Research Unit (MRU) of Colombo University in 1993–94 (de Silva et al. 1994). Part of the motivation for the survey was to assess people's levels of "attentiveness" concerning malarial episodes in order to develop means for reducing the prevalence and impact of the illness through local, community-based approaches.

The MRU maintained health care clinics in the program villages, where they had full records of all the households that had had malaria cases in the past months. From the clinic lists, a random sample of 182 households was chosen, of which 150 households had had at least one malaria case in the past six months and had received treatment at the MRU clinic. The MRU records indicated that nearly half (45%) of the local population had been infected by malaria in the past six months (1993–94).

The interviews at the sampled households were intended to be with the household heads; however, in many cases male heads of household were not available and so the female head of household was interviewed. All the interviews were carried out in April, 1994.

One salient recall question focused on the date of the clinic visit of the malaria case. Researchers were interested in the accuracy of recall, given that all the cases in the sample had happened within the previous six months. It was felt that recall within plus or minus one week of the actual date indicated clear, effective recall, whereas giving dates of more than one week later or more than a week earlier indicated poor recall. As in all such recall studies, the accuracy of recall was strongest in the two most recent months and declined considerably after the third month. Table 13.1 shows the decline in accuracy of recall over the six-month period.

TABLE 13.1 Recall of Approximate Dates of Malaria Events, Based on Interviews in April 1994

Date of Malaria Event (Month)	Number of Cases	Recall Accuracy (%)
1993--October	85	36
November	42	49
December	85	55
1994--January	29	59
February	37	64
March	39	74
April	14	70

Source: Adapted with permission from de Silva et al. 1994: Table 3

In some households the respondent did not recall having a case of malaria in the past six months. The numbers of such "no recall" cases were highest when the elapsed time was five or six months. For the first and second months the "no recall of malaria episode" cases were 14% and 25% respectively; by the fifth and sixth months the numbers had risen to 40% and 44% respectively. Many other studies have reported similar declines in peoples' ability to recall information, even of fairly important events.

The Social Desirability Effect

Trotter and Schensul commented on several studies of informant accuracy (Killworth and Bernard 1976, 1979, and several others), noting that "These studies show that informant reports of behavior are incorrect about half the time, but that the distortions are highly patterned. That is, self-reports of behavior have high validity at the aggregate level when the sources of distortion are known and taken into account" (Trotter and Schensul 1998: 719).

Jeffrey Johnson reported situations in which he directly observed informants lying to researchers during his fishing camp studies in Alaska (Johnson, Avenarius, and Weatherford 2006: 123). However, such cases (of lying for amusement) appear to be rather unusual. Much more usual are "lies" that reflect informants giving "socially acceptable answers."

Concerning the "social desirability effect," Bernard cited an example in which the researchers went to a prominent mid-western American Protestant church and counted the attendance "at the Sunday school." Immediately afterwards they did a survey of the total church membership. The actual attendance observed that Sunday was 115 but, in the survey, 181 persons reported that they had attended on the previous Sunday. Other studies have shown that in America, the survey question "How often do you go to church?" leads to consistent overestimates of actual attendance. This is just one example of the kind of information in which we expect systematic distortion toward "social desirability" (Bernard 2011: 180).

Quality of Data from Participant Observation

The quality of data from participant observation is not always accurate. Johnson and Sackett, in their review of direct systematic observation, commented that "The problem of erroneous description arising from cultural distortion also weakens participant observation as a method of behavioral research" (Johnson and Sackett 1998: 304). They noted that the topics covered in ethnographic reports do not correspond well with the actual frequencies of various activities among different cultural groups around the globe. However, the more general weakness of participant observation is that details of actual observations are seldom given systematically and very little quantification is included.

DIRECT OBSERVATIONS OF PEOPLES' BEHAVIORS: SEMI-STRUCTURED AND STRUCTURED

Much of the research using direct, systematic observation of behaviors is designed to obtain quantitative data, but there are also many examples of relatively systematic observations that were somewhat less structured and were analyzed in a more qualitative style. The basic feature in all of these studies is that the recording (generally in field notes) of the data does not rely on interviews concerning past events and behaviors. The field notes are about ongoing behaviors, as described by trained observers.

Cross-Cultural Comparison of Infant Behaviors

A study of infant behaviors and socialization in Japan and the United States took place a half century ago, and is interesting here as a glimpse into the long history of structured direct observations in ethnographic research. William Caudill initiated the project in 1961. "To begin our study we chose 30 first-born infants, equally divided by sex, all living in intact, urban, middle-class families in Japan. We observed the everyday lives of these infants when they were 3 to 4 months of age. Our observations were made in the homes on two consecutive days" (Caudill 1998: 165).

The first observations (aged three to four months) were followed up with observations at two and a half years and at six years. A comparable sample of 30 middle-class infants was followed in the United States, using the same two-day, intensive observations. In the observations of the infants, "Data were obtained by time-sampling, one observation being made every fifteen seconds over a ten-minute period, and recorded by using a predetermined set of categories concerning the behavior of the mother or other caretaker and the behavior of the infant.... There was a five minute break between observation periods..." (p. 166). The methodological description notes that the system of data recording resulted in a total of 800 observations for each case.

What strikes us immediately in this ambitious project is that basically ethnographic "intentions" were carried out with extremely structured rules of observation. Caudill reported that in the data analysis they found statistically significant differences between the behaviors of the Japanese infants and the American infants. The American infants had more bodily movements, more playing with toys, and more vocalization than the Japanese infants. It appeared that the greater vocalization of American infants coincided with American mothers doing more "chatting" with their babies. The Japanese infants appeared to be more "controlled and reserved in behavior." Caudill wrote, "...I am struck by the fact that the responses of the infants are in line with general expectations for behavior in the two cultures: that in America the individual should be physically and verbally assertive; and in Japan, that he should be physically and verbally restrained" (Caudill 1998: 166).

Direct Observation in School Classrooms

Studies of behaviors in schools have often been carried out through systematic, intensive, direct observations. For example, Margaret LeCompte has described her observations of teacher behaviors in two schools in a community in the western United States (LeCompte 1975; LeCompte and Preissle 1993). One school had predominantly Hispanic students (fourth grade), and the other had predominantly non-Hispanic, "Anglo" students. She described that "In both cases the researcher sat somewhere in the back of the room, usually at a student desk out of the flow of classroom traffic. Observational time was devoted to recording by hand as rapidly as possible, whatever the teacher said" (LeCompte and Preissle 1993: 210).

The observations were carried out for three months in each of the schools. Here's an example of what the researcher wrote down in her notes:

> (Time 9:10) Teacher: "OK, I would like you to pay attention. We've had some problems with money. What's a dollar sign?" (Children shout the answer. She explains how to read numbers as money.) "Now, I want you to pretend you just bought a house. Now, you gotta be careful because houses cost lots of money." (Writes $2856000 on the board. Larry volunteers the decimal placement.) "Darn, I couldn't fool you. Let's see if I can fool this young man." (Does another, he gets it right.) "Who wants a more expensive house—Bernie?" (Does another.) "Let's see. I haven't heard from some of these girls. Aila, that's what I spend at the grocery store." (Does another.)

> (9:15) "Decimal points are very important when we are writing money numbers." (She demonstrates how to add with decimals by using money numbers. She adds them wrong so that the children can correct them, calling out corrections from the classroom.) "One way to help yourself, people, is to make sure that all your dots line up. All right, boys and girls, when you get your answers, be sure to put decimal points in." (LeCompte and Preissle 1993: 211)

In this type of structured observation, the researcher's main aim was to record as much as possible of the teacher's words, plus descriptions of the interactions between teacher and students. Time was noted every five minutes, along the left hand margin of the notebook.

Using these types of observations, for three months each, with two different teachers, LeCompte then analyzed the contents of "what the teachers said," in order to extract main themes and tendencies in the content of their teaching. For example, she was able to show that one of the teachers put more emphasis on "grades" and "sex role conformity" compared to the other teacher.

Although most of the field notes include words from the teachers, these raw data are very different from interview (verbal) materials. In these notes, the speaking of the teachers is not "recall of past behaviors," but is, rather, current verbal behavior, so there is no problem about recall or misrepresentation in the verbal materials, as long as the observer is able to capture most of the verbal output in her note taking.

The large masses of (mainly) verbal materials in the notes were all categorized using a list of codes (content category labels). Those coded categories included content such as "emphasis on grades" and "sex role conformity." After all of the notes were carefully read and coded, one part of the analysis included simple counting (enumeration) of the more theoretically important codes, in the process of examining the differences in the teachers' styles of instruction. Other points in the qualitative analysis were also analyzed using the frequencies of the coded segments.

Direct Observation in Households: Mealtime Food-Serving Behaviors

Joel Gittelsohn carried out extensive, in-depth observations of mealtime food-serving patterns in a remote area of Nepal in the late 1980s (Gittelsohn 1991). His research area was in a hill area in western Nepal. In addition to getting general ethnographic data about agriculture, food use, and other economic activities, he trained his Nepalese research team to carry out systematic observation of household food-serving patterns in six villages. At the time of Gittelsohn's research, the area (Pahargaon) did not have electricity, and people had to walk considerable distances just to get their water from mountain springs. To get to the nearest market town, people from Pahargaon had to walk for a day and a half, as there were no roads.

The local economy was basically subsistence agriculture, and all of the households that Gittelsohn studied had some agricultural lands, though there was considerable variation in the size and quality of their holdings. His research was a combination of nutritional science and ethnographic methods, and included 24-hour dietary recalls, morbidity data, anthropometry, food classification systems, infant feeding practices, and quantified intrahousehold food distribution. For the household observations, Gittelsohn randomly selected 105 households from the six communities he was studying. He wrote:

> The core part of the research consisted of the direct structured observation of meals in 105 households. These observations had two purposes: to record types and quantities of foods consumed by household members during meals, and to record associated behaviors. Meal observations were performed three to four times in each household, during the period of May to August 1987, yielding a total of 318 complete observations. Each meal observation period centered around either the morning meal (*kharcha*) or the evening meal.... (Gittelsohn 1991: 1144)

At the beginning of the household food allocation observations, Gittelsohn assigned his research team members randomly to particular households; those trained observers then continued with the households to which they had been originally assigned. The team members trained themselves to estimate visually the size of servings of food, after they took measurements of the sizes of the serving utensils. At each household, the observer wrote down the name, age, and other information about each household member, and at the beginning of each observation the activities of the household members were noted.

Although the attention of the observers was focused on the actual serving of food to individuals and on noting the sequence in which they were served, they also wrote notes on activities and conversations, with particular attention to food-related discussions. The "meal events" format included the time, actor, and activity, plus the specific food items and quantity of food that was served. In these Nepalese households, the eating area generally is visible from the cooking area, so the observers usually placed themselves in the cooking area in order to see if any self-serving took place in the kitchen.

Based on the carefully recorded data on the sequences of serving different family members, Gittelsohn derived composite "serving order scores" of household individuals by age and sex. The following are some of the interesting results from analysis of those data:

- Children were generally served first, and so the highest "serving order scores" were for children aged 0 to 10 years of age. Contrary to some of the generalizations from other studies in Nepal, there was no discrimination in favor of boys, up the age of 10 years. That is, boys and girls had nearly equal scores concerning serving order.

- After age 10, girls' serving order scores gradually deteriorated, approaching zero by the time a girl was 18 years old (actual score was .15 of a possible 1.00).

- Females aged 18 to 49 were generally the last to be served, after the children and adult men had received their food servings.

- Women older than 50 showed somewhat better scores, as their serving order picked up a bit compared to the younger women.

This study is certainly one of the most thorough, carefully constructed observations of household behaviors that I have seen. The fact that each household was observed more than once is an important feature in the research design, as it is now well established that "reactivity" (people changing their behavior because they are being observed) is generally most pronounced in the first observation situation. It is obvious that the researchers (observers) in a study of this sort would need to be very familiar with the local culture and language in order to "fit in" without being obtrusive and to be able to understand and record all the complex behaviors of large families at meal times.

SPOT-CHECK OBSERVATIONS OF PEOPLE'S ACTIVITIES

Unlike continuous observations over periods of time, such as LeCompte's research in the schools, "spot-check" observations are designed to find out "what are people doing at the moment of first contact." This method, with sufficiently large samples of spot checks, can be used to get good estimates of peoples' time use or "time allocation."

Back in the mid-20th century (1948), as Charles Erasmus and his wife went about the village of Mayo people they were studying in northern Mexico, each time they met with an informant they noted what the person and his or her family members were doing at the moment they met them. During the summer (three months) of field work, they made several thousand such observations of the approximately 200 people whom they met regularly. Thus, because of the large number of contacts at different times of day, they were able to develop frequency tables of amounts of time in different kinds of work, leisure, and other allocations.

Interestingly, the researchers found that males and females had the same percentage of time in "leisure activities," which added up to 30.7 % of the observations for both sexes. However, I note that the researchers placed "eating" in "household activities," whereas I would consider eating to be a leisure activity, and that the men were eating in 9.1% of observations, whereas women had only 3.7% in that category. The other interesting difference in leisure activities was that the men were lying down in 10.9% of observations and women in only 4.%. Rather than lying down, more of the women's leisure activities were "chatting and visiting" (9.1%) and "personal" (6.1%) (Erasmus 1955: 328).

Allen and Orna Johnson did a similar time-allocation study in the 1970s, among the Machiguenga people in the Peruvian Amazon area. They made regular spot checks of 13 households (105 persons) "within reasonable walking distance" of their own location. "Hours were selected in advance with a table of random numbers, and households were visited during the hour specified.... Tabulations show that visits were evenly apportioned by hours of the day and by season. Visits were made on 134 different days, resulting in 3,495 cases (observations of individuals)" (Johnson 1975: 303). The randomizing process used by the Johnsons gives us good assurance that the accumulated data are truly representative of that (small) population and are not biased through lopsided observations of particular households. Also, the randomizing across the daytime hours assures that the observations are a good representation across the daily cycle. We are only left, therefore, with questioning what the people might be doing at night, other than sleeping.

The researchers found that women were engaged in "productive activities" a full hour more per day than the men: 9.5 hours versus 8.5 hours. That difference of one hour reflected the large amount of time in food preparation and child care. Men were observed in "child care" very rarely. In productive activities, women were involved in manufacturing considerably more than the men (women 15.9% versus men 10.4%). The men were mainly involved in woodwork, while the women's manufacturing was devoted to making cotton cloth (Johnson 1975: 307).

Johnson made a special point of how different strategies of classification (e.g., "work") can lead to different conclusions about the relative productive contributions of males and females. Many people, of course, don't classify childcare as "productive work." He also provided a breakdown of activities by age groups, in which we find another interesting male-female difference: among the unmarried adults, there were only 22 observations of males, and 56% of those were coded as "idleness"; in contrast, there were 344 observations of unmarried females, with only 20% categorized as "idleness" (Johnson 1975: 305–306).

Time Allocation and Activities at Night: Papua New Guinea

Most of the time allocation studies in the literature have been restricted to daytime hours, for obvious practical reasons. The Johnsons, for example, said they did not go out after about 6:00 P.M. because (a) it was dangerous to travel at night, and (b) people didn't like anyone to come to their houses at night.

One exception to this general picture is the research by Richard Scaglion in Papua New Guinea (Scaglion 1986). He had done extensive research in the same tribal group previously, so he was well known to the people and knew a great deal about daytime and nighttime behaviors. He decided to do both daytime and nighttime spot-observations among the approximately 100 households in his research village. He randomly selected two households each day and visited them at randomly selected times, day and night. In this manner he had a sample of 153 observations over approximately one month. His nighttime visits encountered several ritual events and considerable hunting activity, and "visiting" came up more frequently at night than daytime. As would be expected, "sleeping" was coded for approximately three-quarters of the nighttime observations.

Spot-Check Observations of Food Sharing

Raymond Hames studied patterns of food-sharing among the Ye'kwana tribal people in the Orinoco river region of Venezuela. The food-sharing data were part of a much larger study of time allocation and adaptations in the tropical environment. Hames and his co-author noted that there have been a number of studies of food sharing, testing hypotheses of "reciprocal altruism" versus ideas based on kinship rules and other theoretical constructs. They reported:

> We examine patterns of meal sharing and find that reciprocal altruism is the strongest predictor of meal sharing between households, whereas hypotheses based on kinship, egalitarian exchange, and tolerated scrounging (theft) fail to be supported. (Hames and McCabe 2007: 2)

COMPARING TECHNIQUES:
SPOT CHECK OBSERVATIONS VERSUS THE DIARY METHOD

Paolisso and Hames (2010) made a systematic comparison of the method of "spot-check" observations (which they refer to as "instantaneous sampling") and the time diary method, for getting time allocation data. Concerning the diary method, they wrote:

> The time diary method has a number of methodological strengths. First, there is a well-established methodological literature available as well as ongoing discussion of the methodological issues of time diary research. With a moderate amount of effort, a novice behavioral researcher can access and even participate in current methodological discussions, all of which should be of great guidance in developing and adapting time diary methods to any particular survey or ethnographic situation. There are also extensive coding schemes and databases of coded behavior available.... (Paolisso and Hames 2010: 372)

The diary method of data gathering has been used in a wide range of different types of research. Examples are presented in Chapter 14.

Concerning the advantages of the "spot check" data-gathering approach, Paolisso and Hames wrote:

> Instantaneous recording has a number of advantages. First, compared to focal follows [sic] or continuous monitoring, it is very economical in terms of an ethnographer's research time. An outcome of this economy is that it permits a large number of different individuals to be sampled. In some cases, over the course of a year, ethnographers working alone have averaged more than 300 observations per person in a village of more than 100..... Finally, it is less obtrusive to subjects, so they are less likely to modify their behavior compared to the constant scrutiny of continuous observation. (Paolisso and Hames 2010: 364-365)

Observations at Special Events: Medical Camps in India

Direct observation of special events is a very different kind of challenge for ethnographic field researchers. Some of the most important examples have been studies of "medical camps," which have been a common practice in South Asia, especially in earlier decades. In some areas "Eye Camps" are still popular, and "STI Camps" (Sexually Transmitted Infections Clinics) have been featured in some HIV/AIDS programs.

The term "camp" here refers to a medical/clinical event that is generally a designated single day of activity, often located in a school building or other available building; although some of the camps are held at government Primary Health Centers (PHCs). The camps are sometimes "donated" by community organizations (such as the Rotary Club) or a prominent industrial organization, in cooperation with government facilities and/or an NGO. Services in the "camps" are usually free, except for "tips" or small charges for transportation.

During the 1990s, sterilization services in India for rural women (laparoscopic sterilization) were often provided in so-called "sterilization camps" (see Figure 13.1) Ramachandar and colleagues have described systematic observations of these special arrangements, at a site in Madhya Pradesh (Ramachandar and Barge 1999). The study was funded by the Ford Foundation in order to assess the quality of care in surgical operations carried out in those, often sub-standard, conditions.

> The research team consisted of six investigators (one male and five females), headed by a project coordinator (the senior author). The investigators were given training in what to observe, observation techniques,

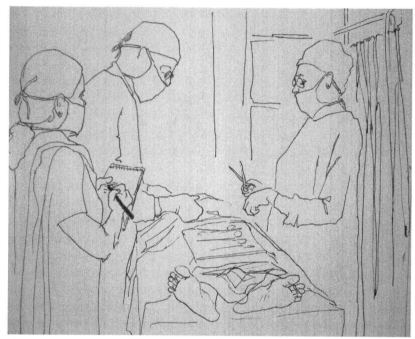

Figure 13.1. Sterilization camp researchers take notes in the operating theater.
© Dunja Pelto 2013.

and how to record their observations. Each investigator was trained in specific functions of the camp and thus was prepared to observe specific tasks associated with that function. Team members were also briefed on how to interact with people at the camps. (Ramachandar and Barge 1999: 275)

In the mid-1990s, the quality of care framework set forth by Judith Bruce (1990) was widely discussed, and the Indian researchers were aware of that framework. However, they were aware that in rural India those standards of care could not be attained, due to the conditions in the health care locations and the lack of modern equipment.

In the pilot phase of observations at a "sterilization camp," Ramachandar and her team experienced difficulties in developing a coherent system for observing all of the different aspects of the clinical operations. They quickly noted that, from the point of view of individual patients, there is a flow or "pathway" through a series of actions from "intake" to "preoperative," then to the operations theater, and finally to "post-operative." Accordingly, the individual team members were each assigned to one sector of the "pathway."

One experienced, trained interviewer gathered information about the patients as they arrived at the site, noting their arrival times. "She also observed the seating arrangements, the discussions that took place among the providers, and the interactions between the clients and health providers" (p. 275). Another researcher observed the actions at the registration site, and a third researcher was stationed at the "preoperative station." Two observers were stationed in the operation theatre, and one researcher was assigned to the "post-operative care" site. The project coordinator (Ramachandar) moved about the area, checking on the situations of the individual observers, and did some spot interviewing, as well as photographing in each of the observation locations.

The research team observed a total of seven sterilization camps, of which five were at temporary locations (school buildings), one was at a PHC and one was at a sub-center (sub-clinic of a PHC). The team documented a number of problems, particularly at the temporary sites, where there were serious problems with maintaining electrical connections, and also serious lapses in sterilization of instruments. Another major problem was in transportation, and they noted that a number of cases were "lost" due to the fact that there was only one vehicle, so that many clients could not be transported to the site of the services.

Counseling was another area with serious problems, and was practically non-existent in most of the camps. The pervasive lack of counseling in most Indian government health services is one of the serious gaps that could be remedied without high additional costs.

The transportation problem was quite severe at almost all the locations. One of the community health workers commented, "I would have brought more cases today, but due to this [vehicle] problem I have lost so many cases" (p. 280).

Similar direct observations of sterilization camps were carried out by another research team in the state of Gujarat (Mavalankar and Sharma 1999). The team observed 10 sterilization camps early in 1994 and reported a large number of deficiencies, particularly concerning maintenance of aseptic standards in the operation theater. The reports from a number of studies of the same type contributed to the decisions to discontinue the sterilization camps in the first years of the 21st century, in most of the Indian states.

The studies of sterilization camps in India, as in the preceding descriptions, can be regarded as "mini-evaluations" (see Figure 13.2). It is notable that a small number of one-day intensive observations, by a well-trained team, can produce large amounts of useful data. Such short-term, intensive observations are particularly suitable for structured programs

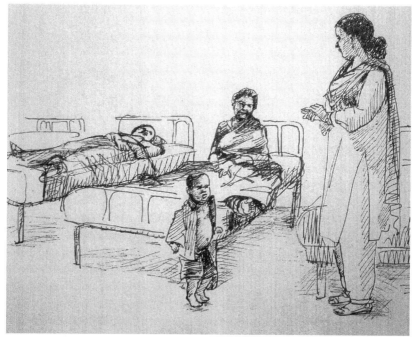

Figure 13.2. Direct observation of the quality of care in health facilities.
© Dunja Pelto 2013.

with very well-defined timetables and activities. The "structuredness" of programs—in health care facilities, schools, and many other settings—allows the researchers to plan for specific, well-defined points of observation. Also, the well-defined structure makes it possible to know how many observers will be needed in the research team.

This type of direct observation, we should note, does not focus on specific individuals, as the unit of analysis is a medical event. If one were to do some sort of systematic sampling, the universe would be "all the scheduled camps"—not a population of individuals. There are many kinds of research questions in which the "universe" can be events or "action sites."

REACTIVITY: CHANGES IN BEHAVIOR DURING DIRECT OBSERVATIONS

An interesting question arises in relation to direct observation: How much do people change their behavior if they know that you are observing them?

As has become clear in the studies described in this chapter, direct observation is an important research tool in many ethnographic studies. Many forms of direct observation have been developed in recent years, partly in response to the criticisms of participant observation and over-reliance on data from interviews, especially "one-shot" interviews.

As pointed out by Bernard (2011), Johnson and Sackett (1998), and many other writers, direct observation is usually regarded as more reliable and valid than the information that people give in interviews. On the other hand, some people (including some policy makers) will argue that the observed data are not completely "credible," because people will change their behavior and "act in socially approved ways" if they know someone is observing them. In our technical language, the people's changed behavior in such situations is referred to as "reactivity."

Fortunately, there have been a number of studies that have tested for the effects of reactivity. In observations of child care practices in a sample of families in rural Nepal, Gittelsohn and his associates were able to assess the effects of their observations on the behaviors they were interested in. They found that reactivity effects were evident on the first day of observations, but after the first days, the families became accustomed to the presence of the observer, and for most categories of behaviors there was little sign of reactivity. Gittelsohn and colleagues concluded that, although overall reactivity was less serious than some people have claimed, "the validity of direct observation studies of behavior can be enhanced by examining and controlling for reactivity effects" (Gittelsohn et al. 1997: 182).

A more recent study of reactivity effects was carried out by Steven Harvey and colleagues (Johns Hopkins Bloomberg School of Health) concerning insecticide-treated bed nets in the Peruvian Amazon (Harvey et al. 2009). During several months in 2000, four observers, including Harvey, carried out nighttime observations, of about 12 hours in each of 60 households to observe the use of the bed nets and other malaria prevention behaviors promoted by the Ministry of Health. Among the educational messages from the Ministry, people were instructed to bathe shortly before going to bed and to go to bed at a rather early hour (around 6:30 P.M.), as the malaria-bearing mosquitoes are especially active just as darkness is falling.

After introduction, the observer asked an index individual—generally the female head of household—to list the name, age, sex and relationship of each household member. The observer next requested a tour of the house, noted the number and type of beds and bed nets, and asked the family member...to indicate which household members slept in which beds. (Harvey et al. 2009: 9)

The observer then took a position in a corner, as inconspicuous as possible, and tried hard to avoid interaction with the family members. The observers told the family that they had been strictly instructed by their superiors to avoid conversation and other interactions and not disturb the family members. Throughout the evening and night (starting around 6:00 P.M.), the observer took careful notes of all the activities of people in the household. Every action that indicated any evidence of "reactivity" was noted. Afterwards, actions were coded into six categories, ranging from 1) salutations and 2) "Adult interacts with observer in a way unrelated to malaria prevention" to 5) "Household member talks with the observer about malaria in a way unrelated to the focus behaviors" and 6) "Reactivity directly related to change in focus behaviors."

In the notes from 60 observations, there were a total of 339 events indicating some kind of reactivity. However, only 25 of the events were in category 5, and only 2 could be assigned to category 6. The researchers concluded, "Our results contribute to a growing pool of evidence that reactivity broadly defined is common in studies that use direct observation, but its impact on validity is often minimal" (Harvey et al. 2009: 19). The researchers noted that there was ample evidence that the presence of the observer had no effect in bringing about "more correct malaria prevention," as the average bedtime continued to be much later (around 8:00 P.M.) than the timing recommended in the prevention messages.

"Mapping" Social Interactions: Street Corner Society

W. F. Whyte has described the use of systematic, repeated mapping for study of small group relations in the Cornerville Social and Athletic Club. (Whyte 1993: 332–336) The club's quarters were right across the street from Whyte's apartment, and he joined the club in order to study more closely the actions and political style of a particular local racketeer.

After spending some time in informal visits to the club, he began to feel a need for some kind of more systematic study of the organizational structure, including identifying the leader(s). "Since I was completely confused in my crude efforts to map the structure, it followed that I must get at the data more systematically" (p. 333). The task was complex, because there were about 50 members in the club—a much larger and more complex body than the small street corner gang he had been studying.

I began with positional mapmaking. Assuming that the men who associated together most closely socially would also be those who lined up
together on the same side when decisions were to be made, I set about
making a record of the groupings I observed each evening in the club.
(p. 333)

He developed a system of dropping in to the club when there was
a lot of action, and then memorizing the groupings of men in the various activities. If there were movements and re-grouping of men from
one table or one activity to another, he focused on who appeared to be
the initiators of the movements. Like many other researchers in similar
settings (in later years), he avoided taking notes overtly, but sometimes
went to the men's room to jot down a few things.

In this manner he accumulated a set of 106 "groupings" that he used
for examining the systems of relationships among the men. He discovered quite early that there appeared to be two main groupings or "factions," and that there were very few instances in his mappings when
groupings included a person who did not "belong" to that faction. In
addition to simply "faction membership," he also developed a system of
noting "events"—situations of change—and who it was that initiated the
change or event.

Whyte's description of his actions and surreptitious data collection
at the Cornerville Social and Athletic Club certainly raises some ethical issues, and he mentions that, at certain points, he acted unethically.
Researchers in the 21st century will need to find ways to seek consent
for observing the actions and behaviors in a social club or other similar
setting. However, researchers in the first half of the 20th century were
somewhat less concerned about "informed consent" and "confidentiality" than is mandatory nowadays.

Provided one has obtained informed consent for intensive observations in a specific physical setting, the systematic "mapping" of social
groups and their dynamics of change over time is a productive way to
develop useful data concerning social networks and interactions. It is
important to notice that W. F. Whyte's "mapping" of the action at the
Cornerville Social and Athletic Club was much more than simply doing
a map or two. For his purposes, it was the repeated mapping over time
that gave him a thorough picture of the social relations and organization within the club. That is why I have placed this famous piece of
data-gathering in the chapter on direct observation, instead of the one
on mapping.

Conclusions

Direct observations of behaviors and events are increasingly important in applied ethnographic research because of researchers' awareness of serious problems in informants' recall of past behaviors. Also, for a variety of reasons, participant observation, used as a primary method for getting systematic assessments of behaviors, has been seen as unreliable and often not amenable to quantitative analysis. Some of the approaches to systematic direct observation have been developed as modifications and extensions of participant observation.

The special ethnographic tool of spot-checks, or spot observations, such as the research by the Johnsons among the Machiguenga tribal people in South America (Johnson 1975), has been found to be especially valuable and practical in getting good estimates of time-use patterns and related information. The spot-checking approach is much less vulnerable to reactivity, and is much less costly in terms of researcher time commitments. On the other hand, the method is not suited to getting complex patterns and sequences of behaviors.

Continuous observation studies (continuous monitoring), such as the household food distribution study in Nepal (Gittelsohn 1991) and the bed-net study in Peru (Harvey et al. 2009), obviously have greater vulnerability to the reactivity of the persons being observed. The lesson here is that "one-shot" direct observation should be avoided. Multiple visits—the more the better—can minimize reactivity, and can also provide ways to correct for biases due to people's sensitivities to being observed.

The example of longer-term ethnographic monitoring in the classroom (LeCompte 1975; LeCompte and Preissle 1993) is a model that can accommodate a wide range of shorter or longer monitoring of some special behaviors and events, such as "testing times." At the same time, the duration of several months of contact with the school(s) gives the possibility for some kind of spot-check component to the research.

Spot-check and continuous observation strategies are not intended to be stand-alone ethnographic studies. The spot observation studies particularly have been integrated with a variety of other data-gathering activities, and the same applies to the continuous observation studies. These methods of direct observation can strengthen the credibility of carefully planned interview data, thus contributing to an effective overall research design.

Using Hypothetical Scenarios, Diaries, and Other Special Techniques

There are a great many ways in which interviewers can increase the depth and credibility of interview data. Some interviewers use pictures or video shots for probing. Multiple interview sessions with each informant can greatly increase the quality of interview data. Some interviewers give small gifts to their informants, although thoughtful field workers are very cautious about giving money for interviews. Innovative ethnographers can invent many ways to get improved, in-depth data in field work.

This chapter examines techniques that have proved their value as ways to enhance interview data. These techniques—the use of hypothetical scenarios, or situations, and of diaries and other record-keeping for getting certain types of information—can be elaborated on in many ways, depending on the topics about which the field researcher wishes to obtain information.

USING HYPOTHETICAL SCENARIOS IN INTERVIEWING

The use of hypothetical scenarios, with or without pictures or other visual aids, is often a productive and "user-friendly" way of getting people to talk about sensitive topics or areas of controversial opinions, and of gathering everyday information concerning personal problems, decision-making, social support, and a wide range of other topics.

Undoubtedly, a great many social scientists have used hypothetical scenarios in the course of interviewing, if people regarded discussion of the topic as politically or spiritually "dangerous." Melville Herskovits went further than most field workers in the systematic use of the "hypothetical situations" strategy, judging from his paper about this method

(Herskovits 1950). He described that, among the West African and African-American communities where he did most of his research, many topics were considered "dangerous" to discuss, because powerful supernatural beings might object, as in the following note about "abnormal childbirths" in West Africa:

> Women are most reluctant, not only to discuss such births, but even to mention actual cases of them. For in the beliefs of this people... especially where actual or sociologically defined abnormalities are concerned, [they] are ascribed to powerful beings, who will visit the same ill fate on those who talk too freely.... However, much of the reluctance to discuss child-birth, especially in its abnormal aspects, disappeared when hypothetical situations were presented, and it was literally only by the use of this method of indirection that data bearing on what proved to be an important aspect of the beliefs and practices of this people could be obtained. (Herskovits 1950: 33)

Herskovits found much the same pattern of secrecy and avoidance of open discussion in research in Brazil, particularly in relation to religious cult groups. He described a particularly interesting interview situation concerning a woman who was establishing a religious cult center:

> Though it would have been a violation of accepted canons of etiquette to have questioned her about a project of this sort, it was not difficult, in discussing cult-procedure of various kinds, to lead the analysis to a point where a hypothetical cult-house was to be founded. Soon, however, the discussion moved from this hypothetical situation, first to the project in which she was actually engaged, and then, again hypothetically, to reestablishing an older center. Here, once more, she moved to the exposition of an actual case. In both instances she cited facts that were so inclusive as even to yield budgetary figures, and in their totality to demonstrate the foresight with which developments of this sort are planned, providing a sense of how carefully financial provisions are made, as well as of the intricacy of the ritual procedures involved. (Herskovits 1950: 37)

He noted that in many of the societies where he did research, "non-Christian" religious practices were strictly banned, and informants were extremely reluctant to discuss these topics. However, in many cases when complex cultural data had been obtained through the "hypothetical case" method, it was then possible to cross-check the findings through direct observation or in informal conversations about actual observed events in the communities he studied. Thus, other data-gathering techniques were used to cross-check and confirm the beliefs and behavior patterns initially brought forth using hypothetical scenarios.

Herskovits commented that "In subsequent field-trips the method of the hypothetical situation was employed repeatedly. Sometimes it was entered as routine field method" (Herskovits 1950: 35).

Considerably earlier than Herskovits, W. H. R. Rivers (a psychologist who became an ethnographer) described using hypothetical examples in probing for information about property inheritance among the Toda people in South India:

> I first obtained an account of what was done in the abstract—of the laws governing the inheritance of houses, the division of the buffaloes and other property among the children, etc. Next I gave a number of hypothetical concrete instances; I took cases of men with so many children and so many buffaloes, and repeating the cases I found that my informant gave answers which were consistent...with the abstract regulations previously given....
> (Rivers 1906: 11; quoted in Bernard 1998a: 12)

Hypothetical Scenarios in Nutrition and Health Studies

The technique of using hypothetical scenarios in semi-structured interviewing has been included in some of the Focused Ethnographic Studies (FES) protocols developed for applied research in nutrition and health areas.

A multi-country project for "community assessment of natural food sources of vitamin A" (a project of the International Union of Nutritional Sciences) included a series of hypothetical cases to learn about people's perceptions of the effects of vitamin A deficiency. The following is one of the scenarios presented to informants, in probing about recognition of night blindness:

> Miguel is three years old. He is a very active little boy who has many friends in the neighborhood to play with. But for the past week, as the day ends and the sun sets, Miguel chooses to stop playing with his friends. He just sits alone. Miguel seems frustrated and sad and is afraid to move around. His mother, Fey, has noticed his recent inactivity at nightfall and wonders what should be done. What do you advise?
> (Blum et al. 1997: 64)

This scenario has usually been most productive in communities where night blindness is relatively common. If there has been specific awareness raising about the symptoms of vitamin A deficiency in the area, the probing can explore for specific items of information from the educational materials. Various additional questions can be added as probes, depending on the cultural context in which the data gathering takes place. The Vitamin A Project manual includes the following suggested probes:

- What do you think is wrong with the child?
- Is there any other information you would like to know about the child before you suggest advice?
- When should the mother (or caretaker) seek care for the child?
- What are some other signs that the mother should watch for?
- Who in your household or neighborhood knows a lot about these kinds of eye problems? (Blum et al. 1997: 65)

Using that scenario, L. Blum found in her research in Niger that people were fairly familiar with night blindness and had some appropriate ideas about remedies.

> Using a story format [the scenario above]...of the child suffering from night blindness, six of the sixteen mother respondents advised that the mother place a piece of uncooked liver on the child's eye so that the eye could absorb the blood from the liver. Subsequent to that, women suggested that the mother feed the child grilled liver. Seven respondents indicated that the child was suffering from hunger, and if the child were fed foods rich in vitamins, such as liver, meat, green leaves, eggs and milk the problem would be resolved. (Blum 1997: 90–91)

Those data showed that the people in that part of Niger are fairly aware of the important sources of vitamin A treatment for night blindness and other eye problems. Blum added, however, that the people may not be able to maintain effective dietary treatment because of their lack of resources. She also noted that the amounts of liver people suggested were often insufficient, and that taking the child to a health care facility was often suggested only as resort after home remedies failed.

Hypothetical Scenarios for Acute Respiratory Infections

The use of hypothetical scenarios is also one feature of the focused ethnographic study (FES) manual developed by the World Health Organization for the study of cultural understandings and behaviors regarding acute respiratory infections (ARI) in young children (see Chapter 16).

However, in some situations, researchers encountered problems with the method. Hudelson reported the following while using the FES guidelines in interviewing mothers in Honduras:

> The intention was to use different illness scenarios...to be able to look at the influence of symptoms, age, and gender on maternal perceptions of appropriate action. However, mothers had trouble remembering the details of the scenarios presented, and even for the more severe illness scenarios would say things like "Well, if the child was really sick, I would...." In the end we decided to ask "What would you do if your child had cough and fever?" and probe a bit more for details about perceptions of severity. (Hudelson 1994: 442)

On the other hand, researchers using the FES guidelines in West Java (Kresno et al. 1994) encountered no difficulties in using the hypothetical scenarios:

> In responding to hypothetical ARI case scenarios, mothers most commonly selected the community health center as the first choice provider for a six-month-old and for a two-year-old with signs of pneumonia; nurse and doctor were the second and third choices. When presented with a case-scenario involving a neonate with signs of pneumonia, mothers most often selected the dukun [traditional healer] for a first consultation. (Kresno et al. 1994: 431)

These researchers found that severe symptoms in newborn infants were often thought to be the work of supernatural agents, which was one of the reasons for choosing the dukun as the first provider.

The set of hypothetical scenarios for ARI illustrates one of the practical uses of the scenario method. The key variable of "age of small child" can be systematically varied in order to identify differences in selection of treatment, reflecting cultural beliefs. The selection of the traditional healer for treating newborn infants reflects cultural beliefs about illness causation that are widespread in South and Southeast Asia.

Use of Hypothetical Scenarios in Interviewing Health Practitioners

The Rapid Assessment Procedures (RAP) for study of women's health (Gittelsohn et al. 1998) recommends the use of hypothetical scenarios in interviewing both practitioners and women informants about treatment modalities. "By casting the questions in the form of hypothetical cases, the intention is to elicit responses about the 'best' or 'most appropriate' course of behavior as the respondent sees it" (Gittelsohn et al. 1998: 93).

The manual goes on to suggest that researchers prepare a series of scenarios for different illnesses. For each scenario, there should be several variations—different ages of patients and different characteristics of the symptoms (for example, vaginal discharge can be varied in color, viscosity, and amount of discharge). Gittelsohn and associates also commented that "Generally, local health practitioners respond well to requests to comment on hypothetical cases...." (p. 94).

The following are additional guidelines about hypothetical scenarios:

1. If you have a considerable number of scenarios, present only three or four to each individual informant. That may mean that you need to interview more informants to get enough responses concerning all the different scenarios.

2. Collect enough responses (from enough informants) so that you can do simple tabulations of the response patterns.

3. Change the sequence of scenarios for each informant. Don't start every interview with the same scenario. One way is to have each scenario on a different card, and shuffle the cards before starting with the next informant.

4. Prepare a simple tabulation format for data analysis (see Table 14.1).

5. Collect sufficient numbers of responses so that there can be some numerical analysis.

TABLE 14.1 Suggested Format for Tabulation Sheet for Illness Scenarios (expand as needed)

Diagnosis	Treatment and Provider (enter for each illness)			
	Scenario 1	*Scenario 2*	*Scenario 3*	*Scenario 4*
White discharge (local term)				
Malaria				
TB				
Local term for witchcraft				
Asthma				

Often it will be most productive if two or more categories of respondents can be compared systematically, for example, older versus younger respondents; traditional healers versus trained modern doctors; informants in "high-prevalence areas" versus "low-prevalence areas." Many other such comparisons can be useful.

Use of Scenarios in the Study of Farmers' Agricultural Knowledge

Soleri and Cleveland (2005) have described the use of "scenarios as a tool for eliciting and understanding farmers' biological knowledge." Their research was carried out in Mexico, Cuba, Mali, Nepal, and Syria. In each location, the researchers conducted extensive interviews and observations with farmers to develop frameworks of language use and agricultural data. Those data were used to invent scenarios involving common, primary crops (maize in Mexico, rice in Nepal, barley in Syria, etc.). The questions about the crops involved the effects of varied environmental conditions, particularly under situations of ample, moderate, and scant rainfall. The scenarios also involved variations in genetic characteristics of the seeds: "variety [of seeds] from community located in relatively favorable environment" versus "variety from community located in relatively difficult environment." In addition, the scenarios included the differences between random selection of seeds and intentional selection of seeds.

The researchers used a variety of visual aids (physical objects) to concretize the various aspects of their questions. For example, "Small rocks or crumpled paper balls of three sizes were used to represent years with high, normal and low rainfall; and for farmers to use in representing a distribution of years defined by rainfall during a typical ten-year period" (Soleri and Cleveland 2005: 292).

The authors noted that in situations where the farmers' predictions or crop expectations are different from those of the agricultural specialists, empirical testing can be carried out. They concluded, "In our experience, carefully constructed scenarios are a valuable tool for understanding...[farmers' knowledge] of fundamental concepts about plant breeding and values concerning other important agricultural policy issues that rarely include input from local people" (p. 298).

This example from a project in agricultural development research is particularly important, as it illustrates the use of hypothetical scenarios in a highly technical field in which framing effective interviewing is particularly difficult. The questions about crop genotypes (variants) interacting with different environmental conditions are extremely difficult to frame in ways that will work in standard interview formats. The study is also an important model that points to the need for extremely careful development and pre-testing of hypothetical scenarios, along with the use of visual aids (including physical objects) to clarify the features of complex questioning.

Use of Diaries to Collect Behavioral Data

Use of the diary method for getting certain types of data has long been particularly popular among psychologists and sociologists. However, until recently, anthropologists have been less interested in collecting information by means of diaries, perhaps because of their traditional reliance on participant observation and key informant interviewing. Also, anthropologists have often studied non-literate populations, for whom the diary method has not been possible in most cases.

P. Sorokin was one of the pioneers in sociology who developed research on people's "time budgets" (Sorokin and Berger 1938). In Sorokin's study, people kept detailed records of the amounts of time spent in their various daily activities. In a review of uses of the diary method in the social sciences, Corti noted:

> Self-completion diaries have a number of advantages over other data collection methods. First, diaries can provide a reliable alternative to the traditional interview method for events that are difficult to recall accurately or that are easily forgotten. Second, like other self-completion methods, diaries can help to overcome the problems associated with collecting sensitive information by personal interview. Finally, they can be used to supplement interview data to provide a rich source of information on respondents' behaviour and experiences on a daily basis. (Corti 1993)

The paper by Corti is particularly useful, as it gives many practical guidelines, including the formatting of diaries to be given out to prospective informants.

Bolger and colleagues have written a comprehensive review of the use of the diary method of data collection, in which they focus mainly on research by psychologists (Bolger et al. 2003). Those studies included family interactions, fathers' interactions with children, mood changes of different categories of persons, students' examination stress, alcohol use, drug use, reactions to stressful life events, social support—the list goes on and on. The paper by Bolger and colleagues is a handy reference for researchers planning a detailed, diary-based methodology, as they review a large number of different diary strategies and note the strengths and weaknesses of each.

According to these authors, diary studies can be classified into three types: (a) regular interval diaries, such as daily or weekly entries; (b) "signal entry" diaries, in which a message is sent to the informant, perhaps at irregular intervals, requesting the informant to please make an entry; and (c) the "event-contingent" system, which depends on the informant making entries whenever a particular type of situation or action occurs (e.g., sign of illness in the newborn, quarrel or violence with spouse, or social support contact from one's social network). The example in our discussion later in this section—gifts of food to pregnant woman in Sri Lanka—illustrates the "event-related diary keeping," whereas the water-use diary research in Bolivia is a good example of a regular interval diary. Diaries used in time allocation studies and food-diet studies are also usually designed as "regular interval entries."

Another aspect of research design is the physical form of the diary itself. In some cases, the informant is simply given a notebook and asked to write down information—give the date, time, etc. In other words, the diary is mainly "open format." In other types of diary–data-collection, the researchers prepare elaborated formats for the data entry.

The reviews of diary use in research point out that, in the great majority of studies, the data from diaries are superior to data from interviews. That point is particularly emphasized in the studies of alcohol use and sexual behaviors. One of the serious difficulties is that the diary method of data collection generally requires careful, time-consuming training of individual informants. Some of the training is essential for explaining the often complex formats provided for writing down the data.

Paolisso and Hames recently compared diary data gathering with direct observation (instantaneous sampling) to assess the strengths and weaknesses of these two specialized methods (Paolisso and Hames 2010). They commented that recent technological developments have created new data-gathering opportunities for social scientists that were not feasible in earlier decades:

> In technologically advanced countries, researchers from different disciplines are using cell phones, pagers, and handheld computers to "beep" respondents at randomly selected times to collect immediate recall data on behavior as well as respondent's emotional and psychological states.... In non-Western settings, anthropologists have trained field

staff to implement instantaneous sampling.... Many of the communities anthropologists once studied are now closely linked to mainstream societies and have higher levels of literacy and thus are more amenable to time diary methods. (Paolisso and Hames 2010: 359–360)

Studies Using Diary-Based Data Collection Methods

The following examples of diary-based methods show that widely varying types of data can be collected using this method, though it is evident that the informants in most such studies need to have at least a moderate level of literacy.

DIARIES OF SEXUAL CONTACTS

Campbell and associates, in their WHO manual (1999) entitled *Social Science Methods for Research on Reproductive Health*, wrote that the diary method has "the potential to record accurate information about relatively frequent events or episodes, such as coitus, breast-feeding or symptoms of illness" (Campbell et al. 1999: 39). They give the example of diaries of sex workers collected by Pickering and colleagues in Gambia (Pickering et al. 1992). The diaries were mainly used to examine the frequencies of condom use and associated factors related to "safe sex." In this example, the researchers assisted the sex workers to compile the diaries. "Field workers visited the prostitutes daily and compiled the diaries for them in which were recorded the type of sexual contact that they had (client or boyfriend), the price paid and whether a condom was used. This technique was used to record 24,000 sexual contacts over a 14-month period" (Campbell et al. 1999: 39).

In that example, it appears that the "diaries" were actually produced through systematic interviewing, as the informants were not themselves literate. We refer to this approach as the "assisted diary method."

DIARY METHOD FOR THE STUDY OF WATER USE IN BOLIVIA

Amber Wutich studied water use patterns in a Bolivian community using the diary method. She randomly selected a sample of 72 households, in which repeated interviews were carried out in four two-month cycles in order to get data on water use across the annual cycle (Wutich 2009). She and her researchers identified 13 different water-use tasks, and then had an artist draw a locally appropriate sketch of each task. The sketches were then incorporated into the fairly complicated water-use diaries given to the families. One key person in each household (usually the mother) filled in the diaries.

Wutich and her researchers had to develop a complex list of different water uses (cooking, washing hair, brushing teeth, drinking water, etc.), and they also had to provide the households with standard measuring containers.

As noted earlier in the this chapter, the diary method is believed by many researchers to be a more accurate and reliable technique than ordinary interviewing, particularly for getting the kinds of data for which people's recall of past events may give distorted results. The method generally requires at least moderate levels of literacy, although Wutich was able to use the method successfully even though literacy levels appeared to be marginal in her sample of families. In analyzing the diary data, she sorted them into two groups: the "more credible" diaries and the "questionable" diaries. Interestingly, she found no statistical differences between the two categories.

In addition to the diaries, the researchers also collected a "prompted recall" and a "free recall" of total water use for the past week. In her statistical analysis comparing the techniques, Wutich found that the diaries gave the most credible data, as checked against available water use records in the community.

FOOD GIFTS FOR WOMEN DURING PREGNANCY (SRI LANKA)

A. de Silva used the diary method to collect data on food gifts received by 35 women during their pregnancies in a rural village in Sri Lanka (de Silva, Lewis, and Pelto 2002). In Sri Lanka, the custom is widespread that members of a pregnant woman's social network (mainly relatives) bring gifts of food to the woman during her pregnancy. As described by de Silva, the gifts of food are seen as manifestations of social support in a basically bilateral kinship system.

The first step in the study was to contact all the women in the rural study area who were in their third and fourth months of pregnancy. From the data kept by community health workers, de Silva was able to identify 45 women who were in early stages of pregnancy. They all agreed to keep diaries about food gifts during their pregnancies. Some of the women went to their natal families during the last two months of pregnancy, and so the sample was reduced to 35 women with diaries. After the initial contact, the women were visited monthly for interviews, during which de Silva went through the diaries and asked about any other gifts of food that might have been missed, also probing for additional information about the contents of the food gifts and related topics. The average number of food gifts reported by the women during six months of pregnancy was 9.1.

The women had written many things in the diaries; the foods they were presented by people, foods they longed to eat but did not get, problems they encountered, relationship issues-particularly with mother-in-law and other in-laws, how her husband has treated her etc., etc. There were many complaints as well. (de Silva 2011)

de Silva also collected systematic data concerning the women's weight gain, and the results showed that the women who received more food gifts gained significantly more weight than the women who received fewer gifts. As expected within the Sri Lankan kinship structure, the number of gifts from the woman's kinfolks was twice that from the husband's kin.

THE DIARY-PLUS-INTERVIEW METHOD

Several researchers who have used the diary method—notably Paolisso and Hames, and also Wutich—found evidence that the "diary-plus-interview" method produces better data than the usual interviewing methods: the respondents are directly involved in the data process through keeping diaries, and the researchers have repeated contacts with the informants. Both of these factors likely increase the level of motivation and thus improve "remembering" among the informants. Many studies have shown serious problems in people's recall of information when, in one-contact interviews, they were asked to remember events, actions, or situations over several months (Bernard 2011; Johnson and Sackett 1998; Killworth and Bernard 1979). Thus, in interviews asking informants to recall details of recent illnesses, psychological feelings, communications with family members, or other topics, it is suggested that the recall period should be up to three months, perhaps six months for some topics, but not longer.

It seems quite obvious that the diary system, particularly with informants who are at least partially literate, is likely to produce much more accurate data, especially in those studies where the researchers return periodically to the informants to "check up" on the diaries and probe for any missing information. At the same time, it is also clear that the process is costly in terms of a researcher's time, so the sample of diary-informants can't be very large. If researchers rely only on the informants' consistent diary-keeping and don't go back and check their work, data may be lost because some informants forget about the record-keeping (de Silva 2011).

The heavy investment of time and effort, including training the diary-keepers, suggests that a sub-sample of diary-keepers should be selected for a simple trial of the method, based on first-round interviews or other systematic data. Local NGO outreach workers could be asked to "nominate" individuals for such a sub-sample.

USING CARD-MARKING METHODS WITH ILLITERATE INFORMANTS

Researchers have often shied away from trying to use card sorting and diary/record-keeping methods with illiterate informants. However, a number of researchers have found that illiterate informants are not as lacking in response skills, as has been supposed. Some ethnographers have found ways to get excellent data by training informants to keep simple records on specially prepared cards.

The data gathering among sex workers in Kolkata reported by Bhattacharya and Senapati (see Chapter 3) is an outstanding example of collecting a type of "diary data" from illiterate female sex workers:

> Because of the inhibitions of the sex workers in disclosing their practice and behaviour, it was thought of designing a self-monitoring card. This was initially handmade and pretested. At the beginning the women had inhibitions in filling up the cards. They were briefed for the purpose and assured of non-disclosure of their individual identity.... (Bhattacharya and Senapati 1994: 549)

The research team in this study did a card-marking exercise with a group of women, whose cards were then dumped into a basket. The women were asked to see if they could find their own individual cards. This exercise proved to the sex workers that even they could not identify their own cards, thus demonstrating the guarantee of anonymity.

> The self-monitoring card was tri-coloured; red for vaginal sex, blue for oral sex; and green for anal sex. The card was designed to record the number of clients and days of the week in columns and rows respectively. A sex act of any type was recorded as safe/unsafe by a tick or a cross mark. This was done because a majority (80%) of the sex workers were illiterate.... The women were asked to fill up the cards daily for a week and drop the same in letter boxes hung up for the purpose. Four such letter boxes were installed at different junctions of the area for easy accessibility.... Initially the card had provision for as many as six clients per day, which was increased to 10 as per the suggestion of the women.... (Bhattacharya and Senapati 1994: 549–550)

The researchers found that, with proper training from the research team, the women were able to fill out the cards effectively without having to write out any words, but simply by entering marks on the cards.

Conclusions

The special data-gathering techniques in this chapter can be valuable, productive additions to your mixed-methods strategy in ethnographic research. The example of card use with illiterate sex workers in Kolkata reminds us that there can be many different strategies for getting useful data in special groups, even if the informants are largely illiterate.

The "hypothetical scenarios" approach has been used in situations of interviewing for sensitive information, but the method has many other uses, including topics that are not sensitive but for which it is difficult to devise meaningful interview questions. These methods are also worth exploring, because they are often more interesting for informants than the usual interview formats.

In most applied ethnographic research situations there are several different sub-populations from which you need to collect data. For example, research in a school-based program will require different forms of data from students, teachers, and parents. In some research situations, you might find that a special sub-group of informants would be appropriate for a diary-based data gathering, whereas other sub-groups should be approached with card sorting or paired comparisons, along with open-ended narratives about key behaviors and experiences. Research teams should explore the feasibility of many different techniques and approaches, in order to strengthen the credibility of the research products.

Mapping: A Powerful Tool in Ethnographic Research

In Chapter 4, I discussed "social mapping" as a participatory rural appraisal (PRA) tool that is especially useful in early phases of ethnographic research. As set forth in that chapter, the aims of social mapping are usually not focused so much on the maps as accurate, detailed products, but as a technique for getting acquainted quickly with the research area and getting data about the different sub-groups, varieties of hamlets and neighborhoods, and other environmental features. There are, however, many other kinds of mapping activities, with different degrees of participation from people in the study communities. In some cases, the maps themselves are the primary products, requiring cartographic skills. This chapter explores some of those more advanced mapping processes.

In the past two decades, various forms of mapping have received increased attention in ethnographic research. The change is a reflection, at least in part, of the increased use of research strategies in which various forms of "participatory mapping" are prominent elements. To some extent, it is useful to divide field research cartographic activities into two distinct categories: (a) ethnographic mapping, and (b) participatory/social mapping. The distinctive feature of the second category is that a large share of the mapping is done by members of the study communities. There are, of course, many mapping operations that are carried out primarily by the research teams, with or without assistance from community people and "local experts."

There are endless important uses for maps. The following list is only a small sample of the possibilities.

- In the past two decades of HIV/AIDS prevention programs, mapping has been essential for locating "target populations" (sex workers, injection drug users, and other vulnerable groups) and places of high risk behaviors such as sex work "hot spots," truck halt places, and drug injection locations. Other examples of mapping high-risk people and areas include clusters of malaria cases, dengue fever areas, cholera outbreaks, areas of industrial pollution, and other environmental threats and special conditions.

■ Survey research in both rural and urban areas often requires preliminary mapping of local subgroups in order to prepare effective sampling strategies concerning ethnic groups, variations in socioeconomic status, and other population characteristics in study areas.

■ Data concerning relationships and other important features among local herding collectives, social networks of entrepreneurs, local political leaders, and other types of social organization can be effectively derived from mapping operations.

■ Micro-mapping of local meetings, weekly market arrangements, recreation areas, and various small-scale activities are excellent ways to gain an understanding of social and economic relationships at local levels. The same principle applies to hospitals and other health facilities, schools, and other public service institutions.

■ Mobility mapping is now recognized as an important data-gathering strategy regarding sex workers and other special sub-groups in HIV/ AIDS programs. It is also a very useful technique for assessing program effectiveness and coverage in projects that depend on spatial coverage by community-based outreach workers.

■ Mapping the home locations from which patients come to special clinics, home neighborhoods of students coming to a special school program, and similar situations can be important tools for assessing the effectiveness of outreach activities in various programs.

ETHNOGRAPHIC MAPPING

Ethnographic mapping, traditionally, has included a wide variety of activities, ranging from small-scale "sketch-maps," to large-scale, multi-community visualizations of significant features of the physical and social environments, often representing the "territory" of the study population. In ethnographic mapping, the construction of the geographical information is carried out by the field researchers, sometimes with the help of hired cartographers and, in most cases, an effort is made to present locations and distances with at least some geographic accuracy.

Quite frequently, the term ethnographic mapping is used to include studies in which a great deal of cultural, economic, and social information is collected and described in connection with the spatial mapping operations. Thus, some ethnographic mapping becomes practically the same thing as a full ethnographic study. On the other hand, many other kinds of small- and medium-scale mapping activities are also included under this general label.

PARTICIPATORY MAPPING — WHERE THE MAPS ARE OF KEY IMPORTANCE

A somewhat separate "sub-species" of mapping is given the label participatory mapping (PM), or sometimes "participatory action research mapping" (PARM). Practitioners such as Peter Herlihy credit Robert Chambers and his associates with contributing to the genre, but they have a much more involved concept of the "participation." In the most fully developed form, persons from the local study communities are trained to do detailed geographic data gathering, and the research is intended for the benefit of the communities where the mapping is carried out. A full picture of participatory mapping is presented by Herlihy and his colleagues in a collection of papers in *Human Organization*. The title of the lead paper gives the flavor of this approach: "Maps of, by and for the Peoples of Latin America" (Herlihy and Knapp 2003). The papers in this collection all describe how teams of indigenous people were trained to carry out extensive mapping operations of their traditional territories, generally connected with indigenous land claims and conservation programs.

Anthony Stocks, an anthropologist, wrote, "As The Nature Conservancy (TNC) technical advisor...I began to document the indigenous territorial claims in March 1994 at the invitation of the leaders of the Mayangna communities of the Waspuk River [Nicaragua]. To do this, I used a participatory methodology in which local communities of each territory named researchers to be trained in the application of a socio-economic survey, in historical cartography, in navigation with Brunton compasses and GPS units, and in data analysis" (Stocks 2003: 350). Stocks did all the training himself, as the area is very remote and so no other technical people were available to come out into the territory.

The indigenous mappers eventually identified six separate territories, and "By 1999, all six indigenous territories in Bosawas were mapped and zoned, and there were ethnohistorical and socioeconomic studies for each territory constructed by the people themselves" (p. 351). While the mapping was progressing, the social organizing of "civil societies" was also taking place, for the purposes of local governance and for negotiating with the central government of Nicaragua concerning their legal standing and other issues. The newly formed local organizations also developed clear boundary markers, and a system of "defense" patrols to keep out "colonialist" settlers. After the local governing organizations had taken shape, the local people, with help from outside technical persons, began to work on plans for resource management, including study of the impact of hunting activities on the wildlife of the area.

The other five studies in this collection all reported similar styles of operations, in which local indigenous inhabitants were recruited for complex mapping and related research. In each study there was heavy reliance on the indigenous knowledge of geography, historical events, and other information needed to put together the full picture of territorial use and economic concerns of the local communities.

From the examples in the *Human Organization* collection, we can see clear differences between their participatory mapping and the social mapping described in various studies by Chambers (1997) and associates. In PRA social mapping, the maps are used to facilitate agricultural development, community health projects, watershed management, and many other practical programs, including, most recently, large numbers of HIV/AIDS prevention programs. Thus, with social mapping in the style of Chambers (as presented in Chapter 4), there is less need for the maps to be highly accurate and fully developed, and the mapping is not intended to document territorial claims. On the other hand, in the work of Herlihy, Stocks, and others, the maps themselves are a primary objective of the research, and the maps are intended to have long-term legal status, for example, in the service of indigenous people's land rights.

Both of these approaches emphasize participation of the community people. Both Chambers and Herlihy (and their associates) put heavy emphasis on getting community people to do the mapping, emphasizing the importance of making full use of the local people's knowledge of their physical and social environments, as well as historical information about changes that have occurred over time in their local environments.

PLACE-NAME MAPPING: A FORM OF ETHNOGRAPHIC MAPPING

Place-name mapping, particularly in indigenous tribal/ethnic areas, is the domain of geographers, linguists, anthropologists, and some folklore specialists. These different types of researchers have somewhat different data-gathering approaches. Full-scale place-name research, like the participatory mapping described in the preceding section, requires extensive participation by local indigenous experts.

The mapping of place names (toponymy) is intended for the benefit of the indigenous peoples whose geographic locations are the locus of the research. The strong participatory nature of toponymic studies was particularly evident in projects carried out with the Inuit in the Canadian Arctic from the early 1970s to the mid-1990s by Ludger Müller-Wille (a professor in the Department of Geography at McGill University in Montréal, Canada), his wife, Linna, (a data-bank specialist and translator), and their team, which included Inuit researchers.

The Müller-Willes had done exploratory place-name research in Naujaat/Repulse Bay (Arctic Canada) in the 1970s. Working with local experts from the older generation of Inuit elders, they mapped 400 locations identified with local Inuit names. Part of the research process included displaying place-name inventories in the local school, where all the community people were invited to inspect and verify the authenticity of the lists. The local population was very enthusiastic about the place-name mapping.

The next step in the process was to present the maps with indigenous place names to the Canadian Permanent Committee on Geographical Names, which is an official government body that must certify all place names for mapping purposes. By 1979, the Committee had approved approximately 150 of the Inuit place names that the Müller-Wille team submitted to them.

In the early 1980s, the Müller-Willes decided to carry out a more ambitious toponymic study. In 1982, they conducted the first surveys in two communities in arctic Québec. Shortly after, they arranged for a meeting with the Avataq Cultural Institute (ACI), which is the official cultural organization of the Inuit people in the Province of Québec. The Avataq leaders were very interested in the place-name mapping project, so they submitted a proposal to the Canadian government for long-term funding. Thus, the research grant was awarded to the Inuit organization, and the researchers from McGill University were contracted by the Avataq Cultural Institute to carry out the study in 12 arctic (Inuit) communities in Québec. The place names project—now called Nuna-Top Project—was carried out in 1984.

This collaborative project required close coordination between the Inuit organization (ACI) and the researchers, who hired two bilingual Inuit field workers to do the face-to-face interviewing. The Inuit organization advertised for "place-name experts" in each community, according to the research schedule provided by the data-gathering team. In each location, at the scheduled times, a number of local "experts" were assembled. Most of the expert informants were older men, whose average age was around 65 years. They were the Inuit with long-term experience and full local-language knowledge of names and other relevant information.

Linna Müller-Wille had devised a special recording system for computerized storage of the data. Personal computers were not available for the first toponymic exploration in 1973, but in the 1980s, projects such as the place-name study were greatly aided by the much easier data storage processes brought by the "computer revolution."

In addition to the names for each given location, the team also collected anecdotes and other cultural and environmental information from the informants about the individual locations. Often, those ethnographic additions dealt with information about hunting particular kinds of game or, in some cases, dangerous features affected by seasonal weather variations.

The final step in each community mapping was the display of the results—the inventory of place names—in a public place. All the local inhabitants were invited to examine the place-name lists and maps and to suggest any additions or alterations. Also, the basic list of names, called a "gazetteer," was submitted to the local municipal council for approval.

In 1987, Müller-Wille published a large gazetteer, with approximately 8,800 Inuit place names (Müller-Wille 1987). The people in the Inuit communities were very pleased that an important segment of their cultural heritage has been recorded, and that at least parts of their indigenous geographic naming heritage had been recognized by the Canadian government. The principle of giving priority to local indigenous place names had been strengthened.

The preservation of indigenous place names, and some of the accompanying cultural lore, is of major significance for the maintenance of indigenous cultural identities, and the Avataq Cultural Institute made that research a priority in their planning. Fortunately for them, the Müller-Wille team was strongly motivated to establish a collaborative project with the Inuit authorities.

The Müller-Willes also wrote a set of guidelines for place name research that incorporates the lessons they learned in nearly three decades of work with the Inuit people in the Canadian Arctic. The following excerpts from their manual (1989) give a clear indication of the basic principles concerning indigenous involvement in the research:

> Assure high quality of accuracy and validity of the information gathered on place names and related information through interviews with indigenous experts.

Provide complete indigenous involvement by having indigenous researchers directing the survey and conducting interview sessions as well as training others in the survey methods.

Direct the survey team to interact closely with the indigenous experts and local authorities.

The authors make it clear that the primary purpose of the toponymic inquiries is to preserve local knowledge and oral traditions for the benefit of the indigenous populations. Unlike most other ethnographic research, they note that the place-name data belong to the indigenous community, as stated in the following:

> It is clearly understood that the information collected is owned by and belongs to the indigenous nation as elements of their common cultural property. It is up to the community to decide which data should remain confidential, be released by express permission of the community and, in the case of private information, of the individuals involved. (Müller-Wille and Müller-Wille 1989: 11–12)

They also warned that cultural knowledge of geographic features is gender-biased, as men generally have much greater freedom of movement in their daily activities. Therefore, researchers should make a special effort to include female informants in the data-gathering system.

The manual gives detailed guidelines for using the maps, in a much more detailed manner than the usual ethnographic map utilization. Geographers, after all, are highly trained in the technical details of working with maps of different scale and different features. The manual even suggests a system of color-coding for various features.

The researchers, with their Inuit counterparts, carried out their ethnographic study of place names in much the same manner as Franz Boas had done with the Inuit a century earlier (1883–84). It is interesting to note that Boas was actually breaking away from Euro-American "exploration" traditions in assigning local indigenous naming on his maps. The usual custom of the "White Man" was to give new names to the areas and features that they explored and mapped, and often those names were intended to honor important political persons of the home country, as well as the explorers themselves (e.g., "Rhodesia").

Boas' ethnographic method was based on recruiting local experts, and asking them to draw sketch maps, on which he marked the Inuit place names as he interviewed the Inuit experts. The volunteer indigenous experts that Boas recruited for his place-name mapping did excellent sketch maps. The locally produced sketch maps were essential because, in the 1880s, very few maps were available for the areas where he carried out his research. The following quote from Boas' writing gives a glimpse of the research process. On November 3, 1883, he wrote:

> The sketch maps are always valuable. The table is opened out and a large quantity of paper laid out on it. We and Mutch lie on the table and then the conversation proceeds, seven-eighths in Eskimo and one-eighth in English. In the morning Pakkak and his kuni [wife] were here, mapping Kignait and I'adli for me. (Quoted in Müller-Wille and Müller-Wille 2006: 222)

There are, of course, other manuals and guidelines for doing systematic place-name mapping, but the set of guidelines prepared by the Müller-Willes is particularly detailed in terms of materials, procedures, and intended products. Also, this manual is especially interesting in its strong focus on involving the people in the indigenous communities. The Nuna-Top Survey Method presented in the Manual has been used for a series of place-name studies in aboriginal communities in various locations in the Canadian Arctic.

Ethnographic Mapping by Professional Research Teams

The label ethnographic mapping is used here to refer to mapping carried out directly by the research team. In most cases, they take the help of local persons (key informants), but the mapping is done by the full-time researchers.

Oliver-Velez and colleagues (2002) have provided a detailed description of ethnographic mapping as carried out by their research teams, with the added feature that they coordinated and combined the mapping of two very different locations—one in Puerto Rico and the other in New York City. The two research teams were composed of both "insiders" and "outsiders." The team in New York City consisted of an ethnographer and two members of the study community, both of whom were Puerto Ricans who had many years of experience in the local Puerto Rican research area. Similarly, the team in Puerto Rico consisted of a senior ethnographer, a local ethnographic assistant and an interpreter; both of the latter were from the study community.

The authors made a distinction between "ethnographic mapping" and "geographic mapping," noting that ethnographic mapping includes a great deal of cultural and other detail, requiring extensive interviewing and interacting with persons encountered in the process of mapping.

Another distinctive feature of their version of ethnographic mapping is that the mappers must walk through, or travel through, all or most of the physical locations that are being mapped.

> Mapping initially took place in 1997 over two to three months in both locations. In East Harlem, geographical boundaries from previous studies had to be reassessed. The team went out each day with a clipboard and a small tape recorder. We walked the avenues and cross streets of East Harlem from 9:00 A.M. to 5:00 P.M. each day.... On some blocks it was possible to take notes as we walked, but on some others the senior outreach worker instructed us not to take notes until we had left. (Oliver-Velez et al. 2002: 265)

The mapping processes described by the researchers continued for a number of months, and actually could be called a "mini-ethnography," as a great deal of information was collected concerning the varied behaviors of drug-dealers, injection drug users, and the many other types of people and physical locations.

The complexities of the data the researchers gathered are partly reflected in some of their guidelines, as well as in the glossary of terminology that was accumulated before and during the mapping activities. One interesting feature was the collection of information about timing. "How drug users perceive time and how they are constrained by the time frames established by institutions, health facilities, and treatment programs contributes to explaining their movements.... Depending on the drugs they are using, their patterns will also differ in time and the use of space" (p. 267).

In the East Harlem (New York City) monthly schedules, the mapping team was aware of interesting local terminology, for example, "Check Day" and "Mothers' Day," which have important effects on drug use behaviors, as those are the days when welfare checks and social security checks are issued, as well as food stamps. Another important day, they found, is "Fed Day," when federal agents come through the area making arrests. The mappers found that Tuesdays and Thursdays are Fed Days.

The mapping resulted in identifying many different kinds of subgroups, including the various different kinds of Puerto Ricans: long-term New Yorkers, recent arrivals, "returnees" (back to Puerto Rico), and various other categories. This information made it possible to develop detailed plans for a quantitative survey.

> Information collected during the mapping process was used to develop lines of inquiry for focus groups, targeted ethnographic interviews, key informant interviews, and the survey instrument. (p. 273)

One of our major conclusions was that the ethnographic mapping process was essential to identifying and understanding influences which can increase or help to diminish risk behaviors.... (p. 273)

ETHNOGRAPHIC MAPPING FOR RAPID ASSESSMENT

In many situations, project planners will need to get some mapping done in just a few weeks; sometimes only a few days are allotted to the task. In many cases, such rapid mapping can be a mixture of social mapping (involving direct mapping by local informants), along with mapping activities carried out by members of the NGO team as they move about the area.

Mapping high risk populations in South Asia has taken many forms. In many areas, extensive mapping activities by NGOs were carried out along highways to identify the truck halt places and other "hotspots" where there are concentrations of sex workers and others involved in high-risk activities (see Figure 15.1). In many urban areas, the sex worker locations are quite scattered, and many sex workers try to maintain secrecy concerning their activities. Similarly, injection drug users are usually "hidden populations" that are difficult to locate and enumerate.

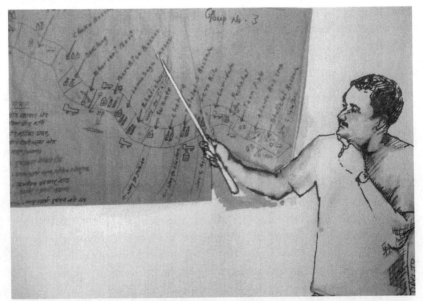

Figure 15.1. An NGO team carrying out detailed mapping of "hotspots" along a highway segment leading from Kathmandu to the China border. © Dunja Pelto 2013.

Situation Assessment of Female Sex Workers and Injection Drug Users in Nepal

Situation assessments for HIV prevention programs in Kathmandu and other locations in Nepal have been carried out by Nepalese research NGOs. Researchers at the Center for Research on Environment Health and Population Activities (CREHPA) in Kathmandu used a combination of mapping and key informant interviewing to identify locations and to get estimated numbers of all the sex workers and injecting drug users and sites in the Kathmandu Valley. Although they used the term, "social mapping," their methods were actually a complex mix, involving many local key informants, some mapping by local people, and intensive visiting by the research teams to all the identified sites.

Two operations—the mapping of sex workers and of injection drug users—plus collecting free listings, ratings, and in-depth interviews, were carried out in four months, in 2001. The work was done by four teams of CREHPA field workers, each comprised of two or three field workers (including both male and female researchers in each team). During the mapping, the teams were accompanied by selected key informants as they visited various sites throughout the Kathmandu valley area.

Concerning the injection drug users (IDUs) they reported:

> In social mapping: altogether 162 sites...in the Kathmandu valley have been identified as drug taking or sharing places....92 locations have been recognized as major concentration areas. The IDUs were mostly seen in public places like open ground, temple street, pool house, riverbank, public toilets, cinema hall, paati and bahal (open space in the middle of a house). (CREHPA 2002: 17)

Basically, the same processes of mapping were carried out for identifying sex worker (SW) locations throughout the Kathmandu valley area.

> Social mapping of SWs was carried out in four stages. The first step included observation visits to different locations that were identified by NGOs and...local key informants (ex-drug users, hotel/restaurant owners, drivers, paan pasales [chewing tobacco/betel leaf sellers], security guards, policeman, crime reporter, owner of medical hall, local dada [informal leader], etc.). After observation, the sites that were mentioned...were triangulated through direct observation or...[sometimes by] mystery client observers. Once the sites were confirmed, plotting of the sites on the base maps was carried out.... The final step included the finalization of the maps by the cartographer. (CREHPA 2002: 66)

From that description we note that their method was a "modified social mapping," in which the identification of locations depended heavily on local informants in various sites but the actual marking on the maps was done by the field researchers. The CREHPA workers found that, unlike the sex worker populations in India, the Kathmandu valley area has a large number of female sex workers located in so-called "cabin restaurants" and "dance restaurants." These are generally young women who work as waitresses and earn extra money through their sex work.

The mapping by the CREHPA teams contrasts with the ethnographic mapping reported by Oliver-Velez and her team (in the preceding description), particularly in the kinds of additional data collected. Whereas the data gathering in the Puerto Rican communities included large amounts of information about the types of activities in various sites and other cultural and social data, the Kathmandu research focused on getting in-depth interview data from individual sex workers and injection drug users. A description of the CREHPA research organization can be found on its website (CREHPA 2013).

Sketch Maps for Understanding Land Use in Brazil

D'Antona and colleagues at the Anthropological Center for Training and Research on Global Environmental Change (Indiana University) developed a system of sketch mapping called "spatial sketch of the property" (SSP), to be completed by interviewers in connection with a questionnaire for collecting data on current land-use patterns in rural northern Brazil, along the Trans-Amazon highway. The interviewers in their team were mainly social science students from universities in the area, plus some local residents who had experience in survey research.

The sketch maps "were only one of several data collection instruments used in field work...as [sketch mapping] was followed by a structured questionnaire covering land use, property characteristics, off-farm labor, and household economic characteristics" (D'Antona, Cak, and Vanwey 2008: 70).

Unlike the relatively free-form mapping of sex work sites described in the preceding section, these mapping activities were intended to be matched up with satellite mapping of the entire development area. Thus the survey format included "...a table for listing registered global positioning system (GPS) coordinates of the property. These coordinates, marking houses and corners where the property touched the road, helped import the sketches into a geographic information system (GIS) for processing and linking data in the SSP with satellite data" (p. 72).

The sketch mapping was put on paper by the interviewers, but much of the information on the sketches required informal interviews with the informants, as well as walking on the lands with informants in order to fill in map features and take GPS readings. That process produced many opportunities for cross-checking information on the maps with the data in the questionnaire.

Despite the technical complexity of the entire data-gathering operation, the interviewers were given considerable freedom to innovate the timing of the sketch mapping. The complex process with each respondent was initiated by showing a large satellite map of the entire region, in order to place the specific land holding into the larger framework. The interviewer also showed the informant two maps of the particular property from previous satellite photos (1996 and 2003).

The amount of time spent in data collection at each property depended a great deal on the number of houses and households on the property. In the cases with several households and complex land use, interviewers sometimes spent an entire day interviewing and sketching at that one location. Altogether during the field work, the team gathered data from 399 properties, which contained 971 households.

Mobility Mapping of NGO Outreach Workers and Outreach Activities

"Mobility mapping" is another under-utilized research tool. The method consists of asking individuals or groups to describe all the places they have visited (and for what purposes) during the past week, past month, or other suitable time unit. Generally, researchers have preferred to do the marking on the maps themselves, while the informant describes their movements.

An NGO in Nepal (in an HIV/AIDS prevention program) developed the innovative idea of asking its outreach educators and peer educators to indicate on a map all the places they had gone for outreach work in the past month. Each individual's movements were marked on the map in a different color. The program officers of the NGO studied the resulting composite map, and found that there were some important areas of high-risk sexual activities that were not covered by the outreach workers' visits, whereas some other areas had received "excessive coverage." Based on this mobility mapping, the NGO people shifted some assignment areas in order to focus more effectively on high priority areas.

Box 15.1 Notes on Mobility Mapping

1. Mobility mapping can be done as a form of social mapping in which you ask the informants to do the mapping of their visits to other locations in the past week or month. In other situations, the mapping can be done by the interviewer by asking specific questions of the informants about their movements.

2. The most productive approach (e.g., for monitoring outreach workers) is to interview systematically about the person's movements "yesterday," and then the previous day. "The past week" is also a useful timeframe. In addition to these short time frames, researchers can probe for additional data concerning "other places and activities in the past month."

3. Interviewers should also explore the possibilities for getting rough estimates of time spent in various activities. In some programs, it would be extremely useful to combine the mobility mapping with information about travel times, time spent with target persons, and other timings. For the time allocation data, a diary method would be useful.

Summary and Conclusions

Mapping is an important component in almost all situation assessments, because all applied programs, regardless of the nature of the program activities, need to have a sense of "Where are the target populations?" "Where are the problem areas?" and "Where are our workers carrying out their activities?" Perhaps the most neglected area of thinking about mapping in many projects is the central importance of developing a clear geographical sampling strategy for data gathering, particularly when a quantitative survey is planned.

In the varied kinds of mapping reviewed in this chapter, and in the earlier discussion of social mapping (see Chapter 4), the quality of the maps themselves has differing degrees of importance. Clearly, mapping indigenous territories (Herlihy and others) and place-name mapping (Müller-Wille and Müller-Wille) call for systematic attention to the correct geographic positioning of places. Sketch-mapping (D'Antona and coauthors) also includes considerable attention to the correctness of the mapping, in order to effectively assess land-use patterns.

Sometimes mobility mapping and sketching of the layout of meetings and other action locations are intended mainly for producing other kinds of data, and the maps themselves do not require careful attention to detail. The ethnographic mapping described by Oliver-Velez and her team appeared to require careful attention to specific map details, but their data gathering was also focused on many other kinds of information. Mapping activities are particularly effective for attracting intensive participation by members of the study community. In some situations, it can be useful to ask community organizations to take charge of the mapping activities. The cartographic data gathering provides rich opportunities for contact and rapport with people in the communities, including some of the experts, who later can become your key informants.

Qualitative Research Guidelines: RAP, PRA, RRA, FES, and Others

In recent decades, a large number of manuals presenting guidelines for conducting applied, relatively short-term ethnographic field research have appeared under interesting labels such as Rapid Appraisal Procedures (RAP), Participatory Rural Appraisal (PRA), Rapid Rural Assessment (RRA), Focused Ethnographic Studies (FES) and others. These products generally provide useful inventories of the main data-gathering tools for ethnographic research on specific topical areas. Most of them have been written for use in applied social science research contexts, and they are often intended to be used in training non-academic field researchers. Labels such as RAP indicate that many of these manuals are intended for relatively short-term field research, thus fitting with the practical needs of intervention projects. Similarly, FES points to a major requirement of applied research—that the data gathering is sharply focused on a specific practical issue, such as a particular category of illness.

This chapter does not contain a complete inventory or systematic evaluation of those manuals, but rather, presents an overview of their key features. Most of these ethnographic guidelines have been designed for formative research, to be followed by specific intervention activities.

These qualitative research guidelines have been especially notable in the area of community health and nutrition, but there is also a considerable number of them intended for applied research in agricultural projects, water and sanitation, and many other areas (Chambers, 1981, 1997).

One of the first manuals for applied qualitative research in health was *Rapid Assessment Procedures for Nutrition and Primary Health Care* (Scrimshaw and Hurtado, 1987). The front cover of the book, subtitled *Anthropological Approaches to Improving Programme Effectiveness,* clearly signals the intended practical applications. This manual popularized the term "RAP," which is widely used today to refer to relatively short-term, focused qualitative studies. The first RAP manual was sponsored by the United Nations University (Tokyo), the United Nations Children's Fund (UNICEF), and the Latin American Center at the University of California, Los Angeles (UCLA).

The same label, RAP, was used for a larger manual, *Rapid Assessment Procedures (RAP): Ethnographic Methods to Investigate Women's Health* (Gittelsohn et al. 1998), sponsored by the Johns Hopkins University School of Hygiene and Public Health. This manual was published by the International Nutrition Foundation, and the development of the publication was connected with a program of technical assistance initiated by the Ford Foundation in India. The manual proposes a timeline based on a nine-week framework. The timeline includes "program applications" in the final four weeks, thus sharply focusing on the applied intentions of the research. The nine-week timeline highlights the "rapid" aspect of the research agenda. In general, all of these qualitative research guidelines present multi-method interview techniques, mapping procedures, direct observations, and training of field workers. The RAP manuals have extensive sections describing data-gathering and data-analysis formats, saving researchers from much of the tedious work of designing data-capture instruments.

A related manual is the World Health Organization's *Social Science Methods for Research on Reproductive Health* (Campbell et al. 1999). This manual differs from some others in that it includes discussion of structured quantitative surveys. It is an excellent example of the qualitative-quantitative mix of research methods.

A manual entitled *Field Research into Socio-Cultural Issues: Methodological Guidelines* (Nkwi, Nyamongo, and Ryan 2001) is of special interest because it was developed mainly by African researchers using African examples. The authors are from Cameroon, Kenya, and the United States, and publication was sponsored by UNESCO. The book has compact, clear sections on structured qualitative methods (e.g., free listing, pile sorting, paired comparisons) and sampling strategies (often neglected in qualitative guidelines), plus a brief discussion of computer software, which is useful even though it is more than 10 years old. It also includes diagrams illustrating such topics as "cognitive map of 29 drugs for management of malaria in Gusii" (a tribal group in Kenya), based on the results of pile sorting, and "a folk model of malaria causation and treatment" (also from Kenya).

Box 16.1 Microcomputers: A Bit of History

The several manuals of RAP guidelines and other similar manuals reveal an interesting glimpse into the recent history of field research. In the first RAP manual (Scrimshaw and Hurtado 1987), there is no mention of the use of computers. However, in the manuals published 10 years later (Gittelsohn et al. 1998; Blum et al. 1997), use of microcomputers is prominently mentioned, and specific software programs for data processing are suggested, although some of those early software programs have since disappeared.

Rapid Rural Assessment (RRA) and Participatory Rural Appraisal (PRA)

RRA and PRA are discussed extensively by Robert Chambers in *Whose Reality Counts?* (1997), as well as in a number of other publications. The two approaches arose primarily in relation to research on agricultural and rural development. The main research methods developed under the RRA heading include strong emphasis on mapping, use of semi-structured interviews, and seeking out local experts for key informant conversations and in-depth interviews. Transect walks (discussed in Chapter 4) are another core component.

As Chambers and others have pointed out, much of the methods inventory of RRA came from earlier work of anthropologists. Thus, in some respects the development of RRA in the 1980s included importing several primary research tools from ethnographic methods, but shortening the expected time frames to make the research process fit with programmatic objectives.

The RRA practitioners, many of whom were university-based researchers, focused mainly on agricultural practices and other aspects of rural development such as water management. In the early phases, they typically did not pay much attention to participatory methods involving the people from local communities, other than as passive informants. The newer research paradigm, PRA, which was developed out of the RRA framework but which incorporates much greater emphasis on "participatory methods," has been adopted by many non-governmental organizations (NGOs) and government agencies. Today, PRA has spread into many other areas of research and organizational practices.

In Chambers' words, PRA puts great emphasis on "handing over the stick" to people in the research communities (Chambers 1997: 117). Although researchers practicing RRA were enjoined to respect the local wisdom and ways of traditional peasant farmers, the field researchers usually expected to draw their own maps and diagrams, based on information given by local informants, plus the data from transect walks and other observations. PRA researchers, on the other hand, "hand over the stick" and the drawing materials to the local people, and insist that they do the mapping, diagramming, and other (especially visual) representations of information. Thus, PRA places much greater emphasis on using the knowledge of local study-area persons, including recruiting them into active research. Various PRA methods are designed to draw out the intrinsic knowledge of local people—into maps, diagrams, ratings of socio-economic resources, and other expressions of local knowledge. A particularly widely known PRA practice involves having a group of villagers draw a map of their village on some flat ground, sometimes using colored powders (in South India), stones, sticks, grains of corn or other materials to mark houses, temples, stores, and other special features.

The degrees and forms of "participation" in PRA methods can vary widely, in part depending on the purposes of the data-gathering activities. Some projects with high degrees of local participation, including data gathering by local community members, are aimed at developing information for empowering local organizations, such as women's groups or youth groups, for specific localized applications. On the other hand, the PRA techniques are also used in a more structured manner for applied research that is intended for advocating policy changes in government agencies or for publication in scientific journals. Campbell and associates have commented that "PRA is more a philosophy and a tool for community development than a research strategy as such. The priority is to generate information for action rather than for the advancement of knowledge as in basic research" (Campbell et al. 1999: 53). This statement, however, applies to many different forms of applied research, not just to PRA studies.

Regardless of the extent to which the methods are intended for immediate, local uses, rather than adding to a broader spectrum of knowledge, the fact remains that the PRA literature now contains an impressive array of specific data-gathering techniques that are amenable to careful quality controls, and hence are suitable for systematic quantitative (scientific) analysis.

FOCUSED ETHNOGRAPHIC STUDIES

FES manuals contain sets of guidelines for multi-method, short-term research strategies. Each FES is focused on a specific research target such as acute respiratory infection (ARI), management of diarrhea in children, or "natural food sources of vitamin A." The strategies have been developed mainly for applied research in community health and nutrition. Some methods in the manuals are the same as those in RAP and PRA, but their tight focus leads to unique topic-specific data-collection components, such as the use of video scenes as prompts to get data about informants' recognition of symptoms of ARI.

The FES for Study of Acute Respiratory Infections

The FES for ARI is the best known and the prototypical item in this category (Pelto and Gove 1992; Gove and Pelto 1994). The "Focused Ethnographic Study of Acute Respiratory Infection" has the following features:

- multiple data-gathering methods, mainly qualitative in nature;
- relatively short time frame for data collection;
- attention to local people's vocabulary concerning the domain of respiratory illnesses in young children, recognition of symptoms, and treatment-seeking options;
- model questions and detailed interviewing instructions; and
- primary focus on information that will be useful for community intervention programs.

Specific questions in the ARI manual are designed to elicit the following:

- people's beliefs about ARI in children, including causes and treatments;
- identification of the factors that facilitate or constrain treatment-seeking;
- description of household management of children with ARI; and
- identification of other cultural characteristics and conditions that are likely to influence responses to the ARI program (Gove and Pelto 1994: 411).

The last item in the foregoing list signals that the manual was developed to serve a specific action program of the World Health Organization (WHO).

Community Assessment of Natural Food Sources of Vitamin A

A FES manual for the study of vitamin A was developed under the leadership of Harriet V. Kuhnlein and Gretel Pelto. The project was sponsored by the International Union of Nutritional Sciences (IUNS) (Blum et al. 1997). Like the ARI manual, the Vitamin A FES consists of a series of qualitative data-gathering tools designed as a flexible package that can answer the following set of specific questions in specific cultural/ ecological settings:

- What are the key foods (staples, fruits, vegetables, animal food, fats/ oils) in the study community?
- What are cultural beliefs about the key foods?
- What are the patterns of food use?
- How is food prepared and stored?
- What signs and symptoms of vitamin A deficiency do the people recognize?
- What remedies do people use for night blindness?

> The study is designed to be conducted in a period of six to eight weeks, including the data analysis and preparation of the report.... The study involves the use of both qualitative and quantitative research methods. (Blum et al. 1997: 10)

Putting Research into Action: Acute Respiratory Infection in Haiti

The Haitian Health Foundation (HHF), a community-based public health program (begun in 1986 in Jeremie, southwestern Haiti), was still in its infancy when the organization was asked to carry out the FES directed at the high rates of infant deaths from pneumonias (ARI). The WHO protocol was newly developed, and the HHF was one of the first organizations to experiment with the WHO guidelines.

The ethnographic explorations with mothers in the rural villages showed that, despite the high rates of infant deaths from pneumonia, most of the rural people were not seeing the connections between the key symptoms and the killer disease.

> Many mothers said that the big belly and chest in-drawing during rapid breathing was because the child had (parasites); the mothers were concentrating on the size of their child's belly rather than their chest and breathing. *Bwonch* was the word mothers used for pneumonia symptoms

and *grip* was a term used for flu-like symptoms. They believed *bwonch* was caused by bathing too late in the day or in cold water.... (Lewis and Gebrian 2009: 24, emphasis added)

Part of the FES ARI data-gathering consists of showing women a video of a child with pneumonia symptoms. Three-quarters of the Haitian women did not recognize the rapid breathing as a symptom of pneumonia. The ethnographic data not only made clear the important areas for training community people about pneumonia signs and symptoms, but also provided the health workers with local language vocabulary to use in meetings with the villagers.

The next phase of the ARI program in the Jeremie area came in 1993, when the Pan American Health Organization (PAHO) initiated an ambitious pneumonia prevention and treatment campaign, with funding from the United States Agency for International Development (USAID) and other sources. HHF was selected to do the pilot testing of the program, which involved extensive training of public health staff, and outreach to community organizations with a well developed protocol based partly on the FES data that had been developed at HHF two years earlier.

Fortunately, the public health program was making good progress with its computerized data system by 1993, so the HHF was able to develop a tracking system for pneumonia cases. The program included data on referrals, follow-up timing, and outcomes. The computerized data system greatly facilitated locating cases for follow-up studies.

The HHF public health program in Jeremie started with intensive training of their own staff concerning the ARI issues, including both the medical perspective and the ethnographic data.

The senior medical and nursing staff members were trained in a two-week program including role-plays, analysis of algorithms, diagnostic processes, documentation, patient teaching, and community education. The training was conducted by a U.S. nurse fluent in Haitian Creole who was a part of the John Snow International REACH project. (Lewis and Gebrian 2009: 25)

The training of the public health program staff was followed by selecting 20 of the Village Health Agents for intensive practical training for carrying out the ARI program in the villages, working with the community organizations. At the same time, the documentation of pneumonia cases was proceeding. Something of the magnitude of this health problem is evident from the fact that the HHF public health program documented 17,000 cases over a three-year period.

One major aspect that highlights the success of the HHF community-based program is that not only did parents in the communities learn to recognize the symptoms (especially rapid breathing and chest in-drawing), but there also was rapid acceptance of the efficacy of medical treatment.

> Many women would bring a child to the health agent saying that this child had *nemoni* (pneumonia) and needed to be treated.... Even though mothers used home treatments, they simultaneously sought treatment quickly. Children sang the pneumonia detection song on their way to school. Fathers in the village groups brought their children to the health agents for care. More and more children were treated and the staff reported that fewer children were dying. (p. 27)

A systematic evaluation of the HHF program in the Grand Anse Region was carried out by researchers from the Center for Disease Control (CDC) in 1997. The data showed that the program had reduced pneumonia mortality rates by half: from 6.2 per 1000 to 3.1 per 1000 during the three years of operation. Those results are an impressive testimony to the effectiveness of the Village Health Agents in the community-based operations (Heffelfinger et al. 2002; Dowell and Heffelfinger 1998).

Complementary Feeding of Infants and Young Children in Ghana

Another FES manual developed recently is aimed at assessing infant and young child (IYC) complementary feeding in low income environments in order to explore possible pathways to nutritional improvements through the introduction of new, low-cost products (Pelto and Amar-Klemesu 2010). The label "IYC" refers to children aged 6 to 24 months of age. Like the other FES manuals, the research guidelines are intended to facilitate practical formative research in multiple environments. To date, the research has been carried out in Ghana, South Africa, Afghanistan, and Kenya.

The first study was conducted in Accra, Ghana, where the researchers came to the tentative conclusion that an intended new product, a special commercial IYC food, would probably not be feasible. The research was carried out over a period of 12 weeks by a team of two senior researchers (an anthropologist and a nutritionist with anthropological training), plus two field researchers.

A central feature of ethnographic research that is particularly important in short-term research projects is that data analysis is started at the very beginning of the project, rather than being initiated after all the data have been collected. Typically, in many research projects of this type, the data from social mapping, key informant interviews, and free lists are compiled at one time, and then decisions must be made quickly about which items to incorporate in any pile sorting, rating, and follow-up interviews. The team in Ghana selected eight different sub-communities in the urban area, from which they selected 30 mothers with children in the age range of 6 to 24 months. The sampling strategy in this study, as in many FES and RAP projects, was a "maximum variation sampling" (Patton 2002), and was chosen in order to have confidence that the research results would apply to a wide range of different urban sub-groups.

Another usual feature in this kind of study is that the researchers go back to the original set of informants for the second phase of data collection. In Accra, the second interview consisted of sorting a set of cards with names of the various complementary foods. The cards were used for collecting ratings concerning the factors that are most important in the selection of foods for the infants and young children. The ratings from the mothers showed that they put the heaviest emphasis on "healthiness" and only medium importance on "cost" and the "child's acceptance of the food." In Accra, as in most other parts of Africa and elsewhere, the usual foods given to infants and young children are various grain porridges—maize porridges that are usually home-cooked and millet porridges that are usually purchased from vendors. One disconcerting note in the data from Accra was the relatively high prevalence of a ready-to-eat product that is produced by a multinational corporation and is extremely widely available, but is costlier than most other foods for IYCs.

This study highlights an important point about sample size in applied formative research. That is, that some research topics—notably infant feeding—have a limited array of basic data in any particular location, and therefore much of that limited range of variation can be captured with quite a small sample—in this case, 30 informants spread around a large metropolitan area. If the research topic had been "adult food intakes," for example, the sample size would have had to be much larger.

FIELD TESTING: A COMPARISON OF DATA-GATHERING METHODS

Bhattacharya and associates at the Child In Need Institute (CINI) in West Bengal (India) conducted a thorough study in West Bengali villages, in which they compared three data-gathering methods for getting information concerning cultural perceptions of acute respiratory infections (ARIs) in children (Bhattacharya 1997). The three different research approaches were (a) a structured quantitative survey, (b) the WHO Focused

Ethnographic Study for ARI, and (c) "traditional" ethnographic methods involving participant observations and key informant interviewing. Bhattacharya noted that the three approaches produce very different kinds of data and have different advantages and limitations.

The structured quantitative survey approach has the advantage of producing numerical results which, if the sample is random, can be statistically analyzed and "generalized" to represent the entire study population. In some situations, policy makers are impressed by numbers and statistics, and so a survey like this might well get the attention of government officials and other policy planners. However, the major drawback of the survey is that contextual details and situational analyses are almost totally lacking. In particular, in most cases structured surveys do not provide data about the language use and special local belief structures that play major roles in patterning people's behaviors.

In contrast, the FES approach permits extensive triangulation of the data, thus greatly enhancing both the reliability and validity (overall credibility and usefulness) of the data. For example, in the FES protocol the viewing of a video of small children suffering from respiratory infections is used to elicit information about symptom recognition, local terminology, and information about treatment alternatives.

In the "traditional" ethnographic research style, the data gathering required many weeks of field work, which would usually make that research approach impractical for intervention projects, as they are likely to have demanding timetables.

The West Bengal researchers compared the time requirements and costs of the three types of research, and found that the FES was a clear winner on all counts. Bhattacharya estimated 17 weeks to complete the quantified survey, 27 weeks for the traditional ethnography, and only 7 weeks to do the FES. The cost estimates also favored the FES, partly due to the shorter time required for field work and data analysis. Although the survey didn't require very much field work time, several weeks were required to develop and test the interview protocol, and the data analysis was very time consuming.

> Among the quantitative survey, the FES, and the ethnography, it is clear that the wealth of data, combined with the time, cost and logistical advantages of the FES make it a powerful tool. (Bhattacharya p. 231)

The research on respiratory illness in children undertaken in Western Java by Kresno and associates also tested the usefulness of the FES ARI manual. Following their data gathering using the FES guidelines, the researchers carried out a large-scale prospective study of cases of acute respiratory illness in a sample of 6,000 children, among whom there were 141 deaths, of which about half were judged to be due to serious respiratory infections. The study included interviews with the mothers, particularly in the cases of morbidity and mortality. The researchers concluded that the data from the FES research were largely confirmed in the epidemiological, quantitative study (Kresno et al. 1994: 433).

The Javanese researchers concluded:

> Thus the current study, based on a rapid and focused assessment with only minor modification from the WHO/FES protocol, in the hands of an experienced field investigator already familiar with the local region, produced results which were not only congruent with other analyses of Javanese culture but were also predictive of significant health outcomes. (p. 433)

CONCLUSIONS

In 1992, Scrimshaw and Gleason produced a 500-page compendium of writings concerning the growing interest in rapid assessment research (Scrimshaw and Gleason 1992). The publication was based on a conference held in 1990 in Washington, D.C. Some of the writers referred to the decade of the 1980s as the period of emergence of this new trend in applied social sciences research. M. M. Cernea, as a senior advisor at the World Bank in 1992, had the lead paper in the publication, in which he discussed major changes in applied social science research, saying:

> THE EXPLOSIVE GROWTH and diversification of rapid assessment procedures (RAP) over the last eight to 10 years has opened up new avenues for social investigation in the service of development work. (Cernea 1992: 11, emphasis in the original)

Cernea outlined the key features of this trend in applied programs, first of all noting that, in terms of ethnographic data-gathering methods, there is a "fast repertoire enrichment: new and imaginative procedures are invented and added to an already respectable inventory" (p. 11). He went on to point out that the ongoing diversification of RAP and RRA procedures was already (by 1990) leading to improved planning of development programs. As a Senior Advisor in the World Bank, he had broad familiarity with the evolving patterns in development programs. He noted that "a decade of RAP work has launched some social sciences on the path of methodological re-tooling" (p. 13).

QUANTIFIED DATA WITHOUT A QUESTIONNAIRE: POTATOES IN NEPAL

R. Rhoades expressed an optimistic assessment about new participatory research methods in his paper entitled "The Coming Revolution in Methods for Rural Development Research" (Rhoades 1992). In particular, he noted the problems in the ubiquitous use of questionnaire surveys for developing information that is relevant for rural development programs, and gave examples of qualitative methods that are more effective in getting the local people's knowledge and attitudes concerning the development of improved agricultural approaches.

In his paper he recounted the story of research in Nepal in the 1980s, in which his team was supposed to carry out a review of the Nepal National Potato Programme. They started with a structured questionnaire, but quickly found that it was not getting good information, and was awkward and boring.

> After debating the problem, the team decided to abandon the questionnaire and go to the local market and buy all the different potato varieties we could find. Local farmers added more to our sack of different varieties. (Rhoades 1992: 67)

The team began a trek through the countryside, and wherever they found groups of farmers, they poured out their collection of potatoes, and the farmers began to comment on the different varieties. The farmers were immediately interested and were enthusiastic about discussing the important characteristics—disease resistance, adaption to different soils and conditions, suitability for different cooking styles, and so on. This is an excellent example of innovative PRA data-gathering.

> We began to see how quantitative data could be obtained about varieties. We built a matrix on the ground where each variety could be related easily, for example, to multiplication rates in farmer terms, uses, barter and sale, disease problems, marketability, and zones. Stones and sticks were used to get at comparative values.... Within a very short time, a tremendous amount of very useful quantified data was collected. (Rhoades 1992: 67)

Many researchers have emphasized the usefulness of the qualitative-quantitative mix of research methods in applied projects. Most experienced applied researchers are clear about the need for an initial period of qualitative research to identify key problems and needs in specific communities, and to learn about the "vocabulary of the problem": "How do the people in the study area conceptualize their needs and problems?" and "What specific words and phrases do they use for discussing those issues?" After researchers have developed a good understanding of locally defined needs assessment, the structured survey can be used to get numerical estimates of frequencies, for example, of the use of different crops, patterns and frequencies of specific problems, and correlations with possible "causal factors."

CLOSING COMMENTS

All of the research manuals and guidelines described in this chapter were developed for applied research. It should be noted that they were not, for the most part, intended to develop nomothetic theory. Rather, the research guidelines and designs are intended to provide concrete data about the patterns of specific problems (in health beliefs and treatment-seeking, farming practices, water management, etc.) and about local people's cultural definitions, terminology, resources and related information that is necessary for the design of intervention programs.

The research results based on guidelines are not weaker in validity, reliability, and overall credibility than the products of more academic, expanded research. Rather, the products of the various RAP, PRA, RRA, and FES styles of research are simply more focused in specific areas— for example, descriptions of local conditions and environments—and less concerned about generalisability and contribution to general theory.

Nonetheless, formative research for applied projects and the ensuing interventions are rich fields for the "discovery of grounded theory." In some cases, the combination of qualitative formative research and specific developments in the action programs has produced rich stores of information that can be mined retrospectively to develop theoretical frameworks that can be tested with further, multi-method research designs.

Research Teams and Training
in Applied Ethnographic Research

Many applied field research projects these days are carried out through partnerships of international NGOs, academic researchers, and/or government agencies with local NGO and/or other local organizations. The structures of research teams depend on many factors, including the scope and duration of the projects. With short-term projects, lasting only a few weeks, "rapid data gathering" may only be possible through collaboration with a local organization that has effective community-based personnel. In such cases, at least some of the field researchers are recruited on short-term or medium-term contract by local NGOs. This is particularly true in some HIV/AIDS research projects, as well as various other types of short-term research in both developing and developed countries.

In practice this situation has meant that research was carried out by local NGO teams of researchers (or local persons that they hired) who were given a few days of special training by outside consultants. The training would have to be focused on a small number of techniques, such as social mapping, semi-structured interviews, and in some cases, interviewing for a quantitative survey.

In a relatively short-term research project concerning "situation assessment of sex workers and intravenous drug users [IDUs] in Kathmandu Valley," the research-oriented NGO recruited additional field workers, who were trained and supervised by the core research staff. (This project is described in Chapter 15). In their report (CREHPA 2002), they listed the study coordinator (principal investigator), team leader, four field coordinators, and ten field researchers. In addition, they had five project support persons, including a cartographer and two "word processors." The field data gathering was carried out in a four-to-five month period. In addition to the team members listed in the report, the researchers also had short-term help from informants/guides recommended by local NGOs that were involved with the sex workers and IDUs.

In some large-scale HIV/AIDS projects (and other multi-site programs) there are sometimes parallel data-gathering operations—large quantitative surveys and qualitative interviews with smaller samples of informants. In some of those projects, the data gathering has been carried out by two entirely separate teams. The multi-site qualitative ethnographic data gathering very often consists of some mapping, followed by individual key informant and case interviews. Very little participant observation takes place, and in most cases the field interviewers are not trained to take "general field notes," as the note taking concentrates on the interviews.

FIELD WORK BY SOLO ETHNOGRAPHERS

Field work by solo ethnographers is becoming less common in applied research. There are still some examples of one-person, solo (applied) ethnographic research, but the practice is increasingly unusual, particularly in applied research in the developing countries. There appear to be several important influences pushing for team research involving several interviewers.

One underlying feature of contemporary applied ethnographic research is the diffusion of the qualitative data-gathering techniques into many other disciplines and organizations outside the orbit of anthropology. In many cases the research personnel from other disciplines have had rather little exposure to the full scope of ethnographic data-gathering methods and principles. As already mentioned, the increasing emphasis on "rapid research" often means that several field researchers must be involved in order to carry out the data-gathering within the tight schedule.

ETHNOGRAPHIC RESEARCH BY NON-ACADEMIC ORGANIZATIONS

Many non-academic organizations are doing ethnographic research. Throughout the developing countries a great many free-standing NGOs do applied research, including increasing numbers of ethnographic studies. Another large category of non-academic NGOs and agencies are the international organizations such as the Ford Foundation, Family Health

International, International Center for Research on Women (ICRW), the Bill and Melinda Gates Foundation, the Aga Khan Foundation, and the many governmental aid agencies such as the Danish International Development Agency (DANIDA), the German Agency for Technical Cooperation (GTZ), the Swedish International Development Cooperation Agency (SIDA), and the United States Agency for International Development (USAID). The United Nations Children's Fund (UNICEF), the Food and Agriculture Organization of the United Nations (FAO), the World Health Organization (WHO), and the World Bank make up another large category of non-academic organizations with major research agendas. This listing is only a small part of the inventory of research-oriented non-academic entities.

There are, of course, many applied projects involving university-based researchers from the developed countries, but those academic "outsiders" are often dependent on the in-country organizations to provide researchers proficient in local languages and cultural settings. The point of all this is to emphasize the large scale of applied research in which non-academic influences are at work to modify the styles and contents of ethnographic data gathering.

In South Asia, among the non-academic organizations, the composition of research teams is quite varied, and few field-research coordinators have had extensive training in ethnographic methods. Many researchers have had experience with quantitative surveys, but the qualitative techniques are often learned in short-term training sessions and through on-the-job experience. In the best research projects, at least some of the field team members have participated in the development and field testing of research guidelines and protocols, so they have learned the basics of research strategies before entering into the actual data gathering.

SMALL-SCALE TEAM RESEARCH: AN EXAMPLE FROM RURAL INDIA

Many short-term ethnographic research projects in South Asia have been initiated by local NGO research teams that received small grants from international sources in connection with intervention programs. In some cases, the research is contracted to an individual research consultant, who develops the data gathering using researchers recruited by the local NGO.

Lakshmi Ramachandar was the contractor for a small-scale project to assess patterns of abortion-seeking and costs of medical termination of pregnancy in a multi-village rural area in Jharkhand state (India). The study was contracted by Family Planning Association–India (FPAI), and was carried out in the local service area of an FPAI clinic during November and December, 2008 (Ramachandar 2009b).

She arrived in the field location in Jharkhand on the 1st of November, and met with the staff people at the FPAI (NGO) hospital. They had already contacted 10 local female college students (in social sciences) as potential candidates for training as interviewers. The following days were taken up with interviewing the candidates and conducting planning meetings with the FPAI staff. Training of the selected interviewers began on the 8th of November.

The plan of the study called for (a) social mapping of health providers in the study area (b) approximately 20 key informant interviews (including several FPAI staff and outreach workers), and (c) in-depth interviews with at least 40 women who had recently experienced planned pregnancy terminations. In the following weeks, the team collected a total of 56 interviews with recent abortion cases (terminations within the past six months). The cases for interviewing were identified by the community-based FPAI outreach workers (local "link persons").

The Research Team

In the terms of the research contract, FPAI provided the training site, a vehicle and driver for transportation to rural villages, and a full-time research coordinator who was familiar with all the locations as well as many of the medical practitioners who were interviewed as key informants. The part-time link persons in local villages and block-level outreach workers also assisted the research. They were all part of the local FPAI outreach system.

Ramachandar selected six local interviewers from among the young women FPAI had tentatively recruited. One had nursing training; the others were undergraduate students in various disciplines. In addition to the basic team of those six interviewers plus the research coordinator and principal investigator, it was necessary to find a local person to translate and transcribe the expanded interview notes into English in the computer. Fortunately a local retired man was identified who was able to transcribe most of the abortion interviews using his personal computer.

Training the Interviewers

The training of the interview team consisted of three days at the NGO site, interspersed with three days of field "practice." The following points were emphasized in the training:

- The interview format consisted of a series of "main points," that was to be treated as a checklist. The interview was to be conducted in a flexible, conversational style. Each main point was allotted two sheets of blank paper for note taking.

- Interviewers were trained to encourage informants to give narratives about the main points, to provide details and context concerning their experiences with pregnancy termination.

- Each interview had to begin with the required "informed consent procedure," during which the interviewers assured informants of their confidentiality, anonymity, and voluntary participation.

- The note takers were encouraged to get as much of the informants' actual words as possible, and to be careful to get key words, and sometimes whole sentences, verbatim. Some of those Hindi language key words and phrases would be preserved in Hindi in the transcriptions to capture the flavor of the women's statements.

- Strong emphasis was placed on extensive, careful expansion of the interview notes, as these would provide the core data for the report.

The initial orientation sessions were followed by role play and practice sessions. For these practice sessions the FPAI outreach workers brought in women who had had recent abortions. After the English language transcriptions were prepared, those "finished" transcriptions were checked against the Hindi notes.

The training sessions were all bilingual, because much of the training material was presented in slides and charts (English language). Each English language section was then described and discussed in Hindi.

The field researchers were trained to do their interviews as two-person teams: one individual did the interviewing while the other took notes in the local Jharkhand Hindi language. One of the teams was able to translate their Hindi notes into rough English and to enter their expanded notes into the computer. The other two teams expanded their notes in Hindi, which were then translated into English by the data-entry person. The principal investigator conducted key informant interviews with some of the FPAI field staff, a sample of private practitioners, and a few attendants in the medical shops.

The schedule of work consisted of interviews on alternate days, with expansion of hand-written notes and review of the expanded notes the day after the interviews. On those alternate days, the principal investigator also wrote out her notes from the key informant interviews.

Examples of Data

Information about household goods, house construction, and family occupations permitted the research team to sort the 56 cases into levels of socio-economic status (SES), with 12 in the "high SES" category, 20 in "medium SES" and 24 in "low SES." Here is an example of "high SES":

Babita Devi [pseudonym] is 26 years old, and her husband is employed as an agent for an insurance company, with a regular salary of at least 3000 rupees per month. She also earns small amounts of income from sewing clothes.

> The family lives in an official quarter allotted to her father-in-law which includes two rooms, a guest room, kitchen, bathroom and toilet. There is a T.V set, a motorcycle, mobile phone, heater, coal-fed smokeless Chula (stove), two ceiling fans, and a table fan. They have to pay Rs. 100/mo for electricity, and Rs. 70 is paid for cable connection per month. There is a kitchen garden near the house having trees of "kathal" (jack-fruit), guava, bananas, papaya and others. They have a cow (Jersey breed) and calf, so the family has supply of milk. (Ramachandar 2009b)

Main Results of the Study

Of the 56 recent abortion cases, the majority (36) received the services of qualified medical doctors: private clinics/small hospitals (18), Dr. F (14), and FPAI (4). Another 10 cases went to small private clinics of trained medical doctors (probably not qualified for abortion services). Fourteen cases were in the hands of unqualified, uncertified practitioners: registered medical practitioners (5), auxiliary nurse midwives (4), traditional birth attendants (dais) (4), and a chemist shop attendant (1). The four dais used a traditional method involving a powerful root ("stick abortion"). Such traditional stick abortions, carried out by the traditional birth attendants, still occur in the more remote villages, though the practice has declined greatly in recent years, according to the informants.

In this form of small-scale ethnographic research, there is little or no possibility for participant observation. Also, the short time frame and recruitment of local persons for the interviewing limits the data-gathering components to simple formats that can be learned in a few days of training. The following are usual features of small-scale research of this sort:

- The entire process of data-gathering was completed in six weeks, followed by another three weeks of data analysis and writing.

- This pattern of quick ethnography is only possible if there is strong support from a local organization (usually a NGO) that has an effective community outreach system in place.

- Although counting the numbers of cases utilizing different types of providers (and procedures) is an essential part of the analysis, most studies of this type use only very simple statistics.

- The reliance on locally recruited interviewers is an essential component, especially in rural areas, as interviewers need to be familiar with local language and related cultural behaviors.

RESEARCH TEAMS FOR FOCUSED ETHNOGRAPHIC STUDIES

FES research protocols (described in Chapter 16) are generally much more complicated than the study described above. The standard research protocol for study of acute respiratory infections, for example, includes key informant interviewing, case interviewing, showing a video and then asking questions about the video, hypothetical scenarios, pile sorting, paired comparisons (choice of providers), and a few other tasks. Generally, that complicated list of different research activities requires quite experienced (well-trained) researchers. In practice those studies often been carried out by teams of two or three persons.

In cases where the field workers have not had experience with all of those ethnographic techniques, training would require many days of both didactic and role-play activities. On the other hand, in many cases, the field coordinator participates fully in the research and can give additional training, along with close supervision. The FES team that studied acute respiratory infections in West Java looks like an ideal model:

> The fieldwork was conducted under the direct supervision of the senior author, who has worked in the...area over a period of several years and is fluent in the local dialect. She was assisted by three full-time female research assistants who were undergraduates in anthropology at the University of Indonesia. (Kresno et al. 1994: 426–427)

LARGER, LONGER-TERM PROJECTS

During 2007–2008, researchers from the Population Council (New Delhi) conducted complex research on "patterns of migration/mobility and HIV risk among female sex workers" in four Indian states (Saggurti et al.

2008). A parallel study of "migration/mobility of male workers" was also part of the project. Each of the states—Maharashtra, Andhra Pradesh, Karnataka and Tamil Nadu—has a different language, so local, state-based organizations were contracted to assemble research teams in their areas, in order to carry out the data gathering. Three or four different commercial research organizations were contracted to do both quantitative surveys and qualitative ethnographic interviewing. For example, in the state of Andhra Pradesh, a marketing research organization (TNS India Private Limited), carried out the main field-interviewing tasks, and one of their ranking staff persons co-authored the published report (Saggurti et al. 2008). In the state of Tamil Nadu, on the other hand, faculty persons from the Department of Population Studies at a large university received a contract and carried out a major part of the research. They are first and second authors in the ensuing research report (Subbiah et al. 2008).

Another recent study by Population Council researchers from New Delhi was carried out in the state of Uttar Pradesh through a combination of contracted NGOs to do the quantitative survey research while an in-house Population Council research team carried out all the ethnographic research (Khan, Hazra, and Bhatnagar 2010). The complex multi-method, multi-site project collected data on aspects of childbirth and postnatal practices affecting both infant and maternal morbidity and mortality. The research team, headed by M. E. Khan, received training in ethnographic research techniques in New Delhi before going out to the rural sites in Uttar Pradesh. In this case, the Population Council team was able to carry out ethnographic research in the various sites because the team members were all fluent in Hindi, the main language in Uttar Pradesh.

A Large-Scale Research Organization in Bangladesh

One of the largest research organizations in South Asia is the International Centre for Diarrhoeal Disease Research, Bangladesh (ICDDR,B), which has an internationally known field base in Matlab (a sub-district of Chandpur District in south-central Bangladesh). The ICDDR,B hospital with research facilities in Matlab was originally the Cholera Research Laboratory, founded in the 1960s with international funding. In the first decades of operations, most research at the Matlab site (and the ICDDR,B headquarters in Dhaka) was focused on medical issues, particularly in relation to cholera and other diarrhoeal disease.

A significant shift of focus occurred at the ICDDR,B Matlab site in 1992, when the large, well-funded Bangladesh Rural Advancement Committee (BRAC) set up operations in the sub-district and entered into a research partnership with the ICDDR,B (Chowdhury, Bhuiya and Ahmed 2007). The BRAC mandate is focused on poverty alleviation, broadly defined, as well as developing a major network of education facilities. This means that issues of access to education, gender inequities, environmental degradation, access to health care, and many other general social problems are part of the BRAC programmatic structure. The joint BRAC–ICDDR,B Research Project was broadly aimed at study of the "social determinants of health," and the effects of the various programs in improving general health and well-being of the low-income families of the region.

Also in the 1990s, the ICDDR,B established the Social and Behavioral Sciences Programme of research within the Community Health Division (Ross et al. 1998). The first head of the new program was James Ross, an American anthropologist, who set up a site in the rural Matlab area for training and data collection concerning women's reproductive health problems. Already in the 1990s, other research units within the ICDDR,B were involved in a variety of studies utilizing both qualitative and quantitative field methods.

Most of the BRAC–ICDDR,B projects relied on cross-sectional survey methodologies, often linked to the highly developed Demographic Surveillance System (DSS), which is a goldmine of demographic and health data concerning the various communities in the Matlab area.

The tendency to include qualitative research in programs of the ICDDR,B was already evident in the late 1970s. A trio of researchers embarked on an ambitious mixed-methods study of "beliefs and fertility in Bangladesh" (Maloney, Aziz, and Sarker 1981). At the time of the study, C. Maloney was a visiting professor at Rajshahi University in the Institute of Bangladesh Studies, P. Sarkar was on the faculty of Rajshahi University (Department of Social Work), and K. M. A. Aziz was an Associate Scientist at the ICDDR,B. This was a highly ambitious study, involving 17 different rural communities in Bangladesh. The authors did a large number of structured survey interviews, but their team members also did participant observation in selected villages, and collected life histories and a number of open-ended interviews. The result was a wide range of data about sexual practices and beliefs, contraception, and other materials related to fertility. The authors commented that this was the first thorough study of sexual beliefs and practices in Bangladesh.

The research team recruited 15 field researchers (7 females and 8 males), who were then trained intensively at Rajshahi University for nine days. Following the training, the field researchers all selected individual village sites, in which they resided for several months to carry out the assigned interviews and observations. All 15 researchers in the selected villages were visited occasionally by a senior member of the team. Thus, because they were each in a field site for at least five months, they were able to do informal participant observation and to become familiar with the local people. In addition to supervising the 15 field workers, both Aziz and Sarkar did extensive interviewing in their own research sites. In addition to the quantitative survey data, the field researchers interviewed a total of 152 informants, including mullas, midwives, healers, teachers, and family planning workers.

A specially trained group of four field researchers did in-depth, life-history interviews with 38 individuals, most of which involved several sessions. The final report (a book) has large numbers of quotes from interviews, illustrating "typical responses" concerning the wide range of topics relating to sexuality, reproduction, and fertility.

This study in Bangladesh was unusual in that the three principal investigators were all anthropologists, one of whom (C. Maloney) was from the United States. However, most of the field researchers were not trained in anthropology.

Qualitative Evaluation Research for Large-Scale HIV/AIDS Program

A large multi-site HIV/AIDS program in the state of Andhra Pradesh, India, contracted for a qualitative evaluation in 2004–2005 to be carried out by a NGO research organization: the Institute of Health Systems (IHS), located in Hyderabad (George et al. 2005). During a two-month period in 2004, the research group, with help from outside consultants, developed detailed guidelines for focus group discussions (FGD) and in-depth interviews. The research team of nine persons (5 males and 4 females) participated in the planning and construction of the interview and discussion guidelines, and then conducted pilot testing of the instruments, so the interviewers were well acquainted with the rationale and aims of the data-gathering. The team received training in qualitative methods from an experienced researcher at the Population Council. The research team received additional training and assistance from other organizations, including significant logistic support from the Academy of Nursing Studies, which provided transcription and translation services. Another outside consultant provided training in the use of the ATLAS/ti software for managing the interview data.

The IHS team carried out research in eight different sites, doing FGDs and individual interviews of female sex workers, men who have sex with men (MSM), people living with HIV/AIDS, NGO personnel, and some "gatekeepers." The team did 16 FGDs of both the sex workers and the MSM, and 32 individual interviews in each of those two categories.

The report (George et al. 2005) presents data on a large number of "themes," for which the data are given in the form of numerous quotes from individuals. However, the report has no tabulations of frequencies of specific responses, and no construction of "variables" in the usual sense. Nonetheless, quantitative statements are given concerning many of the "themes," such as "Significant number of respondents from MSM and FSW groups reported discrimination and violence at the hands of the police" (p. 57). That statement was followed by six verbatim excerpts from interviews. Almost all the sections dealing with various "themes" include quantitative statements. Some of the "themes" report negative characteristics—lack of something, such as "Very few of the respondents reported having had the opportunity to develop any kind of life skills" (p. 68).

TRAININGS FOR ETHNOGRAPHIC RESEARCH

The large changes occurring in the various styles of applied ethnographic research, and the fact that most of the actual data-gathering is done by persons with little or no previous training in ethnographic methods, mean that a great deal of training and re-training is required in connection with the ongoing research needs. As described above, each newly initiated project requires pre-research training. The usual practice is to have at least five or six days of training, with at least two days of field practice. In addition, close supervision during the actual data gathering is highly desirable in order to reinforce the specific skills and understandings that were imparted in the training sessions.

Training Workshops and Technical Assistance for Research and Action Organizations

In addition to the training for individual field teams, a second level of training has been carried out in many areas, in which intervention program staff people, field staff of NGOs, and other individuals have received specific skills training in ethnographic research. For example, from 1990 to 2000, a program developed by the Ford Foundation in India conducted a large number of one-week workshops for training applied-program people in qualitative research methods. The program, "Building Social Science Research Capacity for Women's Reproductive Health in India," mainly recruited participants from NGOs and specialized educational institutes such as the Tata Institute for Social Sciences (Mumbai) and the Jawaharlal Institute of Post-Graduate Medical Education and Research (JIPMER) in Pondicherry. In addition to two workshops each year, the core staff of the project (anthropologists) visited researchers in the participating organizations in order to give individualized assistance and training concerning their research projects. The research projects were funded by the Ford Foundation as part of the overall program of capacity building.

The training sessions and on-site technical assistance have resulted in a number of publications, including the edited collection of studies *Listening to Women Talk about Their Health* (Gittelsohn et al. 1994; second edition 2011) and several papers in another edited collection, *Reproductive Health in India: New Evidence* (Koenig et al. 2008). Another collection of papers, *Sexuality and Sexual Behavior* (Mutatkar et al. 2005), is a series of studies carried out under the auspices of the School of Health Sciences, University of Pune. In addition to such individual papers in various journals and books, other written materials from the network of NGOs are in the form of unpublished reports.

The unusual feature of the Ford Foundation program throughout the decade of the 1990s was that very few academic (university-based) persons were participants in the workshops and other activities. Most were staff people from small and medium-sized NGOs, some of which had significant community health programs such as the Society for Education, Welfare and Action–Rural (SEWA-Rural), an organization in Gujarat, and the Child In Need Institute (CINI) in Kolkata.

DISCUSSION

The examples of ethnographic research teams in this chapter are mainly drawn from South Asia, partly because I am most familiar with the various research activities in that area. South Asia is also a useful example area because of the very wide range of different applied programs that include ethnographic research in their current activities.

In many applied ethnographic projects, in both developed and developing countries, the data gathering is carried out by multi-disciplinary teams of varied composition. In the mapping projects described in Chapter 15, the teams are sometimes a mixture of geographers and "expert" participants from the local population, as in the example of place-name mapping in Arctic Canada by the Müller-Wille team. The mapping projects described by Herlihy and associates in Latin America included some that were headed by geographers and others headed by anthropologists. The various FES-style studies concerning acute respiratory infections and other health and nutrition topics have often involved combinations of clinical practitioners and academic researchers (e.g., from public health backgrounds), along with community based NGO outreach workers.

In those projects, local indigenous people had very important roles. As noted in the descriptions of the various projects, many influences contribute to the composition of research teams, as outlined in the following:

- The pressures for short-term, rapid assessment in some projects make it nearly impossible for one person alone to carry out the required number of interviews and other data-gathering.

- In many cases, the applied research takes place in populations where the local language is different from that of the principal investigator (research director) and the research coordinators. Therefore, local bilingual persons are hired and trained for the interviewing work, which in some cases involves more than one ethnic group.

- The increased preference for participatory approaches has led research teams to include persons from the local communities in their research operations.

- The use of various structured qualitative interview methods (free-listing, pile sorting, etc.) and of research designs based on collecting samples of cases requires contacts with sufficient numbers of informants for at least modest quantitative data analysis. This is, in part, a reflection of increased pressure for improved validity and credibility in ethnographic research.

- Many applied research tasks are multi-site, in situations of changing economic and social circumstances, and thus require more complex sampling and data-gathering. Those factors, in turn, call for more diversified research teams.

- The increased tendency for joint research, involving the practitioners (e.g., health providers or rural development workers) teaming up with "outside researchers," leads to complex research groups.

- The advent of the "computer revolution," which spread rapidly throughout the developing countries in the 1990s and later, led to widespread use of computerized data management. That has facilitated the expansion of data-collection activities while, at the same time, adding the need for experienced computer specialists in research teams.

The continued growth of applied ethnographic research, particularly in developing countries, has increased the need for short-term and longer-term training opportunities, particularly for NGO researchers. Some of that need is met through on-the-job training sponsored by international NGOs and some funding agencies. Nevertheless, many applied research efforts still rely on poorly planned quantitative surveys that could be much improved if researchers included formative ethnographic research in their repertoire.

Writing Ethnography:
Keeping it Grounded and Inductive

In this chapter, I review the main guidelines for writing ethnographic research materials and, as you will note, repeatedly emphasize "stick close to the data," and "present the voices of the people." In the first part of the chapter, I discuss some lessons from two interesting papers—one is written by the well-known ethnographic researcher, Harry Wolcott, re-examining the first lessons in writing an ethnographic paper based on his research entitled "The Man in the Principal's Office" (Wolcott 1973). In the second part of the chapter, I discuss guidelines for writing the different sections of research-based papers and reports.

RECALLING A LESSON FROM A MENTOR

Many years ago, Harry Wolcott did a detailed ethnographic study of a school principal (Wolcott 1973). In a recent paper he reminisced about that ethnographic writing, and described his exchanges with George Spindler (his former PhD adviser), as he struggled with writing a paper from his field notes (Wolcott 2003). Wolcott's review of that learning experience makes for truly interesting reading.

The review of an earlier event is actually a sort of "mini-ethnography"—in this case, about writing a paper, focused particularly on the interactions with the mentor. Fortunately, Wolcott had preserved his original drafts of writing for the Spindler collection, and had Spindler's comments written all over that original, unsatisfactory, first draft:

> On page one of my manuscript he offered a critical examination of my discussion of method:

Pertti Pelto, "Writing Ethnography: Keeping it Grounded and Inductive," in *Applied Ethnography: Guidelines for Field Research*, pp. 295-310. © 2013 Left Coast Press, Inc.

—pp. 1-12. A little meandering. Needs sharper focus—exposition and defense of why as well as how you study only one man and his operational context.

—How do you justify studying one principal in order to understand principals?

—Questions to answer in 1st part: What did you want to find out? Why do you call it an ethnography? Why couldn't you find out other ways?

Further along, where I sing the praises of capturing dialogue but fail to employ any, Spindler asks, "Yes, but what use is the dialogue? Dialogue is good to use, but its relevance should also become clear." (Wolcott 2003: 326)

Wolcott continues, in this vein, to examine the problems in his draft paper and to quote from the comments that his mentor had sent to him in days long before such exchanges could happen rapidly through email.

After some of the problems in the early pages, he notes on page 12, after describing the research methods:

I explained my purpose: "I have chosen to make some rather broad statements, and I have chosen to speak about the elementary school principalship in general rather than restrict my comments only to the specifics of one man over a given period of time." (p. 327) Spindler's response to that was one word: "Why?"

This is the key point that we all need to focus on. Wolcott, like many of our graduate students, was trying to get to "the big generalizations," because he didn't yet grasp the usefulness of detailed, case-by-case inductive data accumulation. On page 31 Spindler commented sharply: "Don't generalize. The heart of ethnography is singularity" (p. 327).

As these sorts of critical comments continued in his mentor's review of the paper, Wolcott recalls that he began finally to understand the core meaning of "ethnography." He had jumped too quickly to "the big picture," before doing justice to the specific, concrete information in his field notes. The message from his mentor was that the strengths of ethnographic research are in the specific, carefully observed data—the actions, dialogue, and language used by the principal that he had observed in detail over many months.

I am reminded, in reading Wolcott's highly informative description, of how many times we have instructed our students and other trainees: "Give the concrete details...." Often it is important to give the person's exact words or exact actions in a situation. Anyone getting into ethnographic research should read Wolcott's essay—to get the core message of how to think about ethnographic field research. The essay is certainly intended to be about "writing ethnography," but the gist of the message needs to be understood before the field work begins. It is interesting that Wolcott was already a skilled field researcher, yet his own description tells us that, at that early stage of his career, he had not yet grasped the full significance, the meaning, of "ethnographic research."

The mentor's message is particularly clear at another point where he instructs:

> The substance of what you found out should be presented inductively, with substantial behavioral slices, and excerpts from oral interchanges, then interpreted briefly. (p. 328)

Wolcott says that that is where he began to realize that he had to re-write the entire paper. He was still trying to write about "school principals," and was resisting his mentor's advice to focus on the actions and words of this one (singular) person. Wolcott writes:

> Apparently I did not really understand how to make my study "ethnographic." Not that I lacked information about principals. But the whole point of ethnography was not sufficiently clear that I recognized or even trusted it. (p. 328)

He gives a great deal of credit to others for his "learning to write ethnographically," and suggests that an important strategy is to ask colleagues to comment on each draft—but that it's important to pick the right persons for that task.

A Couple of Cases Tell the Tale: Math in Cultural Context

The following discussion is about a highly unusual paper, in which the purpose of the ethnographic content is to give a concrete description of the development of a "culturally appropriate math module" for Alaskan native elementary students. Even though the paper describes the videotaping of two teachers' classroom styles and the interactions with the sixth grade children, the purpose of the ethnographic approach is to give a lively and credible view of the "Math in Cultural Context" model.

Jerry Lipka and colleagues at the University of Alaska (Fairbanks) have presented a clear rendition of their ideas concerning culturally appropriate math teaching, utilizing just two case studies (Lipka et al. 2005). The team developed a model for teaching math to native Alaskan students, which they refer to as Math in Cultural Context (MCC). They developed the system through long-term interactions with Yup'ik elders, teachers, and community people.

> MCC is based on Yup'ik cultural knowledge and norms, and it seeks to bridge the culture of the community with that of the school. Our definition of culturally based math education includes math content knowledge (informed by both Western knowledge and that of Yup'ik elders), pedagogical knowledge (informed by school-based practices and community-based ways of teaching, communicating, and learning), and contextual knowledge (ways of connecting schooling to students' prior knowledge and the everyday knowledge of the community). (Lipka et al. 2005: 368)

The math teaching model featured in the case studies is called Building a Fish Rack (a framework for drying salmon). The authors, in developing the module, had video-recorded the step-by-step process as Yup'ik elders did the actual construction of a fish rack. Their paper explained that the measuring processes in fish rack construction formed a nice connection between daily realities in communities and the math concepts they needed to handle in the curriculum. This introduction of a real life activity provides the basis for further, more complex mathematical concepts at later stages in the classroom.

In their study of sixth grade teachers using the fish rack module, the researchers videotaped the interactions of the teachers with their students, as the students simulated the steps in building the structure. One of their "model teachers" was a Yup'ik woman, Doreen, teaching in the school in her native home town. The second teacher, Stacy, was an "outsider," from the "lower 48" (the 48 contiguous states of the United States). The strategy with both teachers (who both had good scores in their students' gains in math knowledge) was that both were first assigned to "control" situations, using the "standard math teaching," and then the two did the MCC "fish rack" teaching. Videotapes of their teaching showed very interesting changes in the teacher-student interactions.

Doreen, the Yup'ik Teacher

The non-MCC video of Doreen was an hour-long session:

> On the tape are a group of 15 sixth graders sitting in three even rows facing the board and the teacher. After modeling one example of finding the perimeter of a square, Doreen handed out a homemade

worksheet saying, "OK, today we are going to have some fun with perimeters." The worksheet had several problems in which the students were to find the perimeter of various geometric shapes (e.g., a girl, a butterfly, a house) on graph paper. (p. 372)

The authors' critique of the videotape points out that the sequence is very teacher-centered, and there was very little dialogue. In fact, most of the hour was almost totally silent, as the students worked on the assignment. Only the inaudible whispering was heard, as Doreen worked with individual students when they were having difficulties. After that first task there was supposed to be a more interactive exercise, but time ran out. During the first 15 minutes, as Doreen explained the processes, and then asked questions, the answers came generally as "choral responses," as several students gave the answers in unison.

The next videotape of Doreen was at her home village of Beluga Bay, and she was using the "fish rack" teaching module for her sixth graders. The class was in the gymnasium, and students were running around, having fun. Then they settled down in pairs, and each pair worked at constructing a rectangular "fish rack" using a piece of string as a measuring device. Doreen was moving around from group to group, and asking the students "How do you prove it's a rectangle?"

The "fish rack session" then moved into the classroom, where there were photos of children climbing on fish racks in Beluga Bay. Doreen asked the students to go to the board and explain what they had done in the fish rack exercise. There was a lot of interaction and interest—a much different situation from her earlier (non-MCC) teaching scene.

The "ethnographic method" used by Lipka and colleagues consisted of what they referred to as "co-analysis," in which they had Yup'ik cultural "experts" and professional researchers working together in the analysis of the videotapes. They also had a number of discussions and interviews with the two teachers featured in the videotapes. In the interview with Doreen, she at first stated that her teaching style had not changed much when she used the "fish rack module." However, later she admitted:

> Now that I watch the videotape and took notes and mental notes I do see a lot of differences. Like one difference was in the fish rack module I notice I had the students take more control of what they were doing, and I was more the moderator, just making sure that they were pretty much on task, but they were in control of communication between each other... they were communicating mathematically more with the fish rack unit....(p. 375)

Stacy, the Outsider Teacher

The descriptions of Stacy's teaching style emphasized two features: first, she is a "natural teacher" who encouraged much interaction among the students and showed a very high degree of understanding students' needs and interests in learning; second, she didn't have full knowledge of the local native culture, so she lacked a frame of reference for her math teaching. It appeared from the videotapes that Stacy was able to create a much more interactive learning environment in the classroom, even though her teaching was lacking in "local cultural content." When she did the fish rack module, the approach fit right in with her natural teaching style and provided a good framework for the math content, which she didn't have earlier.

In interviews Stacy told the researchers that in teacher training they were instructed not to call on individual students to answer questions, as "it puts them on the spot." Nonetheless, when she had achieved good trust among her students, she had initiated the practice of calling on individual students. However, she had a subtle agreement with some students—they would let her know if they needed help and then they would not be called on. For example:

> Zach and I had an agreement that he would initiate the move for me to give him help. These were nonverbal cues like flipping through the pages of his book—this translated that he didn't know what was going on. Another was a look at me and he would shake his pen or pencil. This was a signal that he needed help. (p. 380)

Doreen and Stacy were quite different in their teaching styles. In addition, their classroom environments were also different. Stacy's was a multi-age student group, in which she was with the same students for three years. That gave her a large opportunity to build up the kind of friendly and cooperative relationships that prevailed in her classroom. There appeared to be much more active cooperation and communication among the students, even in the "control" situation where she was not using the MCC fish rack module.

The researchers concluded with a statement that illustrates the main purpose of the paper:

> This curriculum is unique in that it is locally and culturally based while meeting both the state of Alaska's cultural standards and the national standards of the National Council of Teachers of Mathematics (2000). We believe this curriculum holds great promise to improve Alaska Native students' mathematical understanding while bridging the culture of the schools to that of the community. (p. 383)

DISCUSSION

The University of Alaska research team had carried out a quantitative evaluation of their MCC module, by comparing the pretest-posttest statistics of "treatment" (MCC module) to the "controls." They reported statistically significant results favoring the MCC module teaching (Lipka and Adams 2004). Doreen and Stacy were chosen for the "two-case ethnographic presentation," in part because their students showed good posttest progress in the math tests.

This paper, "Math in a Cultural Context: Two Case Studies of a Successful Culturally Based Math Project," is an excellent model for presenting the description and analysis of larger projects. Obviously the two cases do not by themselves constitute a complete piece of research. In fact, the paper does not even mention how many teachers they included in the qualitative ethnographic study. However, in the context of teaching math in the sixth grade, the two cases serve to illustrate the nature of the innovation (the fish rack module), as well as pointing out the main elements of what the researchers consider to be appropriate pedagogy—how to get students more fully involved and thinking about (conceptualizing) components of mathematics.

The researchers emphasized the extent to which the MCC teaching increased communication and cooperation among the students, and reduced the "teacher-centered" tendencies in the usual "standard" teaching styles. The examples of the two teachers, using the culturally familiar "construction of a fish rack," also served to highlight the emphasis on linking in-school teaching to the daily life of the (Yup'ik) community. The researchers felt that the use of the MCC module encouraged the students to "take ownership" of the project, and to communicate effectively with each other.

This is a very unusual paper, as the objective is to present the intervention product, the math teaching module (MCC). However, instead of doing a description in the usual, pedestrian manner, the authors used the ethnographic style, including quotes from student-teacher interactions, descriptions of action in the videotapes, and other very concrete action. These ethnographic excerpts were used to highlight what they believe to be the strengths of the math education module they had developed.

MAIN POINTS IN WRITING YOUR ETHNOGRAPHIC PRODUCTS

The following three basic rules should be remembered throughout the writing process.

Rule One

Ethnographic writing should, in most cases, follow an inductive, "discovery of new information" style, as noted in Wolcott's essay discussed above. You should try hard to present data in a very concrete, richly descriptive form. That is, you write about individual case materials. Where some of the data are analyzed and presented in quantitative formats with statistical analysis, it is often useful to first present raw data from in-depth interviews, including variations in important variables or themes, followed by the quantitative tables and explanatory analysis.

Rule Two

Remember that a major purpose of in-depth interviewing is to bring out the "voices of the study people." That means that writing should include a number of small and not-so-small quotes from the key informants and individual cases, sometimes giving the local language (local vocabulary). In many cases it will be useful to include a glossary of the most important vocabulary items relating to the central topic of your research.

Rule Three

In presenting ethnographic materials, leave much of the literature review and theoretical discussion to the end of the paper or report, with only brief introductory "setting the stage and objectives," at the beginning of the writing.

Writing Your Introduction

Introducing your research focus and primary concerns (objectives) is the beginning of your paper or report, but it is not necessarily the first thing you start writing. The introduction is often the most difficult part of the writing, and I have sometimes advised my students to start their writing with something easier. For example, start by describing your research site(s), study population, and data-gathering methods. That's usually an easier piece of writing. Sometimes you can write most of the rest of your report, and then go back and write the introduction.

Conventionally the introduction to a study is supposed to be in the form of the "literature review." This task often arouses fear and trembling for even the boldest writers, especially for people who have little previous experience in writing for publication. Many writers fail to mention that there are previous studies about the same subject matter, even from the same region. On the other hand, some papers that I have seen mention dozens of research papers that somehow touched on the topic, and referred vaguely and somewhat randomly to studies in other parts of the world. Many times I become impatient because the citations are all over the place; in many journals they are in the form of tiny numbers, for example [1, 3, 8, 9].

Even in the more sensible journals where the citations are rendered as (Smith 1996, Jones 1997, Wilson 2001), the references all by themselves tell us nothing about the contents of those studies, their locations, and why they are cited here in this paper. That is why I believe that you should include only a few references, and then make clear why they are important, including what population they refer to and what they found out. In some cases it is also useful to include a comment about their methodology.

The studies cited in the introduction should have direct relevance to your particular study. Cite mostly the literature closest to your research area, and for each study give the location and a bit of detail about the study. For example, if your data are about teenagers in certain communities in West Africa, it doesn't do much good to cite recent studies in California. Rather, your introduction could include something like this:

> Smith's very original research on teenagers in Senegal (Smith 1996) found that (details) ... On the other hand, Jones, in similar communities in Nigeria, reported a quite different pattern (Jones 1997), which could reflect differences in the research design, with unusual sample selection (details of how it is different).... There are, of course, large variations in behaviors of adolescents due to religion, local economic conditions, and other factors. Mukebe's comparisons between East and West African teenagers (Mukebe 2002) showed.... [Both the text and the citations in this example are hypothetical to illustrate my point.]

Sometimes your introduction will include statements such as "....The data in the Nigerian study, however, were from one-shot interviews with school-going teenagers in an urban area, whereas Smith's informants, in a notably different environment, were contacted more than once for in-depth interviews, which contributes to better validity and reliability."

Each study that you cite should refer to issues close to the topical area of your research. Also, your mention of particular studies should always say where they were conducted. If you find contradictory results in some earlier studies, it is then particularly interesting if your study resolves some of the conflict.

I realize that most journal publications impose severe word limitations, so you don't have the luxury of a detailed discussion of the literature. Nonetheless, the descriptions of previous research by others should set the stage and give a framework that tells the reader how your study relates to the literature on this topical area.

It is often useful to cite a general, macro-level paper that deals with your central topic in the region. For example:

> The general picture of malnutrition in small children in Southeast Asia shows that often the female caretakers' workloads and social situations are important factors (Jones 2002; Moritz 2005). [hypothetical example]

Then, introduce your particular focus, at a more local level:

> When we focus on issues of women's work in relation to child care and feeding in (specific research area), some special features about women's work, family structure, child malnutrition... (Jones 2007). [hypothetical example]

If possible, pick one or two of the studies that are the closest to your own research topic, and show how "These studies raise important further questions...." or "Their conclusions are useful, but need greater depth, with more careful analysis of the specific environmental factors...."

Objectives of your Study

After the introduction referring to important previous studies, you should state your objectives in clear, concrete language.

Too vague and general: "Our main objective in the study was to describe and understand sources of conflict in the two communities."

Better: "The objectives of the study were to examine the differences and similarities in sources of conflict in the two communities in order:

- to identify main factional cleavages and conflict areas in the two communities;

- to determine the importance of religious and ethnic differences, neighborhood fault lines, and other factors contributing to intra-community conflict;

- to understand the relationships of macro-level political processes to local political cleavages in the communities; and

- to examine the extent to which socio-economic stratification contributes to the factions and conflict situations in the communities."

Methods of Data Gathering

Here's where ethnographically oriented people need to be very concrete, sophisticated, and thorough in the writing. The epistemological discussions in the social sciences—the conflicts about postmodernism, neo-positivism, realism and the other "isms"—have all raised questions about data-gathering styles, including concerns about the ethical issues of maintaining confidentiality and avoiding psychological or social harm to study communities. Thus, many factors have contributed to the importance of clear, thorough descriptions of research actions.

Box 18.1   Main Points to Cover in Your Description of Data Gathering

1. Selection of specific research sites. Language situation—languages spoken in the communities. Ethnic, social, and cultural diversities in the communities.

2. Collaboration, if any, with local NGOs, health facilities, school authorities, and other organizations.

3. Recruitment of research assistants/interviewers. Their qualifications and characteristics.

4. Training of the locally recruited researchers.

5. Mapping. Description of the specific methods used in mapping activities. Organization of any social mapping, including number of participants (informants), and social mapping sessions.

6. Key informants. Their characteristics. Number of times you contacted and discussed the project with main key informants.

7. Cases selected for interviewing. Sample selection processes.

8. Table giving main characteristics of the cases—ages, education, any other salient variables.

9. Interview protocol development. Description of the check list, including whether it was semi-structured or open-ended, and how was it developed. Process for pilot testing the interview format.

10. Note taking, audio-recording (if any), photography, etc.

11. Expansion and processing of the notes from note taking. Transcribing of interviews from recording devices. Indication of who wrote the expanded data into computer files.

12. Coding, cleaning, further processing.

13. Analysis of the data, including both qualitative and quantitative procedures.

A simple, one-variable table can give a good summary of an important feature. Some useful univariate tables include "tabulation of physical abuse by husband as reported by wives" and lists of "recent illnesses reported by women," "providers to whom sex workers went for treatment," and many others. Of course, the results of free listing are generally presented in a simple table, showing the frequencies of the items listed.

CATEGORIES OR "TYPES" OF INDIVIDUALS IN YOUR SET OF CASE INTERVIEWS

In many applied research projects, two or three different categories of individuals were interviewed. Perhaps your sampling of cases consisted of 20 individuals from each of Ethnic Groups A, B, and C. You should explain your reasons for comparing the three groups, and something about their characteristics and locations.

On the other hand, perhaps the categories emerged from your data analysis. For example, in a study of women's income generating activities, you might get systematic data to compare (a) "successful, well organized, earning good income"; (b) "well organized, but not much income"; and (c) "poorly organized, losing money." In most studies your sample of cases can be sorted or subdivided into three or four (sometimes more) categories.

In those situations, you should carefully describe your methods for assigning people to specific categories, giving examples of individuals and showing why that person was categorized as "high" or "low," or whatever category labels you are using.

Presentation of Main Themes, Patterns, Relationships, and Other Descriptive Materials

When the research design is a comparison between two or three communities/groups, the ethnographic discovery processes will often reveal important secondary features or variables (systematic differences) that may be more interesting and fruitful than the initial focus of the analysis. For example, studies of sex workers in India have frequently compared three categories—brothel-based, home-based, and street-based—in the analysis of sex workers' vulnerabilities to violence, risk of HIV, and other important variables. In some studies, however, sex-worker mobility has been discovered to be a key feature, and so the sex worker informants were re-grouped into "high mobility including out-of town assignments," "medium mobility," and "fixed local contacts only" (Saggurti et al. 2008).

Many discussions about ethnographic field work emphasize the inductive aspects of the research. Even when researchers begin with some observed features of the study community, and perhaps some tentative hypotheses, there are still new discoveries, new insights, and other "inductive moments" in the research. As a result, the writing about research methods will often have an inductive "flavor." That means that you can include statements, for example, "During the early phases of the research we discovered that...." or "Soon after we began the research, the local authorities changed the practice of _____, so we had to re-design our sampling strategy accordingly." Many parts of your reporting may provide such opportunities to report "discoveries," "unexpected results," and other products of the inductive side of ethnographic research.

For each "theme" or main topic, give quotes from informants, and give some frequencies for each theme. Also, look for possible cross tabulations between particular themes and sub-groups, or for relationships among the key variables. For example, the study of Cambodian students in a California school (Chhuon and Hudley 2010) described in Chapter 9, showed clear differences in "preferences of ethnic identity" between students in the "more prestigious" and "less prestigious" academic clusters (academies). In that paper, the authors could have included a table showing the cross-tabulation of the two variables, along with the quotes from the interviews.

Avoid using complex technical terminology and academic-sounding vocabulary wherever possible. Especially in applied research writing, the language should be easily read by non-specialists.

It is often useful to present contrasting case interviews. As described earlier, in 2005, Ramachandar interviewed medical doctors in a South Indian district concerning the recently introduced practice of medical abortion (using the "abortion tablets"), particularly with reference to rural women. Some of the doctors were quite negative about medical abortion for rural women. Ramachandar quoted one doctor, who said:

> This method is not appropriate for rural women. They are less knowledgeable, lack awareness and are not cooperative with the doctors....
> (Dr. Minusha (pseudonym))

On the other hand, doctors who were positive about the benefits of medical abortion seemed more positive about the level of awareness and cooperativeness of rural women.

> In my experience, [rural] women are opting for medical abortion and there is a rising trend for medical abortion. Women come and demand "the new tablet for having an abortion." They have knowledge about the

new pills. (Dr. Lalitha (pseudonym)) (Ramachandar and Pelto 2005: 59)

EXAMPLE: STUDY OF WOMEN'S PERCEPTIONS OF
ABNORMAL VAGINAL DISCHARGE (GOA)

Patel and associates in Goa (western India) (Patel, Andrew, and Pelto 2008) interviewed 42 women concerning their explanations and beliefs about abnormal vaginal discharge (AVD). The sample for qualitative interviewing was a purposive selection of AVD cases from a large quantitative survey. The researchers found that a majority of the women (28) linked the AVD to an important reproductive event, such as childbirth, sterilization, insertion of IUD, or problems during menarche. The article quoted some of the women mentioning the purported cause.

Another factor (theme) that emerged in various interviews was the common belief that AVD is caused by anxieties and tensions, including family conflicts. The authors presented a series of excerpts from some of the in-depth interviews, such as the following quotes that focus on "tensions:"

> White discharge started due to tension because my husband was drinking alcohol. I can't tolerate a person who drinks, I get very angry. If you tell me to starve for 10 days, I will do it but I can't tolerate a person who drinks.

> When we have sexual relationship, discharge is more. I think women get white discharge because of tension. When you think too much, it happens. It happens due to thinking. We women have a lot of tension in our head....

> If there is more tension, the flow of white discharge is more. I have noticed it many times, when I have tension [due to] my children['s] mischievous behavior or when I have tension [due to] my sister's marriage, I get more discharge.

This paper is of special interest because the authors included an unusually large number of excerpts from the interview materials. Concerning the reported treatment seeking, for example, statements from six different women are presented.

According to the researchers, the array of causal explanations given by the women in the Goan study represents a relatively "modern," eclectic mix of "lay medical beliefs," including considerable mention of ideas reflecting modern biomedicine. These data are different from the results of studies reported from traditional rural areas, such as the work of Bang and Bang (1994) in eastern Maharashtra. In their study, the women's causal explanations focused on the concept of "heat," (*garmi* in Hindi), including "heaty foods," along with other traditional Ayurvedic concepts.

In summarizing their data, Patel and associates stated that:

> Many women entertained multiple causal models; biomedical and alternative causal explanations were typically found together. These narratives indicate that we may best understand the etiology of this complaint through an amalgamation of women's reproductive experiences, their social context, and their psychological health. (p. 260)

Writing the Conclusions

In ethnographic writing much of the citing of other studies should be left to the concluding section, after the more or less inductive, descriptive presentation of the qualitative and quantitative data in the main body of the paper.

Although some of the introduction needs to refer to previous studies, the results of this kind of study call for comparisons and possible theory-building arising from these new findings. Returning to the example of Patel and associates, their concluding discussion cites 19 publications in order to make a number of comparisons and statements relating this study to other research results, as well as to implications of the findings.

In the conclusions, you should be especially careful to refer to other studies showing similar results, as well as pointing to contradictory or different patterns in other areas. For example, Patel notes that the traditional beliefs in garmi ("heat") as a causal factor in vaginal discharge, which are prominent in other parts of India, are only weakly evident in the Goan women's explanations of their symptoms.

Programmatic Recommendations

Your concluding section should also suggest possible solutions to problems, and perhaps some policy measures for dealing with perceived issues in local and regional programs. If your research was particularly directed to assessment of weaknesses in intervention programs, your final section of program recommendations should suggest possible solutions for the gaps or issues in the interventions. In many studies, certain kinds of problems may be more serious in one or two sectors of the local community, or certain kinds of families, or in a specific ethnic group. Thus, some very specific "remedial actions" might be suggested that could be brought to the attention of the people in charge of the intervention or program about which you have collected the data.

Notes on the Research Report

Quite often, your main writing task is to prepare a report for the program that sponsored your research. In writing such reports it is appropriate to follow the same basic outline as you would in writing a paper for publication. Generally, however, you won't have any serious limitations placed on the length of your report. Therefore you can include more detail about steps in your research methods and a relatively full explanation of the "discoveries" and "changes in data-gathering strategy" made during the research process.

In most cases, a research report should have a section entitled Executive Summary at the beginning of the report. That summary should follow the same outline of information as the main report, but is much shorter. A report of an FES study of acute respiratory infections (ARI) carried out in North India is slightly over 100 pages, with five pages devoted to the Executive Summary. On the other hand, the report by the Institute of Health Systems (Hyderabad), submitted to the Population Council (George et al. 2005) runs to 135 pages, with 13 pages devoted to the Executive Summary. (See Chapter 17 for a description of that study).

When writing a report of your research for the contracting agency, you should consult with those sponsors concerning their expectations about the length and style of the reporting. In some cases they may not require that you do an Executive Summary.

Past, Present, Future:
Notes on the History and Future
of Applied Ethnography

In this book I've tried to present the main tools and strategies for data gathering in applied ethnographic research. The patterns of research now, in the 21st century, are much different from the usual ethnographic studies of 50 or more years ago. There are many different stories and different influences at work, so my selection of materials is an opportunistic and incomplete sampling from a complex global panorama.

Robert Chambers, in *Rural Development: Putting the Last First* (1983), his first major publication concerning programs of rural development, presented a rather provocative picture of applied social science research in developing countries. Although his portrayal of the various actors in applied research was, in my view, somewhat over-stated, there are enough credible points in his argument to provide a framework for identifying important features in the ongoing transformations in applied programs.

The Three Cultures

In *Rural Development: Putting the Last First*, Chambers wrote about applied social science research in which two "outside cultures" ("negative academics" and "positive practitioners") interact with the third culture—"rural people in a particular place."

Chambers' portrayal noted that both the "academics" and the "practitioners" were outsiders who often had little understanding of the local culture in which they were intent on promoting rural development, health programs, and/or other changes. In his chapter "Two Cultures of Outsiders," he emphasized frequent cleavages between the two "outsider cultures."

The physical, linguistic and experiential distance between these two groups, each with its own culture and mores is wide; and often there is little sympathy or communication between them. (Chambers 1983: 29)

One of the main factors, as he presented it, has been that academic social scientists are accustomed to criticizing, and their research is often misdirected and theoretical. "Academics are trained to criticize, and they are rewarded for it" (p. 30). Another persistent problem has been that the research process has been slow, with results becoming available too late to be of any use in improving the development program being studied. The "culprits" from academia, in this version, were often doctoral students who came to the site of the "third culture" (local rural people), collected data, and then disappeared back to their urban, university environments for many months of data analysis and writing.

The practitioners in rural development projects were depicted as more positive, because they saw themselves as immediately accountable for their practical actions in the development programs.

Practitioners have a sense, too, that their actions or non-actions make a difference. So while academics seek problems and criticize, practitioners seek opportunities and act. Academics look for what has gone wrong; practitioners for what might go right. (p. 33)

Much has changed in the 30 years since Chambers presented those negative views about applied social sciences in the field of rural development. One influence for positive change has been the development of participatory research methods, including the PRA data-gathering techniques fostered by Chambers and his colleagues at the University of Sussex, UK. The examples in this book include several strategies for involving people from the study populations as active participants in data-gathering processes.

The participatory rural appraisal (PRA) field methods that Chambers and his colleagues have promoted were designed particularly to:

- get useful data much faster than is possible with traditional survey research techniques;
- use participatory data-gathering techniques that more effectively and accurately utilize the knowledge and understanding of the local community people, and are more responsive to their needs; and thereby
- develop more accurate information, making it available to the practitioners (and policy-makers) in a timely manner.

ENHANCED PARTICIPATION FROM STUDY COMMUNITIES: MAKING ACTIVE USE OF LOCAL PEOPLE'S CULTURAL KNOWLEDGE

Many of the studies cited in the previous chapters are positive examples of two closely interrelated elements: (a) enhanced degrees of participation by people from the study populations; and (b) development of research methods that effectively capture, and make use of, local people's cultural knowledge. The projects on mapping activities (Chapters 4 and 15) are particularly striking examples in which the "local cultural knowledge" was centrally important, and "local experts" were fully empowered researchers—putting together the relevant information for the benefit of the indigenous communities in ways those people found useful and relevant.

The PRA research methods, which Chambers and his colleagues have propagated in many topical areas and geographic locations, are another manifestation of this impressive change in relationships to the study populations (the "third culture"). There is considerable intellectual overlapping between the research approaches from RRA/PRA circles, and those I have labeled "structured qualitative interviewing." The two most prominent research tools in that category are free-listing and pile-sorting. Both methods are designed to learn about local cultural knowledge and behaviors using interesting interview styles. The examples of free-listing women's illnesses and men's sexual health problems—as carried out in a number of studies in South Asia—have produced practical information about people's cultural ideas and behaviors that have contributed directly to health programs.

Another factor contributing to closer and better relationships with the study populations, at least in some areas, has been the increased practice of hiring and training local researchers to carry out much of the data collection, as described in Chapter 17.

A great many of the short-term, applied research projects—whether RAP, PRA, FES, or whatever—have the practical effect of requiring researchers to hire local persons as researchers in many studies. At the same time, short-term research relies heavily on working closely with local NGOs or other organizations, particularly those which have good outreach systems in the study communities. These factors, in turn, contribute to increased communication and understanding between the research teams and community people.

AN UNUSUAL FORM OF PARTICIPATION: COMMUNITY WORKSHOPS

Smucker and colleagues, in the LUCID network (Land Use Change: Impacts and Dynamics) doing research on land use patterns in Kenya, have described the development of an interesting system of community workshops (also referred to as "feedback workshops"), which they have conducted in various research communities after completing a round of data collection and preliminary analysis.

> The workshops have three purposes: (1) to help ensure that the researchers are correctly interpreting the data and information that they have gathered, (2) to return to the community information that has been gathered by the project, and (3) to discuss interpretations of the causes of change and consider the social, environmental, and policy implications. (Smucker et al. 2007: 392)

Their descriptions of a number of community workshops demonstrate that this unusual type of participatory method has, in some cases, led to important modifications and additions to the research conclusions, as well as having an impact on local political and economic decision-making. With that system, it appears that the local community does not have to wait for months and months while the researchers complete their data analysis and write-up.

I believe that ethnographic researchers (including many academic social scientists) have made significant advances in developing good relations with research communities, and also in developing better tools for getting and making effective use of the local cultural knowledge and behavioral expectations.

BETTER RELATIONS BETWEEN THE TWO OUTSIDER CULTURES

The misunderstandings and intellectual differences between academics and practitioners that Chambers wrote about have also seen considerable modification. There are now increased numbers of applied research situations in which the academics and practitioners have very close working relationships. The example of the community health program in Jeremie, Haiti, (the Haitian Health Foundation) is one of the impressive examples of strong relations between outside researchers and the local practitioners. That program highlights a significant trend, in which the academic researchers are welcomed by the practitioners, and the latter often participate actively in the research. There is now a growing list of publications based on research at the Jeremie site of HHF, and many of those publications include both academic and health program persons as authors. I believe that there is a large increase in that kind of academic-with-practitioner joint publishing of research results (though I don't have hard data for that belief).

In the HHF program there has also been considerable contact between the "outsiders" (researchers) and the "third culture"—the local people. A major contributor to closer and better relationships with the study population is the involvement of community organizations (such as Fathers' Clubs) directly in research activities. The health workers, who are referred to as *agents de santé* (ADS) (agents of health) and who are members of local communities, play major roles in some of the research projects, including locating cases (e.g., children with pneumonia) and, in some projects, doing informant interviews.

FOCUSED ETHNOGRAPHIC STUDIES PROMOTE COMMUNICATIONS WITH PRACTITIONERS

Focused ethnographic studies (FES) research projects are also examples of effective collaboration between academics and practitioners. The FES research packages are designed to get practical, useful information for dealing with serious health problems in the specific study sites. The research is not "criticism," and it does not take long for the researchers to deliver the resulting information to the local health practitioners. In fact, the structure of the FES for acute respiratory infections (ARI) looks as if it were designed by and for the practitioners. The aims of that FES are referred to as "getting answers to the program manager's questions." In several ARI studies, practitioners were actively involved in the research. In her description of the ARI study in Honduras, Hudelson commented:

> Although the FES manual provides structured guidelines for conducting the study, program managers are encouraged to add to the list of Programme Managers' Questions as appropriate, and researchers are instructed to adapt data collection techniques to suit local needs and conditions. (Hudelson 1994: 437)

In addition to the many examples of close collaboration between outside researchers and practitioners in the various rapid assessment studies, the wide range of HIV/AIDS programs is another field of action that has fostered effective researcher-practitioner communication. My feeling is that the special situation of HIV/AIDS programs, which must develop strong interactions with hard-to-reach, hidden sub-populations, has caused many practitioners (program managers and others) to seek contacts with the "third culture," as well as with the academic researchers. For example, the researcher (Kulkarni) in the study of MSM individuals, mentioned in Chapter 8 (Sampling and Counting), is a medical doctor who is head of a large clinic, in addition to being involved in a variety of research projects. Those community-oriented attitudes among a growing number of practitioners are evident in many health care environments, as well as in education and community development.

Non-Academic Institutions and Organizations Doing Ethnographic Research

A large number of non-academic organizations have extensive research agendas in agricultural and community development, education, community health, environmental issues, gender equity projects, poverty issues, and many other topical areas. In earlier decades, the standard research tools were very often quantitative surveys, supplemented with focus group discussions and various government statistics. More recently, however, ethnographic research methods have been taken up by many or most of those organizations, including widespread adoption of varieties of participatory methods.

A particularly instructive example is the research conducted by the Bangladesh Rural Advancement Committee (BRAC) in Bangladesh. This example is important, as BRAC is the largest NGO in the world, with (reportedly) nearly 20,000 staff people. They operate over 37,000 informal schools for children who are unwilling or unable to attend regular schools. In connection with their very wide range of projects—microfinance for poor women, water and sanitation projects, health services, and others—they have developed a sophisticated research system that includes qualitative and quantitative methods of formative and evaluation research. One especially impressive ethnographic study focused on issues of corruption in emergency rural relief in a rural area. The data-gathering, in ten villages, consisted mainly of key informant interviewing with poor farmers who were the victims of the corrupt practices. After five months of field work, the researchers quickly wrote up a comprehensive report (BRAC 1980). This study was particularly interesting, as the researchers were themselves practitioners in the BRAC rural development program. As a result, the information from the research was put to immediate use by the BRAC workers and some of the poor farmers in the ten study villages (see also Chambers, 1983: 69–73).

I believe that the three cultures model described by Chambers in his early writing identified many needed changes in the structures of research, and that the resulting new developments are happening at a rapid pace among both academic and non-academic research groups. In particular, the serious lack of communication between the two outsider cultures—(academic) researchers and the practitioners—has been considerably reduced, due to a series of influences. A major factor leading to this change, I believe, is that now, in the 21st century, there has been a large increase in the numbers of non-academic researchers and research teams. Many of these are international foundations, organizations supported by the foreign aid programs of European and North American governments, and small and medium-sized NGOs in the developing countries.

ETHNOGRAPHY HAPPENS IN MANY DISCIPLINES

As described in Chapter 1, ethnographic research was already a significant research orientation in sociology early in the 20th century, and researchers in various aspects of education were actively using ethnographic techniques in the middle of the last century. In recent times, however, elements of ethnographic methods have spread widely into other disciplines, particularly in applied research. The diffusion of ethnographic methods among non-academic research groups has contributed to this growing diversity.

THE ELECTRONIC REVOLUTION AND APPLIED ETHNOGRAPHY

It is very clear that the "computer revolution" and the "mobile phone revolution," are having powerful effects on many aspects of ethnographic research. Beginning in the early 1980s, the advent of personal computers (PCs) had the immediate effect of greatly increasing field researchers' output of field notes and other written materials. However, in small and medium-sized NGOs and other groups in South Asia, the newly available personal computers did not immediately affect field research very much, as few groups were able to buy computers until after 1990.

I remember clearly an occasion in 1995 or 1996, when I participated in making arrangements for the purchase of the first computer for a women's studies program at a large university in Baroda (now Vadodara), in western India. That program had a number of faculty persons and many students, but no computers. Even then, in the mid-90s, the plan was to purchase only one computer.

A small, private research NGO in Baroda in those same years had several computers, and a team of three or four data entry persons. Their contract research was carried out by five field researchers, who usually hired local research assistants in their project areas. All field data were gathered on various types of printed protocols, and qualitative data were of course hand written. Also, field researchers wrote out their field reports by hand, and gave those handwritten materials to the computer center for transcribing into the computers. Naturally, there were many times when the computer people were overloaded with entering data in addition to writing correspondence for the director, so the researchers' reports were often delayed due to the conflicting demands at the computers.

In our network of participating research groups in the Ford Foundation "technical assistance" program, almost nobody had email addresses until 2000. Communications within the network were by phone or telegraph. Email communication among multisite researchers, between field workers and their "headquarters," and other computerized communications did not develop among the small and medium-sized NGO researchers until approximately 2000, and some of the smaller organizations did not begin to use email until about 2004–2005. By the year 2000, the situation was changing rapidly. Laptops were becoming more affordable, and much more portable and versatile. I remember a training workshop in 2003 or 2004 for a group at the University of Pune, in which I was surprised to see about eight laptop computers positioned at the conference table.

Until the development of the Internet, people in field sites and most researchers in developing countries had very little access to published research materials. The small and mid-sized NGOs have only minimal research libraries, and even the larger academic institutions in developing countries can afford only small numbers of publications. In addition, the research and action programs in South Asia, Africa and elsewhere publish most of their research results in locally printed reports. Those reports make up a vast "grey literature," which the NGOs and other organizations distribute by mail to the people who are fortunate enough to be on their mailing lists.

By the last decade of the 20th century, many research organizations in developing countries had begun to have computers, which had been the restricted domain of the "specialists" in the "computer center." That monopolizing of computer operations has practically disappeared with the advent of low-cost laptop computers. Now, in the second decade of the 21st century, the use of personal computers, including laptops and other portable equipment, is spreading rapidly to even the small research groups in South Asia and elsewhere in developing countries. At the same time, access to research literature online has expanded dramatically. On the Internet of 2012–2013, a vast amount of research literature is available using various computer search engines. Many of the small and medium-sized Indian NGOs now have attractive websites and other Internet informational outlets, and many can also be found on Facebook and Twitter.

The widespread networking possible online is certainly having an effect on various research programs and field data-gathering. All the research programs that I know of in South Asia now use computers for entering and managing both qualitative and quantitative data. For researchers in developed countries, that is a long established practice, but in South Asia and other developing areas, it has only come about in the 21st century.

The Internet connections that became ubiquitous in the past decade, even among relatively poorly funded NGOs and other research groups, have greatly increased the possibilities for research groups to gain access to research reports, methodological guidelines, direct advice from peers, and other sources of information.

The "mobile phone revolution" is almost entirely a creature of the 21st century. The ramifications—including the strikingly intense interaction between computers and cell phones—are only now (2012–13) being worked out, and the effects on people's communication strategies are still changing. Unlike the advent of personal computers, mobile phones are much less costly, so their use has spread rapidly in many developing countries such as India.

MOBILE PHONES AND ETHNOGRAPHY

In India, the spread of mobile phones has been particularly striking in recent years. In 2005, there were 52 million mobile phones, and by 2009, the number had reached 392 million (Ganju et al. 2010). Newspaper accounts in 2012 mentioned numbers of around 500 million mobile phones registered in the nation. In the ethnographic and quantitative survey studies carried out by the Population Council in 2008–2009, the researchers found that slightly more than half of rural households (55 percent) possessed mobile phones. The negative side of the data is that the phones are overwhelmingly in the hands of men, as only 9 percent of women reported that they had a cell phone. The Population Council research team quoted a typical woman's response:

> I do not have a mobile but I use my husband's mobile phone. Whenever I want to talk I ask him to dial the number." (Ganju et al. 2010: 89)

Most important from the applied point of view is the finding that 60 percent of the village health workers and 83 percent of village-based private practitioners in the rural study sites have mobile phones. Interviews with the frontline health workers found that the mobile phones are frequently used in work communications, such as messages about meetings, reports, and other administrative matters. Some phone communications with families concerning health matters was also reported. The study by the Population Council team in India's Uttar Pradesh was focused on ways in which the spread of mobile phone use is likely to affect health care communications and treatment-seeking.

Researchers are interested in the interactions between ethnographic research and mobile phone/computer technology on (at least) two different levels. First, some researchers are using regular in-depth interviewing and observations to examine the ways in which the new technology has affected people's patterns of communication, for example, in factories, government institutions, and other organizations. The second important area for research is to explore the ways in which the new technology results in innovative new research techniques and strategies. One rapidly developing technique is the use of mobile phones to call informants, for example to ask, "What are you doing right now?" That is, the mobile phone is being used as part of a "spot check" approach to gathering behavioral data. Similarly, phone calls are being used to tell diary-keeping informants to "make an entry in your activity record." A casual search through Internet entries suggests that many of the ethnography-oriented materials concerning the use of mobile phones and other electronic devices are related to marketing research (see also Masten and Plowman 2003; Fitzgerald 2005).

CONCLUSION

Ethnography, in all its many manifestations and data-gathering methods, has a very long and complex history, which I have only touched on lightly. One major assumption in my writing is that the practices of applied ethnographic work are continuing to change and are developing many new approaches and techniques, due to a variety of influences. My examples from South Asia, to which I have devoted considerable attention, illustrate rapid developments in resource-poor areas. Many of the changes taking place are related to the extensive involvement of non-academic organizations in ethnographic research. Among the non-academic entities doing ethnography, many of us are surprised to find a large presence of corporate, commercial interests participating in these activities. In India, some of the involvement of private, corporate entities in ethnographic research has come about because the government has mandated that private corporations must "donate" a certain fraction of their income in social programs. Also, the growth of "public-private partnership" (PPP) arrangements, in health care programs and other sectors, has added to these trends.

However, at least in South Asia, but very likely in many other developing countries, the not-for-profit NGOs are a large and growing presence in ethnographic field research. In the past decade, a large demand for ethnographic research has arisen from HIV/AIDS programs in most parts of the globe. Along with that major focus, many other health programs—on malaria, tuberculosis, and other infectious diseases; heart disease and diabetes control; nutrition/malnutrition; and a wide spectrum of sexual and reproductive health issues—have all seen expanded interest in ethnographic approaches to seeking solutions to practical problems. Community development and poverty-alleviation programs are putting increasing emphasis on ethnographic data-gathering techniques, including various participatory approaches. Some people in community development programs have experienced disappointments in the information from highly structured quantitative surveys, and have put greater reliance on ethnographic methods. In most cases, however, the increasingly common strategy is to use various "mixed methods" approaches. In some of these studies, ethnographic techniques are used in early phases of research, in order to more intelligently and carefully structure the quantitative surveys. Other mixed-methods approaches involve more complex interrelating of the qualitative and quantitative research activities.

Other important programs with a strong interest in ethnographic research methods are focused on the empowerment of women and the promotion of gender equity. These programs are often linked to projects dealing with water management, agricultural improvement, soil conservation, and other environment-oriented activities.

SUMMING IT ALL UP

The many-branched entity—21st century applied ethnography—is a complex mixture of structured and less structured methods, in which distinctions between qualitative and quantitative are elusive and often misleading. The part that is most qualitative is the data-gathering tools, which are a mixed bag of techniques. Many data-gathering strategies are a combination of direct observation and interviewing, designed to get people's verbal descriptions and explanations. Other ethnographic approaches are a loose mixture of highly structured and relatively unstructured interview techniques.

The analysis and presentation of ethnographic products use various combinations of qualitative descriptive materials, interrelated with quantitative treatment of the data. In some cases, "extremely qualitative" raw data—such as people's free-form narratives—can be examined quantitatively, using word-counts, developing ordinal scales (variables), or sorting into major categories, in preparation for statistical analysis. Certain topical areas of applied ethnography, for example, nutrition studies, generally require quantitative analysis in order to be useful. In other topical areas, simple tables of frequencies (e.g., of different severities of domestic violence) may be sufficient quantification, in the midst of plenty of qualitative description. Additionally, some qualitative sets of data, such as collections of case interviews, can be usefully examined with complex multivariate statistics.

Sampling strategies in applied ethnographic research still need improvement. Many "opportunistic samples" are really careless, haphazard samples and can easily lead to biased, misdirected results. Also, some "quota samples" are poorly designed, without the necessary attention to useful categories or variables in assigning "quotas."

The good news is, however, that most ethnographic studies now pay attention to issues relating to sampling. Many contemporary studies are now concerned also with having adequate sample sizes for producing credible, quantitative statements on key features of the topical area. Fortunately, many ethnographic techniques—free listing, pile sorting, etc.—require only small samples. Thirty informants can be enough for some important pieces of data.

A great many applied ethnographic studies are now structured around small or mid-sized samples of case interviews. Studies of abortion-seeking, migrant male workers' sexual behaviors, students' use of cell phones, effects of gender equity intervention in schools, and many other topics are best done with in-depth interviews (sometimes multiple sessions) with samples ranging from 30 to 60 cases or more, depending on the specific target population and the resources of the research organization. Of course, in larger, multi-site studies, small-sample ethnographic research is often coupled with a large-sample quantitative survey.

Most applied ethnographic reports include extensive quoting from both key informants and case interviews in order to present the "voices" of the study populations. Many of the newer ethnographic tools are intended to explore more fully the vocabularies, background knowledge, and reasons for action in the study communities. For planning interventions or understanding problems in an ongoing program, ethnographic studies are developing better techniques for making the best possible use of the "local knowledge and practices" of target communities.

The picture of basic applied ethnographic data-gathering methods that I have presented in this book will not change drastically because of the introduction of ever-newer electronic equipment. What is changing rapidly, especially in developing countries, is the management of the ethnographic data and the computer-based tools for analysis of those materials. Also, communications in complex field teams are now much better developed, and will continue to improve with the newer technology of both Internet use and mobile telephones. The basic face-to-face actions of ethnographic data-gathering will be much less affected by the technological innovations.

REFERENCES

Abboud, L. N. and P. Liamputtong (2007) The experience of childbirth and hospital stay amongst Arabic-speaking immigrant women in Australia. In: *Reproduction, Childbearing and Motherhood: A Cross-cultural Perspective*, edited by P. Liamputtong, 175–194. New York: Nova Science.

AIMS (Asian Institute for Marketing Studies) (1997) Male Sexual Behavior in Orissa. Unpublished Research Report.

Allport, G. (1943) *The Use of Personal Documents in Psychological Science.* New York: Social Science Research Council.

Asia Market Research (2012) Ethnographic Research. http://www.asiamarket research.com/ (accessed May 2012)

Australian School of Business (2011) The Rise of Ethnography: How Market Research Has Gone Gonzo. http://knowledge.asb.unsw.edu.au (accessed April 2012)

Bang, R. and A. Bang (2011) Women's perceptions of white vaginal discharge: ethnographic data from rural Maharashtra. In: *Listening to Women Talk About Their Health: Issues and Evidence from India.* 2nd ed. Edited by J. Gittelsohn, M. E. Bentley, P. J. Pelto, M. Nag, S. Pachauri, A. Harrison, and L. T. Landman, 109–124. New Delhi: Ford Foundation and Har-Anand.

Beals, A. R. (1998, first published in 1976, University of California Press) Strategies of Resort to Curers in South India. In: *Asian Medical Systems: A Comparative Study,* edited by C. Leslie, 184–200. Delhi: Motilal Banarsidass.

Belton, S. (2010) Violence, poverty and 'weakness' the interpersonal and institutional reasons why Burmese women end a pregnancy. In: *Abortion in Asia: Local Dilemmas, Global Politics,* edited by A. Whittaker, 78–101. New York: Berghahn Books.

Belton, S. (2012) Personal Communication.

Bernard, H. R. (1998a) Introduction: On Method and Methods in Anthropology. In: *Handbook of Methods in Cultural Anthropology,* edited by H. R. Bernard, 9–38. Walnut Creek and London: AltaMira.

Bernard, H. R., Editor. (1998b) *Handbook of Methods in Cultural Anthropology.* Walnut Creek and London: AltaMira.

Bernard, H. R. (2002) *Research Methods in Anthropology: Qualitative and Quantitative Approaches.* 3rd ed. Walnut Creek and New York: AltaMira.

Bernard, H. R. (2011) *Research Methods in Anthropology: Qualitative and Quantitative Approaches.* 5th ed. Lanham, MD: AltaMira.

Bernard, H. R., P. J. Pelto, O. Werner, J. Boster, A. K. Romney, A. Johnson, C. R. Ember, and A. Kasakoff (1986) The construction of primary data in cultural anthropology. *Current Anthropology* 27: 382–396.

Bhattacharya, K. (1997) Key Informants, pile sorts, or surveys? Comparing behavioral research methods for the study of acute respiratory infections in West Bengal. In: *An Anthropology of Infectious Disease: International Health Perspectives,* edited by M. C. Inhorn and P. J. Brown, 211–238. London: Routledge.

Bhattacharya, S. and S. K. Senapati (1994) Sexual practices of the sex workers in a red light area of Calcutta. *The Indian Journal of Social Work* 55(4): 547–556.

Bhuiya, A. and A. M. R. Chowdhury (2007) *Tackling Social Determinants of Health; Fifteen years of learning from BRAC-ICDDR,B project in Matlab, Bangaladesh.* Volume 1. Dhaka: BRAC and ICDDR,B.

Biradavolu, M. R., S. Burris, A. George, A. Jena, and K. M. Blankenship (2009) Can sex workers regulate police? Learning from an HIV prevention project for sex workers in southern India. *Social Science & Medicine* 68: 1541–1547.

Blum, L. (1997) Community assessment of natural food sources of vitamin A in Niger: The Hausas of Filingue. In: *Culture, Environment, and Food to Prevent Vitamin A Deficiency,* edited by H.V. Kuhnlein and G. H. Pelto, 71–95. Boston: International Nutrition Foundation for Developing Countries.

Blum, L., P. J. Pelto, G. H. Pelto, and H. V. Kuhnlein (1997) *Community Assessment of Natural Food Sources of Vitamin A: Guidelines for an Ethnographic Protocol.* Boston: International Nutrition Foundation for Developing Countries.

Bolger, N., A. Davis, and E. Rafaeli (2003) Diary methods: Capturing life as it is lived. *Journal of Personality and Social Psychology* 92: 458–475.

Borgatti, S. P. (1993) *ANTHROPAC 4.05.* Columbia, SC: Analytic Industries.

Borgatti, S. P. (no date) ANTHROPAC 4.98 (for Windows). http://www.analyt ictech.com/anthropac/apacdesc.htm

Borgatti, S. P. (1999) Elicitation techniques for cultural domain analysis. In: *Enhanced Ethnographic Methods. Ethnographer's Toolkit No 3,* edited by J. J. Schensul, M. D. LeCompte, B. Nastasi, and S. P. Borgatti, 115-151. Walnut Creek, CA: AltaMira.

Boster, J. S. (1987) Agreement between biological classification systems is not dependent on cultural transmission. *American Anthropologist* 89: 914–920.

BRAC (1980) *The Net: Power Structure in Ten Villages.* Dhaka: Bangladesh Rural Development Committee.

Brewer, D. D. (2002) Supplementary interviewing techniques to maximize output in free listing tasks. *Field Methods* 14(1): 108–118.

Brink, P (1984) Value orientations as an assessment tool in cultural diversity. *Nursing Research* 33(4): 198–203.

Bruce, J. (1990) Fundamental elements of the quality of care: A simple framework. *Studies in Family Planning* 21(2): 61–91.

Burton, M. L. (2003) Too many questions? The uses of incomplete cyclic designs for paired comparisons. *Field Methods* 15(2): 115–130.

Business Dictionary (2011) Definition of ethnography. http://businessdiction ary.com/definition/ethnography.html (accessed November 2011)

Butte College (tip sheet) (2011) Deductive, Inductive and Abductive Reasoning. http://www.butte.edu/departments/cas/tipsheets/thinking/reasoning.html (accessed November 2011)

Campbell, O., J. Cleland, M. Collumbien, and K. Southwick (1999) *Social Science Methods for Research on Reproductive Health.* Geneva: World Health Organization.

Castrén, M. A. (1857) *Nordiska Resor och Forskningar, IV.* Helsingfors (cited in Niiranen 1992).

Caudill, W. (1958) *The Psychiatric Hospital as a Small Society.* Cambridge: Harvard University Press.

Caudill, W. (1998, first published in 1976) The cultural and interpersonal context of everyday health and illness in Japan and America. In: *Asian Medical Systems: A comparative study,* edited by C. Leslie, 159–177. Delhi: Motilal Banarsidass.

Caulkins, D. D., C. Trosset, A. Painter, and M. Good. (2000) Using scenarios to construct models of identity in multiethnic settings. *Field Methods* 12(4): 267–281.

Cernea, M. M. (1992) Re-tooling in applied social investigation for development planning: some methodological Issues. In: *RAP: Rapid Assessment Procedures,* edited by N. Scrimshaw and G. Gleason, 11–24. Boston: International Nutrition Foundation for Developing Countries (INFDC).

Chakravarthy, J. B. R, S. V. Joseph, P. J. Pelto, and D. Kovvali (2012) Community mobilisation programme for female sex workers in coastal Andhra Pradesh, India: Processes and their effects. Swagati Project. *Journal of Epidemiology and Community Health* 66: ii78-ii86.

Chambers, R. (1981) Rapid Rural Appraisal: Rationale and repertoire. *Public Administration and Development* 2(2): 95–106.

Chambers, R. (1983) *Rural Development: Putting the Last First.* London and New York: Longman Group Limited.

Chambers, R. (1997) *Whose Reality Counts? Putting the First Last.* London: Intermediate Technology Publications.

Char, A., M. Säävälä, and T. Kulmala (2010) Influence of mothers-in-law on young couples' family planning decisions in rural India. *Reproductive Health Matters* 18(35): 154–162.

Chhuon, V. and C. Hudley (2010) Asian American ethnic options: How Cambodian students negotiate ethnic identities in a U.S. urban school. *Anthropology and Education Quarterly* 41(4): 341–359.

Chowdhury, A. M. R., A. Bhuiya, and S. M. Ahmed (2007) Introduction and overview. In: *Tackling Social Determinants of Health: Fifteen Years of Learning From BRAC–ICDDR,B Project in Matlab, Bangladesh.* Volume 1, edited by A. Bhuiya and A. M. R. Chowdhury, 1–12. Dhaka: BRAC and ICDDR,B.

Collier, J. (1967) *Visual Anthropology: Photography as a Research Method.* New York: Holt, Rinehart and Winston.

Collings, P. (2009) Participant observation and phased assertion as research strategies in the Canadian Arctic. *Field Methods* 21: 133–153.

Collumbien, M. and S. Hawkes (2000) Missing men's messages: Does the reproductive health approach respond to men's sexual health needs? *Culture, Health, and Sexuality* 2(2): 135–150.

Cornish, F. and R. Ghosh (2007) The necessary contradictions of 'community-led' health promotion: A case study of HIV prevention in an Indian red light district. *Social Science & Medicine* 64: 496–507.

Corti, L. (1993) Using diaries in social research. *Social Research Up-Date* Issue 2. University of Surrey. http://www2.surrey.ac.uk/sociology/ (accessed October 2011)

CREHPA (Center for Research on Environment, Health and Population Activities) (2002a) *Situation Assessment of Intravenous Drug Users in Eastern Terai.* Unpublished report to Family Health International, Kathmandu.

CREHPA (2002b) *Situation Assessment of Sex Workers and Intravenous Drug Users in Kathmandu Valley.* Unpublished report to Family Health International, Kathmandu.

CREHPA (2013) Institutional Profile. http://www.crehpa.org.np/institutional_profile.html (accessed February 2013)

Cumming, R. G. (1990) Is probability sampling always better? A comparison of results from a quota and a probability sample survey. *Community Health Studies* 14(2):132–137. www.ncbi.nlm.nih.gov/pubmed/2208977 (accessed February 2012)

D'Antona, A. D. O., A. D. Cak, and L. K. Vanwey (2008) Collecting sketch maps to understand property land use and land cover in large surveys. *Field Methods* 20(1): 66–84.

de Silva, M. W. A., K. Millawithanachchi, A. Herath, S. Weerasinghe, R. Wickremasinghe, J. Pinikahane, R. O. Thatil, and K. N. Mendis (1994) Recall of malaria incidents as a measure of health attentiveness of women in rural Sri Lanka. Paper presented at the Annual Meeting of the Sri Lanka Association for the Advancement of Science, Colombo, Sri Lanka. (SLAAS, A12: 10–11).

de Silva, M. W. A., J. Lewis, and P. J. Pelto. (2002) Food gifts, kinship and weight gain during pregnancy in rural Sri Lanka. *The Sri Lanka Journal of the Humanities*, XXVII & XXVIII (Numbers 1 & 2): 38–58. University of Peradeniya, Sri Lanka.

de Silva, M. W. A. (2011) Personal communication.

Devin, R. B. and P. I. Erickson (1996) The influence of male care givers on child health in rural Haiti. *Social Science and Medicine* 43(4): 479–488.

DeWalt, B. R. (1979) Drinking behavior, economic status, and adaptive strategies of modernization in a highland Mexican community. *American Ethnologist* 6(3): 510–530.

DeWalt, K. M. and B. R. DeWalt (2010) *Participant Observation: A Guide for Fieldworkers.* Walnut Creek and New York: AltaMira.

Douven, I. (2011) "Abduction." *The Stanford Encyclopedia of Philosophy. Spring 2011,* edited by Edward N. Zalta. http://plato.stanford.edu/archives/ spr2011/entries/abduction/ (accessed October 2012)

Dowell, S. F. and J. D. Heffelfinger (1998) RE: Consultation in Jeremie, Haiti (December 13 to December 19, 1997). Unpublished memo to Drs. Bette Gebrian, Lloyd Feinberg, Elizabeth Holt, dated January 19, 1998.

Dressler, W. W. (2007) Meaning, measurement, and ethnography. Paper presented at the 106th Annual Meeting of the American Anthropological Association. Washington, D.C., Nov 28–Dec 2, 2007.

Dressler, W. W., C.D. Borges, M.C. Balieiro, and J. E. Dos Santos (2005) Measuring cultural consonance: Examples with special reference to measurement theory in anthropology. *Field Methods* 17(4): 331–355.

Eldredge, N. (2005) *Darwin: Discovering the Tree of Life.* New York: Norton.

Eliot, S (2010) Taking notes vs. recording interviews. (blog post) *The Listening Resource.*

http://www.qualitative-researcher.com/interviews/taking-notes-instead-of-recording-the-interview (accessed October 2012)

Erasmus, C. J. (1955) Work patterns in a Mayo village. *American Anthropologist* 57: 322–333.

Erickson, F. and G. Mohatt (1982) Cultural organization of participation structures in two classrooms of Indian students. In: *Doing the Ethnography of Schooling: Educational Anthropology in Action,* edited by G. Spindler, 132–175. New York: Holt, Rinehart, and Winston.

Ethnographic Insight, Inc. (2011) *Our Services and Methods.* www.ethno-insight.com/ourservices.html (accessed November 2011)

Ethnography and Education. http://www.ethnographyandeducation.org (accessed July 2012)

Fitzgerald, M. (2005) Corporate Ethnography. *Technology Review* Nov 17, 2005. Cambridge, MA: MIT http://www.technologyreview.com/news/404920/corporate-ethnography/ (accessed August 2012)

Fluehr-Lobban, C. (1998) Ethics. In: *Handbook of Methods in Cultural Anthropology,* edited by H. R. Bernard, 173–202. Walnut Creek and London: AltaMira.

Free Dictionary (2011) Definition of ethnography. www.thefreedictionary.com/ethnography (accessed November 2011)

Freilich, M. (1977) Mohawk heroes and trinidadian peasants. In *Marginal Natives: Anthropologists at Work,* edited by M. Freilich, 185–250. New York: Harper and Row.

Ganju, D., I. Bhatnagar, A. Hazra, S. Jain, and M.E. Khan (2010) Reach of media and interpersonal communication in rural Uttar Pradesh. *Journal of Family Welfare* 56 (Special Issue): 83–91.

George, C. K., B. S. Kavitha, N. S. Reddy, and B. Srikanthi (2005) Frontiers Prevention Program outcome evaluation: qualitative baseline of the India Program. Report submitted to International HIV/AIDS Alliance. Hyderabad: The Institute of Health Systems.

Gittelsohn, J. (1991) Opening the box: Intrahousehold food distribution in rural Nepal. *Social Science and Medicine* 33(10): 1141–1154.

Gittelsohn, J., M. E. Bentley, P. J. Pelto, M. Nag, S. Pachauri, A. D. Harris, and L.T. Landman (2011) *Listening to Women Talk about Their Health.* 2nd ed. New Delhi: Har-Anand Publications / Ford Foundation.

Gittelsohn, J., A.V. Shankar, K. P. West Jr., R. Ram, and T. Gnywali (1997) Estimating reactivity in direct observation studies of health behaviors. *Human Organization* 56(2): 182–189.

Gittelsohn, J., P. J. Pelto, M. E. Bentley, K. Bhattacharya, and J. L. Jensen (1998) Rapid Assessment Procedures (RAP): Ethnographic Methods to Investigate Women's Health. Boston: International Nutrition Foundation. http://archive.unu.edu/unupress/food2/UIN01E/UIN01E00.HTM (accessed November 2012)

Glaser, B. G. and A. Strauss (1967) *The Discovery of Grounded Theory. Strategies for Qualitative Research.* New York: Aldine.

Glasser, I. (2012) *Anthropology of Addictions and Recovery.* Long Grove, IL: Waveland.

Gotschi, E., R. Delve, and B. Freyer (2009) Participant photography as a qualitative approach to obtain insights into farmer groups. *Field Methods* 21 (3): 290–308.

Gove, S. and G. H. Pelto (1994) Focused ethnographic studies in the WHO programme for the control of Aacute respiratory infections. *Medical Anthropology* 15(4): 409–424.

Gravlee, C. C., S. N. Zenk, S. Woods, Z Rowe, and A. I. Schulz (2007) Handheld computers for direct observation of the social and physical environment. *Field Methods* 19(4): 382–397.

Hames, R. and C. McCabe (2007) Meal sharing among the Ye'kwana. *Human Nature* 18: 1–21.

Hammersley, M. (1992) *What's Wrong with Ethnography?* London and New York. Routledge.

Handwerker, W. P (2001) *Quick Ethnography.* Walnut Creek and New York: AltaMira.

Harvey, S. A., M. P. Olortegui, E. Leontsini, and P. J. Winch (2009) They'll change what they're doing if they know that you're watching: Measuring reactivity in health behavior because of an observer's presence—a case from the Peruvian Amazon. *Field Methods* 21(1): 3–25.

Hawkes, S. (1998) Why include men? Establishing sexual health clinics for men in rural Bangladesh. *Health Policy and Planning* 13(2): 121–130.

Hawkes, S. and G. Hart (2003) Reproductive Health: men's roles and men's rights. In: *Reproductive Tract Infections and Other Gynaecological Disorders,* edited by Jejeebhoy, S., M. Koenig and C. Elias, 82–105. Cambridge: Cambridge University Press.

HEAT (2012) Health Equity Alliance of Tallahassee. http://www.healthequity-alliance.org/ (accessed September 2012)

Heffelfinger, J. D., T. E. Davis, B. Gebrian, R. Bordeau, B. Schwartz, and S. F. Dowell (2002) Evaluation of children with recurrent pneumonia diagnosed by World Health Organization criteria. *Pediatric Infectious Disease Journal* 21(2): 108–12.

Helitzer-Allen, D. M., M. Makhambera and A.M. Wrangel (1994) Obtaining sensitive information: The need for more than focus groups. *Reproductive Health Matters* 3: 75–81.

Henley, N. M. (1969) A psychological study of the semantics of animal terms. *Learning and Verbal Behavior* 8: 176–184.

Herlihy, P. H. and G. Knapp (2003) Maps of, by, and for the peoples of Latin America. *Human Organization* 62(4): 303–314.

Herskovits, M. J. (1950) The hypothetical situation: A technique of field research. *Southwestern Journal of Anthropology* 6(1): 32–40.

Hossain, S. M. I., M. E. Khan, M. Rahman, and U. Rob (n.d.) Sexual health problems and treatments: street-based and newspaper advertising by "sexologist" practitioners in Bangladesh. In: *Sexuality, Gender Roles and Domestic Violence in South Asia* This completed manuscript has been submitted for publication.

Hudelson, P. M. (1994) The management of acute respiratory infections in Honduras. *Medical Anthropology* 15(4): 435–446.

Izugbara, C. O. and J. K. Ukwayi (2007) The hospital as a birthing site: Narratives of local women in Nigeria. In: *Reproduction, Childbearing and Motherhood: A Cross-Cultural Perspective*, edited by P. Liamputtong, 143–158. New York: Nova Science.

Johnson, A. (1975) Time allocation in a Machiguenga community. *Ethnology* 14: 310–321.

Johnson, A. and R. Sackett (1998) Direct systematic observation of behavior. In: *Handbook of Methods in Cultural Anthropology*, edited by H. R. Bernard, 301–331. Walnut Creek and London: AltaMira.

Johnson, J. C., C. Avenarius and J. Weatherford (2006) The active participant-observer: Applying social role analysis to participant observation. *Field Methods* 18(2): 111–134.

Jordan, B. and B. Dalal (2006) Persuasive encounters: Ethnography in the corporation. *Field Methods* 18(4): 359–381.

Joshi, A., M. Dhapola, and P. J. Pelto (2008) Gynaecological problems: Perceptions and treatment-seeking behaviours of rural Gujarati women. In *Reproductive Health in India: New Evidence*, edited by Koenig, M. A., S. Jejeebhoy, J. C. Cleland, and B. Ganatra, 133–158. Jaipur and New Delhi: Rawat.

Kaplowitz, M. D. (2000) Statistical analysis of sensitive topics in group and individuals interviews. *Quality & Quantity* 34(4): 419–431.

Kendall, C., E. Leontsini, E. Gil, E. Cruz, P. Hudelson, and P. J. Pelto (1990) Exploratory ethnoentomology. *Cultural Anthropology Methods* 2(2): 11.

Khan, M. E. and A. Aeron (2006) The prevalence, nature and determinants of violence against women in Bangladesh. *The Journal of Family Welfare* 52 (Commemorative Issue in memory of Mrs. Avabai B. Wadia): 33–51.

Khan, M. E., A. Hazra, and I. Bhatnagar (2010) Impact of Janani Suraksha Yojana on selected family health behaviors in rural Uttar Pradesh. *The Journal of Family Welfare* 56(Special Issue): 9–22.

Kiley, D. (2005) Shoot the focus group. *Business Week*, November 14: 120–121.

Killworth, P. D. and H. R. Bernard (1976) Informant accuracy in social network data. *Human Organization* 35: 269–286.

Killworth, P. D. and H. R. Bernard (1979) Informant accuracy in social network data III. *Social Networks* 2: 19–46.

Kis, A. D. (2007) An analysis of the impact of AIDS on funeral culture in Malawi. *Napa Bulletin* 27: 129–140.

Koenig, M. A., S. Jejeebhoy, J. C. Cleland, and B. Ganatra, Editors. (2008) *Reproductive Health in India: New Evidence*. New Delhi and Mumbai: Rawat.

Kresno, S., G. Harrison, B. Sutrisna, and A. Feingold. (1994) Acute respiratory illnesses in children under five years in Indramayo, West Java, Indonesia: A rapid ethnographic assessment. *Medical Anthropology* 15(4): 425–434.

Kuhnlein, H. V. and G. H. Pelto (1997) *Culture, Environment, and Food to Prevent Vitamin A Deficiency.* Boston: International Nutrition Foundation for Developing Countries (INFDC).

Kulkarni, V., S. Kulkarni, and K. R. Spaeth (2004) Men who have sex with men: A study in urban Western Maharashtra. In: *Sexuality in the Time of AIDS: Contemporary Perspectives from Communities in India,* edited by R. K. Verma, P. J. Pelto, S. L. Schensul, and A. Joshi, 195–216. New Delhi and London: Sage.

LeCompte, M. D. (1975) Institutional constraints on teacher styles and the development of student work norms. Doctoral dissertation. University of Chicago.

LeCompte, M. D. and J. Preissle (1993) *Ethnography and Qualitative Design in Educational Research.* 2nd ed. San Diego and New York: Academic Press.

LeCompte, M. D., D. Millroy, and J. Preissle (1992) *The Handbook of Qualitative Research in Education.* San Diego and New York: Academic Press.

LeCompte, M. D. and J. J. Schensul (1999) *Designing and Conducting Ethnographic Research. Vol 1. Ethnographer's Toolkit.* Walnut Creek, CA: AltaMira.

Leininger, M. M., Editor. (1985) *Qualitative Research Methods in Nursing.* New York: Grune & Stratton.

Leininger, M. and M. McFarland (2002) *Transcultural Nursing: Concepts, Theories, Research and Practice.* 3rd ed. New York: McGraw-Hill.

Lewis, J. and B. Gebrian (2009) No family left behind: The example of community-based pneumonia care in Haiti. *Journal of Health Care for the Poor and Underserved* 20: 22–30.

Lieberman, D. and W. W. Dressler (1977) Bilingualism and cognition of St. Lucian disease terms. *Medical Anthropology* 1: 81–110.

Lipka, J. and B. Adams (2004) Some evidence for ethnomathematics: Quantitative and qualitative data from Alaska. Paper presented at the 10th International Congress on Mathematical Education, Copenhagen, Denmark.

Lipka, J., M. P. Hogan, J. P. Webster, E. Yanez, B. Adams, and S. Clark (2005) Math in a cultural context: Two case studies of a successful culturally based math project. *Anthropology and Education Quarterly* 36(4): 367–385.

McFarland, J. (2001) Margaret Mead Meets Consumer Fieldwork. *Harvard Management Update.* http://hbswk.hbs.edu/archive/2514.html (accessed April 2012)

Maginn, P. J. (2007) Negotiating and securing access: Reflections from a study into urban regeneration and community participation in ethnically diverse neighborhoods in London, England. *Field Methods* 19(4): 425–449.

Malinowski, B. (1961, first published 1922) *Argonauts of the Western Pacific.* New York: E. P. Dutton.

Malinowski, B. (1989, first published 1967) *A Diary in the Strict Sense of the Term.* Stanford: Stanford University Press.

Maloney, C., K. M. A. Aziz, and P. C. Sarker (1981) *Beliefs and Fertility in Bangladesh.* Dhaka: International Centre for Diarrhoeal Disease Research, Bangladesh. Monograph No. 2.

Maman, S., T. Lane, J. Ntogwisangu, S. P. Modiba, H. van Rooyen, A. Timbe, S. Visrutaratna, and K. Fritz (2009) Using participatory mapping to inform a community-randomized trial of HIV counseling and testing. *Field Methods* 21(4): 368–387.

Markovic, M (2006) Analyzing qualitative data: Health care experiences of women with gynecological cancer. *Field Methods* 18(4): 413–429.

Mascarenhas, J. (1990) Transects in PRA. *PRA-PALM Series Paper* 4E. Bangalore: MYRADA. http://myrada.org/myrada/pra4e (accessed July 2012)

Mascarenhas, J. (1992) Participatory rural appraisal and participatory learning methods: Recent experiences from MYRADA and South India. In: *RAP: Rapid Assessment Procedures,* edited by N. Scrimshaw and G. Gleason, 307321 Boston: International Nutrition Foundation for Developing Countries (INFDC).

Masten, D. and T. M. P. Plowman (2003) Digital ethnography: The next wave in understanding the consumer experience. *Design Management Journal* 14(2) Reprint #03142MAS75. http://www.dmi.org/dmi/html/interests/research/03142MAS75.pdf (accessed August 2012)

Mavalankar, D. and B. Sharma (1999) Quality of care in sterilization camps: Evidence from Gujarat. In: *Improving Quality of Care in India's Family Welfare Programme: The Challenge Ahead,* edited by M. A Koenig and M. E. Khan, 293–313 New York: The Population Council.

Maxwell, J. A. (2004) Using qualitative methods for causal explanation. *Field Methods* 16(3): 243–264.

Mead, M. (1977) *Letters from the Field 1925–1975.* New York: Harper Colophon.

Morse, J. M. (1991) The structure and function of gift giving in the patient-nurse relationship. *Western Journal of Nursing Research* 13(5): 597–615.

Morse, J. M. (2012) *Qualitative Health Research: Creating a New Discipline.* Walnut Creek, CA: Left Coast Press, Inc.

Morse, J. M. (2013) The development of qualitative nursing research. In: *Routledge International Handbook of Qualitative Nursing Research,* edited by C. T. Beck, Routledge (forthcoming).

Morse, J. M. and P. A. Field (1996) *Nursing Research: The Application of Qualitative Approaches.* 2nd ed. London: Chapman and Hall (Reprinted in 2002 by Nelson Thomas Ltd., Cheltenham).

Morse, J. M. and L. Niehaus (2009) *Mixed Method Design: Principles and Procedures.* Walnut Creek, CA: Left Coast Press, Inc.

Müller-Wille, L. (1984) The legacy of native toponyms: Towards the establishing of the Inuit place name inventory of the Kativik region (Québec). *Onomastica Canadiana* 65: 2–19.

Müller-Wille, L. (1987) Inuit place names of Nunavik: The making of the gazetteer. In: *Gazetteer of Inuit Place Names in Nunavik (Quebec, Canada),* Müller-Wille, L. in conjunction with the Inuit Elders of Nunavik and Avataq Cultural Institute. Inukjuak: Avataq Cultural Institute. 1–23.

Müller-Wille, L. (Editor) (1998) *Franz Boas among the Inuit of Baffin Island 1883-1884. Journals and Diaries.* Translated by William Barr. Toronto, Buffalo, London: University of Toronto Press.

Müller Wille, L. and L. Weber Müller-Wille (1983) Inuit place name inventory of Northeastern Québec Labrador. Presented by Avataq Cultural Institute Inukjuak. *McGill Subarctic Research Papers* 37: 151–222. Montréal: Centre for Northern Studies and Research, McGill University.

Müller-Wille, L. and L. Weber Müller-Wille (1989) Toponymic inquiry and oral tradition. The Nuna-Top method: Surveying indigenous geographical names in Canada. Manuscript prepared for the Canadian Permanent Committee on Geographical Names, Ministry of Energy, Mines and Resources, Ottawa, Canada. (Also partially published as Guide to the Field Collection of Native Geographical Names. Ottawa, 1992). http://geonames.nrcan.gc.ca/pdf/native_field_guide_e.pdf (accessed June 2012)

Müller-Wille, L. and L. Weber Müller-Wille (2006) Inuit geographical knowledge one hundred years apart: Place names in Tinijjuarvik (Cumberland Sound), Nunavut. In: *Inuit Studies in an of Era Globalization,* edited by Stern, P. and L. Stevenson, 217–229. Lincoln, NE: University of Nebraska Press.

Mutatkar, R. K., P. J. Pelto, N. Mawar, A. Kaulagekar, and H. Apte, Editors. (2005) *Sexuality and Sexual Behaviour: Social Science Perspective.* Pune: University of Pune.

Myntti, C. (1993) Social determinants of child health in Yemen. *Social Science and Medicine* 37(2): 233–240.

Naroll, R. (1962) *Data Quality Control: A New Research Technique.* New York: Free Press.

Niiranen, T. (1992) Pioneers of Finnish Ethnology. In: *Pioneers: The History of Finnish Ethnology. (Studia Fennica/Ethnologia* 1), edited by M. Räsänen, 21–40. Helsinki: The Finnish Literature Society.

Nkwi, P. N., I. K. Nyamongo, and G. W. Ryan (2001) *Field Research into Sociocultural Issues: Methodological guidelines.* Yaoundé, Camaroon: International Center for Advanced Social Science Research and Training (ICASSRT).

Ogbu, J. U. (1974) *The Next Generation: An Ethnography of Education in an Urban Neighborhood.* New York: Academic Press.

Oliver-Velez, D., H. A. Finlinson, S. Deren, R. R. Robles, M. Shedlin, J. Andia, and H. Colon (2002) Mapping the air-bridge locations: The application of ethnograpic mapping techiques to a study of HIV risk behavior determinants in East Harlem, New York, and Bayamon, Puerto Rico. *Human Organization* 61(3): 262–276

Paolisso, M. and R. Hames (2010) Time diary versus instantaneous sampling: A comparison of two behavioral research methods. *Field Methods* 22(4): 357–377.

Patel, P. (2011) Illness beliefs and health-seeking behaviour of the Bhil women of Panchamahal district, Gujurat state. In: *Listening to Women Talk About Their Health*. 2nd ed., edited by J. Gittelsohn, M. E. Bentley, P. J. Pelto, M. Nag, S. Pachauri, A. Harrison, and L. Landman, 85–96. New Delhi: Ford Foundation and Har-Anand.

Patel, V. and N. Oomman (1999) Mental health matters, too: Gynaecological symptoms and depression in South Asia. *Reproductive Health Matters* 7(14): 30–38.

Patel, V., G. Andrew and P. J. Pelto (2008) The psychological and social contexts of complaints of abnormal vaginal discharge: A study of illness narratives in India. *Journal of Psychosomatic Research* 64(3): 255–262.

Patton, M. Q. (2002) *Qualitative Research and Evaluation Methods*. 3rd ed. Thousand Oaks, CA: Sage.

Paul, B. (Editor) (1955) *Health, Culture and Community*. New York: Russell Sage Foundation.

Pelto, G. H. and S. Gove (1992) Developing a focused ethnographic study for the WHO Acute Respiratory Infections Control Program. In: *Qualitative Methodologies for Planning and Evaluation of Health Related Programmes*, edited by Scrimshaw, N. and G. Gleason, 215–226. Boston: International Nutrition Foundation for Developing Countries.

Pelto, G. H. and M. Armar-Klemesu (2011) Balancing nurturance, cost and time: Complementary feeding in Accra, Ghana. *Maternal and Child Nutrition* 7(Suppl. 3): 66–81.

Pelto, G. H., M. Armar-Klemesu, J. Siekmann, and D. Schofield (2013) *The Focused Ethnographic Study 'Assessing the Behavioral and Local Market Environment for Improving the Diets of Infants and Young Children 6 to 23 Months Old' and its use in three countries*. In press.

Pelto, P. J. (1958) Unpublished field notes (typewritten).

Pelto, P. J. (1970) *Anthropological Research: The Structure of Inquiry*. New York: Harper and Row.

Pelto, P.J. (1994) Focused ethnographic studies of sexual behaviour and AIDS/ STDs. *The Indian Journal of Social Work* (Special Issue on Sexual Behaviour and AIDS in India): 589–602.

Pelto, P. J. (2006) *Frontiers prevention project (FPP): Triangulating the qualitative and quantitative data sets from the baseline studies.* Report submitted to the International AIDS Alliance (UK).

Pelto, P. J. and J. Cleland (2003) Integrating qualitative and quantitative methods in research on reproductive health. In: *Reproductive Tract Infections and other Gynaecological Disorders,* edited by S. Jejeebhoy, M. Koenig, and C. Elias, 360–390. Cambridge: Cambridge University Press.

Pelto, P. J. and G. H. Pelto (1978) *Anthropological Research: The Structure of Inquiry.* 2nd ed. Cambridge: Cambridge University Press.

Pentikäinen, J. (2002) Northern ethnography. In: *Styles and Positions: Ethnographic Perspectives in Comparative Religion,* edited by T. Sakaranaho, T. Sjöblom, T. Utriainen, and H. Pesonen, 20–45. Helsinki: Department of Comparative Religion, University of Helsinki.

Pickering, H., J. Todd, D. Dunn. J. Pepin, and A. Wilkins (1992) Prostitutes and their clients: A Gambian survey. *Social Science and Medicine* 34(1): 75–88.

Poggie, J. and P. J. Pelto. 1969. Matrilateral asymmetry in the American kinship system. *Anthropological Quarterly* 42: 1–15.

Pollnac, R. B. and J. M. Hickman (1975) Abduction and statistical inference of interaction patterns: An analysis of data from Peru, Uganda, and Iron Age France. *Sociologus* 25(1): 28–61.

Quinlan, M. (2005) Considerations for collecting freelists in medical ethnobotany. *Field Methods* 17(3): 219–234.

Quintero, G., K. Young, N. Nier, and S. Jenks (2005) Perceptions of drinking among Hispanic college students: How qualitative research can inform the development of college alcohol abuse prevention programs. *Journal of Drug Education* 35(4): 291–304.

Ramachandar, L. (2003) *Decision-making and women's empowerment: Abortion in a South Indian community.* Doctoral Dissertation. The Key Centre for Women's Health in Society. The University of Melbourne, Australia.

Ramachandar, L. (2008) Recent changes in MTP using Mifepristone-Misoprostol in Dharmapuri District, Tamil Nadu. Report submitted to the Directorate of Family Welfare, Chennai, India.

Ramachandar, L. (2009a) Unpublished field notes. Bellary District, Karnataka.

Ramachandar, L. (2009b) Costs of abortions and their impact on the rural/tribal households in Gomia (Bokaro District), Jharkhand. Report to Family Planning Association of India, Mumbai. 62 pages (with photographs).

Ramachandar, L. (2010) Unpublished field notes. Bellary District, Karnataka.

Ramachandar, L. and S. Barge (1999) The quality of services at Laparoscopic Sterilization Camps in Madhya Pradesh. In: *Improving Quality of Care in India's Family Welfare Programme: The Challenge Ahead,* edited by M. A Koenig and M. E. Khan, 273–292. New York: The Population Council.

Ramachandar, L. and P. J. Pelto (2005) Medical abortion in rural Tamil Nadu, South India: A quiet transformation. *Reproductive Health Matters* 13(26): 54–64.

Ramasubramanian, S. and M. B. Oliver (2003) Portrayals of sexual violence in popular Hindi films, 1997–1999. *Sex Roles* 48(7–8): 327–336.

Rashid, S. F. (2007) Durbolata (weakness), chinta rog (worry illness) and poverty: Explanations of white discharge among married adolescent women in an urban slum in Dhaka, Bangladesh. *Medical Anthropology Quarterly* 21(1): 108–132.

Reichardt, C. S. and T. D. Cook (1979) Beyond qualitative versus quantitative methods. In: *Qualitative and Quantitative Methods in Evaluation Research,* edited by T.D. Cook and C. S. Reichardt, 7–32. Beverley Hills, CA and London: Sage.

Rhoades, R. E. (1992) The coming revolution in methods for rural development research. In: *RAP: Rapid Assessment Procedures,* edited by N. Scrimshaw and G. Gleason, 61–78. Boston: International Nutrition Foundation for Developing Countries (INFDC).

Rivers, W. H. R. (1906) *The Todas.* New York: Macmillan.

Robbins, M. C. and J. M. Nolan (2000) A measure of semantic category clustering in free-listing tasks. *Field Methods* 12(1): 1–28.

Rocha, J. (2005) Measuring traditional agro-ecological knowledge: An example from peasants in the Peruvian Andes. *Field Methods* 17(4): 356–372.

Romney, A. K., S. C. Weller, and W. H. Batchelder (1986) Cultural consensus: A theory of culture and informant accuracy. *American Anthropologist* 88: 313–338.

Romney, A. K., W. H. Batchelder, and T. Brazill (1995) Scaling semantic domains. In: *Geometric Representations of Perceptual Phenomena: Essays in Honor of Tarow Indow,* edited by R. D. Luce, M. D'Zmura, D. Hoffman, G. Iverson, and A. K. Romney, 267–294. Mahway, NJ: Lawrence Erlbaum.

Romney, A. K. and R. G. D'Andrade (1964) Cognitive aspects of English kin terms. *American Anthropologist* 66(3, pt.2): 46–70.

Ross, J. L., S. L. Laston, K. Nahar, L. Muna, P. Nahar, and P. J. Pelto (1998) Women's health priorities: Cultural perspectives on illness in rural Bangladesh. *Health: An Interdisciplinary Journal for the Social Study of Health, Illness and Medicine* 2(1): 91–110.

Ross, N. and D. L. Medin (2005) Ethnography and experiments: Cultural models and expertise effects elicited with experimental research techniques. *Field Methods* 17(2): 131–149.

Rubin, R. J. and I. S. Rubin (1995) *Qualitative Interviewing: The Art of Hearing Data.* Thousand Oaks and London: Sage.

Saggurti, N., R. K. Verma, H. Reddy, N. Ramarao, A. K. Singh, V. S. Mahendra, and A. Jain (2008) *Patterns of Migration/Mobility and HIV Risk Among Female Sex Workers.* Andhra Pradesh 2007–2008. New Delhi: Population Council.

Sanjek, R. Editor. (1990) Fieldnotes: The Making of Anthropology. Ithaca, NY: Cornell University Press.

Scaglion, R. (1986) The importance of nighttime observations in time allocation studies. *American Ethnologist* 13:537–545.

Schensul, S. L., J. J. Schensul, and M. D. LeCompte (1999) *Essential Ethnographic Methods. Vol 2. Ethnographer's Toolkit.* Walnut Creek, CA: AltaMira.

Schweizer, T. (1998) Epistemology: The Nature and Validation of Anthropological Knowledge. In: *Handbook of Methods in Cultural Anthropology,* edited by H. R. Bernard, 39–88. Walnut Creek and London: AltaMira.

Scrimshaw, N. S. and G. R. Gleason (Editors) (1992) *RAP: Rapid Assessment Procedures: Qualitative Methodologies for Planning and Evaluation of Health Related Programmes.* Boston: International Nutrition Foundation for Developing Countries (INFDC).

Scrimshaw, S. C. M. and E. Hutado (1987) *Rapid Assessment Procedures for Nutrition and Primary Health Care: Anthropological Approaches to Improving Programme Effectiveness.* Tokyo: The United Nations University, UNICEF and Los Angeles: UCLA Latin American Center.

Silverman, S. F. (1966) An ethnographic approach to social stratification: Prestige in a central Italian community. *American Anthropologist* 68(4): 899–921.

Sloand, E., N. M. Astone, and B. Gebrian (2010) The impact of fathers' clubs on child health in rural Haiti: Field action report. *American Journal of Public Health* 100(2): 201–204.

Smith, J. J. (1993) Using ANTHROPAC 3.5 and a spreadsheet to compute a free-list salience index. *Cultural Anthropology Methods Newsletter* 5(3): 1–3.

Smucker, T. A., D. J. Campbell, J. M. Olson, and E. E. Wangui (2007) Contemporary challenges of participatory field research for land use change analyses: Examples from Kenya. *Field Methods* 19(4): 38–406.

Sokolova, Z. P. (1992) On the role of the Russian Geographical Society and its Department of Anthropology as well as of the Academy of Sciences of Russia in the Development of Studies in the Peoples Kindred to the Finns. In: *Pioneers: The History of Finnish Ethnology.* (Studia Fennica/Ethnologica 1), edited by M. Räsänen, 9–20. Helsinki: The Finnish Literature Society.

Soleri, D. and D. A. Cleveland (2005) Scenarios as a tool for eliciting and understanding farmers biological knowledge. *Field Methods* 17(3): 283–301.

Sorokin, P. A. and C. Q. Berger (1938) *Time Budgets of Human Behaviour.* Cambridge, MA: Harvard University Press.

Spindler, G. (Editor) (1982) *Doing the Ethnography of Schooling: Educational Anthropology in Action.* New York: Holt, Rinehart and Winston.

Spradley, J. P. (1979) *The Ethnographic Interview.* New York: Holt, Rinehart and Winston.

Stocks, A. (2003) Mapping dreams in Nicaragua's Bosawas Reserve. *Human Organization* 62(4): 344–356.

Subbiah, A., S. Ramachandran, A. K. Ravi Shankar, N. Saggurti, R. K. Verma, A. Jain, S. Rama-Rao, S. N. Swain, and A. K. Singh (2008) *Migration/Mobility and Vulnerability to HIV among Male Migrant Workers, Tamil Nadu.* Chidambaram: Annamalai University and New Delhi: Population Council.

Tamang, A., B. Nepal, M. Puri, and D. Shrestha (2001) Sexual behaviours and risk perceptions among young men in border towns in Nepal. *Asia-Pacific Population Journal* 16(2): 195–210.

The Hindu (2010) Street, home-based sex workers on the rise in state. The Hindu. Hyderabad, Jan 2010. www.hindu.com/2010/01/06/stories/2010010654500400.htm (accessed July 2012)

Thompson, E. C. and Zhang Juan (2006) Comparative cultural salience: Measures using free-list data. *Field Methods* 18(4): 398–412.

Tiilikainen, M. and P. H. Koehn (2011) Transforming the boundaries of health care: Insights from Somali migrants. *Medical Anthropology: Cross-Cultural Studies in Health and Illness.* 30(5): 518–544.

Tiilikainen, M. (2002) Homes and fields, friends and informants. In: *Styles and Positions: Ethnographic Perspectives in Comparative Religion,* edited by T. Sakaranaho, T. Sjöblom, T. Utriainen, and H. Pesonen, 272–289. Helsinki: Department of Comparative Religion. University of Helsinki.

Trotter, R. T. (1981) Remedios caseros: Mexican-American home remedies and community health problems. *Social Science and Medicine* 15B: 107–114.

Trotter, R. T. and J. J. Schensul (1998) Methods in Applied Anthropology. In: *Handbook of Methods in Cultural Anthropology,* edited by H.R. Bernard, 691–736. Walnut Creek and London: AltaMira.

Vasan, A. (2010) Films and TV: Viewing patterns and influence on behaviours of college students. *Health and Population Innovation Fellowship Program Working Papers* No 13. New Delhi: Population Council.

Verma, R. K., G. Rangaiyan, S. Sharma, and P. J. Pelto (1999). Cultural perceptions and categorization of male sexual health problems by practitioners and men in a Mumbai slum population. *Ford Foundation Working Papers in Reproductive Health.* New Delhi: Ford Foundation.

Verma, R. K., P. J. Pelto, S. L. Schensul, and A. Joshi, Editors. (2004) *Sexuality in the Time of AIDS: Contemporary Perspectives from Communities in India,* New Delhi and London: Sage.

Wang, C., M. A. Burris, and X. Y. Ping (1996) Chinese village women as visual anthropologists: A participatory approach to reaching policy makers. *Social Science and Medicine* 42(10): 391–400.

Wang, C. and M. A. Burris (1997) Photovoice: Concept, methodology and use for participatory needs assessment. *Health Education and Behavior* 24(3): 369–387.

Wax, R. *Doing Fieldwork: Warnings and Advice.* Chicago and London: University of Chicago Press.

Weitzman, E. and M. Miles (1995) *Computer Programs for Qualitative Data Analysis.* Thousand Oaks, CA: Sage.

Weller, S. C. and A. K. Romney (1988) *Systematic Data Collection.* Newbury Park and London: Sage.

Whyte, W. F. (1993) *Street Corner Society: The Social Structure of an Italian Slum.* 4th ed. Chicago and London: University of Chicago Press.

Whyte, W. F. and K. K. Whyte (1984) *Learning from the Field: A Guide from Experience.* Beverley Hills, CA: Sage.

Williams, R. L. *Traditional and herbal treatments of ARI.* Presented at: Student Research Day Presentation, University of Connecticut School of Medicine, Farmington (CT), Feb 2000.

Wolcott, H. F. (1973) *The Man in the Principal's Office: An Ethnography.* New York: Holt, Rinehart and Winston.

Wolcott, H. F. (1974) The elementary school principal: Notes from a field study. In: *Education and Cultural Process,* edited by G. D. Spindler, 176–204. New York: Holt, Rinehart and Winston.

Wolcott, H. F. (2003) Reflections from the field: A "natural" writer. *Anthropology & Education Quarterly* 34(3): 324–338.

Wutich, A. (2009) Estimating household water use: A comparison of diary, prompted recall and free recall methods. *Field Methods* 21(1): 49–68.

Young, J. C. (1981) *Medical Choice in a Mexican Village.* New Brunswick: Rutgers University Press.

INDEX

ABOUT THE AUTHOR

Pertti J. ("Bert") Pelto is of Finnish-American background, born in Portland, Oregon. He grew up in western Washington, received his B.A. degree at Washington State College (now WSU), and a doctorate in anthropology at the University of California, Berkeley (1960).

In 1954–55 he studied at the University of Helsinki, and returned to Finland in 1958 for doctoral research among the reindeer herding people in northeastern Lapland. His doctoral thesis *Individualism in Skolt Lapp Society* (1962) was published in Finland.

Dr. Pelto has taught at Cornell University, the University of Minnesota, Washington University, and the University of Connecticut (1969–1992), from which he retired in 1992. At the University of Connecticut he founded the Program in Medical Anthropology.

His book *Anthropological Research: The Structure of Inquiry* (1970), in which he argued for a comprehensive qualitative-quantitative mix of methods, was the first methodology textbook in socio-cultural anthropology. Pelto's main interests have centered on research methods, and he has written a number of papers and book chapters on ethnographic field work. Other publications include *The Snowmobile Revolution* (1973) and several jointly edited books, including *Technology and Social Change* (1983) with H. R. Bernard, and *Sexuality in the Time of AIDS* (2004) with R. Verma, S. Schensul, and A. Joshi. For the past 20 years Dr. Pelto has spent most of his time in India, where he has participated in training and advising various research groups, in HIV/AIDS projects and in other applied programs.